Early Praise for *The Ray Tracer Challenge*

Following in the footsteps of his book, *Mazes for Programmers*, Buck once again takes a challenging concept, presents it in an easy-to-understand format, and reminds us that programming can be both fun and rewarding.

➤ **Dr. Sebastian Raaphorst**
Gemini Observatory

This is a problem domain that I've always wanted to get into but have struggled to find anything approachable for someone who doesn't know or isn't good at all with C or C++. This book is a godsend.

➤ **Danielle Kefford**
Software Engineer

This book is devious. Little by little, a test here and a test there, you'll create an incredibly sophisticated ray tracing library. Because each change is so small, your ray tracer will sneak up on you. That's the devious part: by the end you'll have built an amazingly complex piece of software, but it will never feel difficult!

➤ **Cory Forsyth**
Founding Partner, 201 Created, Inc.

In *The Ray Tracer Challenge* Jamis Buck tames a difficult topic using an entertaining, practical approach that even the mathematically averse will enjoy. The test-driven approach challenges and rewards the reader with experiences and artifacts that remind even the grizzled software curmudgeon of the joyful moments in software development that inspired us to pursue engineering in the first place.

➤ **Justin Ball**
CTO, Atomic Jolt

Creating a ray tracer is a rite of passage that I recommend all developers endeavor to complete. Jamis does a great job presenting complex topics simply and allowing the reader to focus on the most interesting parts of the project. Working through this book is almost guaranteed to bring your programming skills up a notch.

➤ **Jason Pike**
  Director, Software Engineering, Atlas RFID Solutions

The Ray Tracer Challenge is a delightful introduction to 3D lighting and rendering through ray tracing. Yes, there is math, but Jamis provides great examples, and the exercises illustrate concepts in a style that is way more fun than any math class I took in college!

➤ **Matthew Margolis**
  Director, Software Engineering

Taking the Ray Tracer Challenge was so much fun. Starting with some short tests, you'll create beautifully rendered images with just a little bit of math and code.

➤ **Justin Weiss**
  Senior Software Engineer, Aha!

With this book, I can use what I learned at the university thirteen years ago, and it's now fun! *The Ray Tracer Challenge* gave me back my joy for pet projects. I recommend it to everyone!

➤ **Gábor László Hajba**
  Senior IT Consultant

One of the tricks to avoiding programmer burnout is to find a passion project. In this book, you'll find exactly that: an awesome personal project that you can tackle regardless of your language background. Jamis's *The Ray Tracer Challenge* shows us that the best passion projects are shared.

➤ **Kevin Gisi**
  Senior UX Engineer

The Ray Tracer Challenge

A Test-Driven Guide to Your First 3D Renderer

Jamis Buck

The Pragmatic Bookshelf

Raleigh, North Carolina

Many of the designations used by manufacturers and sellers to distinguish their products are claimed as trademarks. Where those designations appear in this book, and The Pragmatic Programmers, LLC was aware of a trademark claim, the designations have been printed in initial capital letters or in all capitals. The Pragmatic Starter Kit, The Pragmatic Programmer, Pragmatic Programming, Pragmatic Bookshelf, PragProg and the linking *g* device are trademarks of The Pragmatic Programmers, LLC.

Every precaution was taken in the preparation of this book. However, the publisher assumes no responsibility for errors or omissions, or for damages that may result from the use of information (including program listings) contained herein.

Our Pragmatic books, screencasts, and audio books can help you and your team create better software and have more fun. Visit us at *https://pragprog.com*.

The team that produced this book includes:

Publisher: Andy Hunt
VP of Operations: Janet Furlow
Managing Editor: Susan Conant
Development Editor: Brian P. Hogan
Copy Editor: L. Sakhi MacMillan
Indexing: Potomac Indexing, LLC
Layout: Gilson Graphics

For sales, volume licensing, and support, please contact *support@pragprog.com*.

For international rights, please contact *rights@pragprog.com*.

ISBN-13: 978-1-68050-271-8
Book version: P1.0—February 2019

Contents

Acknowledgments

This book exists because my son wanted to learn how to write software. I'd tinkered with ray tracers years ago, hacking on POV-Ray and writing my own simple renderers, so when he asked for my help, my first thought was to walk him through writing one of his own. From that experiment was born an idea, which became an outline, which became a book proposal, which became this book.

So—thank you, Nathaniel!

Enormous thanks go to my wife, Tessa. She not only endured this project but actively encouraged me in it, even while she was neck-deep in her own journey toward a second bachelor's degree. There's no way I could have written this book without her support.

Thanks also go to the small army of reviewers who sacrificed their time (and maybe sanity!) to double-checking my prose, tests, and pseudocode. Specifically: Nathan Anderson, Justin Ball, David Buck (who also graciously provided the foreword!), Cory Forsyth, Kevin Gisi, Jeff Holland, Gábor László Hajba, Javan Makhmali, Matthew Margolis, Bowen Masco, David Owen, Jason Pike, Sebastian Raaphorst, Lasse Skindstad Ebert, Bruce Williams, and Justin Weiss. This book would be infinitely poorer without your comments, corrections, and suggestions.

I certainly can't sign off without thanking my editor, Brian Hogan, who was tireless (merciless?) in helping me turn my idea into something polished and presentable. His name deserves its place on the cover of this book every bit as much as my own.

And finally, thanks go to my publisher, the Pragmatic Bookshelf, for taking a chance on my idea. They truly are fantastic to write for.

Foreword

My adventures in ray tracing began in 1986. I owned an Amiga computer, and a friend came over with a floppy disk containing the C source code for a ray tracer written for Unix. I thought it would be interesting to try it out, so I got it to compile on my Amiga and rendered my first picture. It produced a black and white image of spheres over a flat plane. I was instantly mesmerized. The thought that a computer program was able to draw such a realistic picture was amazing to me. I adapted the program to render color images instead of just black and white and I found the result even more spectacular.

My journey into ray tracing led me to write my own ray tracing program called DKBTrace, which I released as freeware. I figured that I'd had fun writing it and I wanted other people to have fun using it. DKBTrace started to become quite popular in the late 1980s, so I worked with a group of developers to transform it into a ray tracer called POV-Ray. POV-Ray is now the most popular freeware ray tracing program available today. Although I haven't done any development on POV-Ray since the early 1990s, the POV-Ray team has transformed it into a top-notch ray tracer capable of producing truly stunning images.

Now, Jamis Buck (no relation) has written a book showing how to write a ray tracing program of your own. His explanations are clear and fun to follow. He leads you through the development by writing tests first, then getting the tests to run. The book is programming language agnostic so you can write the ray tracer in any programming language you like. In fact, I wrote all of the exercises in Smalltalk—my favorite programming language. I was able to relive the excitement and the joy of building up a ray tracing program from scratch and viewing images I'd created by my software. This isn't a book that you just read through. It's a book that guides you to write your own programs. It takes you on a fun journey and gives you the satisfaction of creating your own stunning images.

Now I invite you to follow us on the journey. Along the way, you'll learn about computer graphics and software development. You'll learn the basic techniques used to render movies like *Ice Age* and *Cars*. Most important, though, you'll enjoy the satisfaction of writing your own software that can amaze you. This book lays out the path and leads you along. Now it's time for you to take the first steps. Enjoy the journey.

David Buck
Author of DKBTrace and Coauthor of POV-Ray

Getting Started

Okay. You are officially awesome. You're one of *those* programmers, the ones who actively seek out new ways to apply their craft and tackle challenges for the thrill of it. You're in good company!

With this book, you're going to build a 3D renderer from scratch. Specifically, you'll build a *ray tracer*, casting rays of light backward into a scene and following their paths as they bounce around toward a light source. It's generally not a very fast technique (and so isn't well-suited for real-time rendering) but it can produce very realistic results. By the end of this book, you'll be able to render scenes like this one:

And you don't have to be a mathematician or computer scientist to do it!

Beginning at the bottom, you'll build a foundation of basic routines and tools. You'll use those to bootstrap other routines, making light rays, shapes, and functions to predict how they'll interact. Then things start moving quickly, and within a few chapters you'll be producing realistic images of 3D spheres. You'll add shadows and visual effects like geometric patterns, mirror reflections, and glass. Other shapes follow—planes, cubes, cylinders, and more.

By the end of the book, you'll be taking these primitive shapes and combining them in complex ways using set operations. There'll be no stopping you!

The specific algorithm you'll implement is called *Whitted ray tracing*,[1] named for Turner Whitted, the researcher who described it in 1979. It's often referred to as *recursive* ray tracing, because it works by recursively spawning *rays* (lines representing rays of light) and bouncing them around the scene to discover what color each pixel of the final image should be. In a nutshell, the algorithm works like this for each of the image's pixels:

1. Cast a ray into the scene, and find where it strikes a surface.

2. Cast a ray from that point toward each light source to determine which lights illuminate that point.

3. If the surface is reflective, cast a new ray in the direction of reflection and recursively determine what color is reflected there.

4. If the surface is transparent, do the same thing in the direction of refraction.

5. Combine all colors that contribute to the point (the color of the surface, the reflection, and refraction) and return that as the color of the pixel.

Over the course of this book, you'll implement each of those steps, learning how to compute reflection vectors, how to approximate refraction, how to intersect rays with various primitive shapes, and more. Sooner than you might think, you'll be rendering awesome 3D scenes!

Who This Book Is For

Ultimately, this book is for anyone who loves writing code, but you'll get the most out of it if:

- You have prior experience writing software (perhaps a year or more).
- You've written unit tests before.
- You like tinkering and experimenting with code and algorithms.

It really doesn't matter what programming environment or operating system you prefer. The only code in this book is pseudocode. Admittedly, the explanations *do* tend toward imperative, procedural, and object-oriented languages, but the concepts and tests themselves are translatable to any environment you wish.

---

1. en.wikipedia.org/wiki/Ray_tracing_(graphics)#Recursive_ray_tracing_algorithm

How to Read This Book

Each chapter is presented as a series of tests covering a small piece of the overall ray tracer. Since each one builds on previous chapters, you'll be most successful if you read them in sequence.

You'll implement your ray tracer in test-first style, writing a few tests at a time and making them pass by implementing the corresponding functions and features in code. The first half of the book is structured to take you smoothly from test to test, but as you get into the second half of the book, the pace picks up. With greater experience comes greater responsibility! You'll still be given the tests, but there will be less hand-holding, and the tests will be presented in a more linear fashion, almost like a checklist.

Each chapter introduces one or more new features, discusses how the feature works at a high level, and then walks you through the tests and how to make them pass. The tests are posed as Cucumber scenarios,[2] but it is absolutely *not* necessary to use Cucumber to implement them. Please feel free to use whatever system you prefer to write your tests!

Typically, Cucumber is used to describe high-level interactions between a user and an application, but the tests in this book use it differently. Here, you'll see it used to describe lower-level interactions, like how various inputs to a specific function might affect the function's output. This lets the book walk you through the construction of an API, step by step, rather than just showing you the high-level behavior that you need to try to emulate. For example, consider the following hypothetical specification which describes the behavior of concatenating two arrays.

```
Scenario: Concatenating two arrays should create a new array
  Given a ← array(1, 2, 3)
    And b ← array(3, 4, 5)
  When c ← a + b
  Then c = array(1, 2, 3, 3, 4, 5)
```

It's structured like any Cucumber scenario, but describes low-level API interactions:

- It begins with two assumptions ("Given…And"), which must be true to start. These use left arrows (←) to assign two arrays to two variables, a and b.

---

2. Technically, the tests are written in Gherkin, which is the language in which Cucumber specs are written. See cucumber.io.

- After everything has been initialized, an action occurs ("When"). The result of this action is what is to be tested. Note that this also uses the left arrow, assigning the result of concatenating a and b to another variable, c.

- Finally, an assertion is made ("Then"), which must be true. This uses the equals operator (=) to assert that the variable c is equal to the given array.

Your job as the reader is to implement each test, and then make each pass. You're welcome to do so in Cucumber if you like—in fact, the Cucumber tests may be downloaded from the publisher,[3] to save you the effort of keying them all in by hand. But if Cucumber isn't your thing, you can be just as successful by translating the Cucumber scenarios into whatever testing system you prefer. Honestly, part of the puzzle—part of the fun!—is translating each specification into a working unit test. The scenario tells you what the behavior should be. *You* get to decide how to make it happen.

While working through this book, you're going to discover that an implementation that worked for one test might not work well (or at all) for a later test. You'll need to be flexible and willing to refactor as you discover new requirements. That, or read the entire book through before beginning your implementation so you know what's coming up.

Also, be aware that I've made many of the architectural decisions in this book with the goal of being easy to explain. Often, there will be more efficient ways to implement a function, or to architect a feature. You may disagree with the book at times, and that's okay! This book is a roadmap, describing just one of many possible ways to get to the goal. Follow your own aesthetic sense. Make your code your own.

Lastly, at the end of each chapter is a section called "Putting It Together." This is where you'll find a description of something that builds on the code you wrote for that chapter and gives you a chance to play and experiment with your new code. Sometimes it will be a small project, and other times a list of possible things to try or directions to explore. It's certainly possible to skip those sections if you're in a hurry, but if you do you'll be missing one of the most enjoyable parts of the journey.

Things to Watch Out For

A ray tracer is math-heavy. There's no getting around it. It works its magic by crunching numbers, finding intersections between lines and shapes, computing reflections and refractions, and blending colors. So, yes, there will

---

3.   pragprog.com/book/jbtracer/the-ray-tracer-challenge

be a great deal of math here, but I will mostly give it to you, ready to implement. You'll find little or no focus on where the math comes from, no derivations of formulas, no explanations of why an equation does what it does. You'll see the formulas and, where necessary, walk through how to implement them, but you won't wade through proofs and derivations. If the proofs and derivations are what you particularly enjoy, you can always find a great deal of information about them online.

Also, number-crunching tends to be fairly CPU-intensive. A ray tracer offers a lot of opportunities to optimize code, but that's not the focus of this book. If you follow along and implement just what is described, your code will probably not be very efficient or very fast—but it *will* work. Think of optimization as a bonus exercise!

Other things to watch out for, in no particular order, are these:

Comparing floating-point numbers

Especially in tests, you'll need to be able to compare two floating-point numbers to determine if they are approximately equal. The specifications in the book represent this loose comparison with a simple equals sign. In practice, you'll need to be more explicit and test that the two numbers are within an error value that the book refers to as *EPSILON*, something like this: $|a - b| < EPSILON$. In practice, using a tiny value like 0.0001 for EPSILON is generally fine.

Comparing data structures

As with comparing numbers, it's also assumed that you'll need to compare data structures to see if they are equal. For example, you'll need to be able to see whether two points are the same. These comparison routines aren't explicitly described in the book, but you'll need to implement them all the same. It wouldn't hurt to add tests for these routines, too, despite them not being given in the book.

Representing infinity

In later chapters, like Chapter 12, *Cubes*, on page 167, and Chapter 13, *Cylinders*, on page 177, you'll need to be able to compare numbers with infinity. If your programming language can represent infinity natively, that's great! Otherwise, you can usually fake it by using a very large number instead. (Something like 1×10^{10} is usually plenty. In many programming languages, you can write that as 1e10.)

Use your own names and architecture!

The names of functions and variables given in the book are just recommendations. The functions are designed so that the first argument is the "responsible party," or the entity with responsibility for the domain in question. In object-oriented terms, the first argument would be the self object. But don't let this stop you from reassigning those responsibilities if you prefer. You should always feel free to choose names more appropriate to your own architecture.

Also, the ray tracer will be described imperatively, but you should look for ways to adapt these descriptions to the strengths and idioms of your programming environment. Embrace your classes, modules, namespaces, actors, and monads, and make this ray tracer your own!

A lot of work has gone into making sure everything in this book is accurate and error-free, but nobody's perfect. If you happen to find a mistake somewhere, please let me know about it. You can report errata on the book's web site.[4] And be sure to visit the book's discussion forum,[5] where you can ask questions, share tips and tricks, and post eye candy you've rendered with your ray tracer. This forum is purely my own and is not affiliated with the Pragmatic Bookshelf in any way.

With all that out of the way, brace yourself—we're going to jump right in and get started. This is going to be fun!

---

4. pragprog.com/book/jbtracer/the-ray-tracer-challenge
5. forum.raytracerchallenge.com

## CHAPTER 1

Tuples, Points, and Vectors

A sphere sits alone in a room with checkered walls and floor. It reflects light from a bulb somewhere above it. In fact, it reflects just about everything: the checkered wall behind the camera, the ceiling above, and even (if you look closely) its own shadow.

Mmmm. Isn't that gorgeous? Don't you just want to touch that sphere? Well, step in close and let me tell you a little secret. You ready?

You'll be rendering scenes like this with software you wrote yourself before you're half done with this book.

It's the truth. Cross my heart. It's all just modeling light and objects and how they interact.

But before you can model things like light and objects, you need to be able to represent fundamental concepts like *position* and *direction* and *distance*. For example, that sphere must be located *somewhere* in a scene before your renderer can draw it. Realistic shading relies heavily on the direction from a surface to the light source, and reflections are all about following the change of direction of a ray of light.

Fortunately, these concepts—position, direction, and distance—are neatly encapsulated in a little thing called a tuple.

Let the first chapter begin!

Tuples

A *tuple* is just an ordered list of things, like numbers. That's pretty abstract, though, so let's use the concept of position to illustrate it.

Let's say that you're walking in a park one day. You go forward four meters, and suddenly the ground falls out from beneath you. Down you go, landing four meters later. There you discover a mysterious tunnel to the left, which you crawl along for three more meters. At that point, you discover a chest full of gold coins, and you celebrate. Yay!

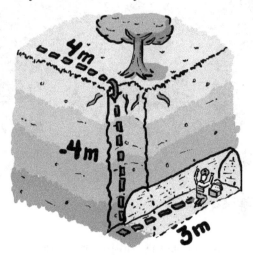

Let's say your first four meters were in the x direction, the second four (when you fell), in the negative (downward) y direction, and the last three (in the tunnel) in the z direction. Those three distances, then, can represent the position of the treasure, in which case we would write them like (4, -4, 3). This is a tuple, and this *specific* tuple is also called a *point* (because it represents a point in space).

Left-Handed vs. Right-Handed Coordinates

With the y axis pointing up, and the x axis pointing to the right, the z axis can be defined to point either *toward* you, or *away from* you.

This book uses a *left-handed* coordinate system. If you take the thumb of your left hand and point it in the +x direction, and then point the fingers of the hand in the direction of +y, you'll find that if you curl your fingers toward your palm, they'll curl away from you. That's the direction of the z axis for the purposes of this book.

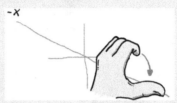

Many sites, documents, articles, books, and APIs use a *right-handed* coordinate system, in which the z axis points toward you. There's nothing wrong with either approach. I've chosen to stick with the left-handed system because it's used in some popular renderers, including Pixar's RenderMan system,[a] the Unity[b] game engine, and the open-source POV-Ray ray tracer.[c]

---

a.   renderman.pixar.com
b.   unity3d.com
c.   www.povray.org

Directions work the same way. Let's say you're standing next to the (now-empty) treasure chest, getting your bearings. You take a moment and mentally draw an arrow pointing from your current position, to where you started. This line will point *negative* four meters in the x direction, *positive* four meters in the y direction, and *negative* three meters in the z direction, or (-4, 4, -3). This tuple—a *vector* now—tells us not only the direction in which to look, but also how far to go in that direction. Pretty cool!

But looking at (4, -4, 3) and (-4, 4, -3), it's impossible to know that one is a point and the other is a vector. Let's add a fourth component to these (x, y, z) tuples, called w, to help us tell them apart. Set w to 1 for points, and 0 for vectors. Thus, your point becomes (4, -4, 3, 1), and your vector becomes (-4, 4, -3, 0).

Now, the choice of 0 or 1 for w probably seems arbitrary just now, but sit tight! It'll make more sense when you get to Chapter 3, *Matrices*, on page 25, where it turns out to be rather important for multiplying matrices and tuples.

This is all pretty fundamental stuff, so it's important that it work correctly. To that end, you're going to write some tests—preferably before you write any actual code—to make sure it comes out right.

 Avoid complex data types as much as possible as you implement your tuples. For instance, you should prefer native floating point numbers over arbitrary-precision abstractions. These tuples are going to be some of your ray tracer's workhorses, so you'll want them to be lean and fast!

Use the following two specifications to guide your tests. The first one shows that a tuple is a point when w is 1, and a second shows that a tuple is a vector when w is 0. Use these tests to demonstrate how your implementation accesses the individual components of the tuple, as well.

```
features/tuples.feature
Scenario: A tuple with w=1.0 is a point
  Given a ← tuple(4.3, -4.2, 3.1, 1.0)
   Then a.x = 4.3
     And a.y = -4.2
     And a.z = 3.1
     And a.w = 1.0
     And a is a point
     And a is not a vector

Scenario: A tuple with w=0 is a vector
  Given a ← tuple(4.3, -4.2, 3.1, 0.0)
   Then a.x = 4.3
     And a.y = -4.2
     And a.z = 3.1
     And a.w = 0.0
     And a is not a point
     And a is a vector
```

You'll use this distinction a lot, so it might make sense to have some factory functions to make it easier to create these two types of tuples. Write two more tests, one to show that a function point(x,y,z) creates points, and another to show that a function vector(x,y,z) creates vectors.

```
features/tuples.feature
Scenario: point() creates tuples with w=1
  Given p ← point(4, -4, 3)
   Then p = tuple(4, -4, 3, 1)

Scenario: vector() creates tuples with w=0
  Given v ← vector(4, -4, 3)
   Then v = tuple(4, -4, 3, 0)
```

Nice! That gives you a solid foundation for creating tuples, points, and vectors. Next, let's look at some of the things you can do with them.

Comparing Floating Point Numbers

Beware of comparing floating point values using simple equivalency. Round-off error can make two numbers that *should* be equivalent instead be slightly different.

When you need to test two floating point numbers for equivalence, compare their difference. If the absolute value of their difference is less than some value (called EPSILON), you can consider them equal. Pseudocode for this comparison looks like this:

```
constant EPSILON ← 0.00001

function equal(a, b)
  if abs(a - b) < EPSILON
    return true
  else
    return false
  end if
end function
```

Operations

Now that you have these tuples, you're faced with the question of how to use them. Ultimately, these will be the bedrock of your ray tracer—they'll crop up in calculations everywhere, from computing the intersection of a ray with objects in your scene to figuring out how a particular point on a surface ought to be shaded. But to plug these vectors and points into your calculations, you need to implement a few basic operations on them.

Let's start with some familiar operations from arithmetic.

 If you haven't already, take a minute to write a function that will compare two tuples for equality. It'll save you some duplication! As you do so, keep in mind the comments on floating point comparisons in *Comparing Floating Point Numbers,* on page 5.

Adding Tuples

Imagine that you have a point (3,-2,5,1) and a vector (-2,3,1,0), and you want to know where you would be if you followed the vector from that point. The answer comes via *addition*—adding the two tuples together. Go ahead and write a test that demonstrates this, like the following:

```
features/tuples.feature
Scenario: Adding two tuples
  Given a1 ← tuple(3, -2, 5, 1)
    And a2 ← tuple(-2, 3, 1, 0)
  Then a1 + a2 = tuple(1, 1, 6, 1)
```

You make a new tuple by adding the corresponding components of each of the operands—the x's sum to produce the new x, y's to produce a new y, and so forth.

And check out how that w coordinate cooperates. You add a point (w of 1) and a vector (w of 0), and the result has a w of 1—another point! Similarly, you could add two vectors (w of 0) and get a vector, because the w's sum to 0. However, adding a point to a point doesn't really make sense. Try it. You'll see that you get a tuple with a w of 2, which is neither a vector nor a point!

Subtracting Tuples

Subtracting tuples is useful, too. It'll come in handy when you get to Chapter 6, *Light and Shading*, on page 75, when you need to find the vector that points to your light source.

Add the following test to show that subtracting tuples works by subtracting corresponding elements of the tuples.

```
features/tuples.feature
Scenario: Subtracting two points
  Given p1 ← point(3, 2, 1)
    And p2 ← point(5, 6, 7)
  Then p1 - p2 = vector(-2, -4, -6)
```

Isn't that cool? The two w components (both equal to 1) cancel each other out, and the resulting tuple has a w of 0—a vector! Specifically, it's the vector pointing from p_2 to p_1: (-2, -4, -6).

Similarly, you can subtract a vector (w of 0) from a point (w of 1) and get another tuple with a w of 1—a point. Conceptually, this is just moving *backward* by the given vector. Add this next test to demonstrate this.

```
features/tuples.feature
Scenario: Subtracting a vector from a point
  Given p ← point(3, 2, 1)
    And v ← vector(5, 6, 7)
  Then p - v = point(-2, -4, -6)
```

Lastly, subtracting two vectors gives us a tuple with a w of 0—another vector, representing the change in direction between the two. Write another test to show that this works.

features/tuples.feature
```
Scenario: Subtracting two vectors
  Given v1 ← vector(3, 2, 1)
    And v2 ← vector(5, 6, 7)
  Then v1 - v2 = vector(-2, -4, -6)
```

As with addition, though, not every combination makes sense. For instance, if you subtract a point (w = 1) from a vector (w = 0), you'll end up with a negative w component, which is neither point nor vector. Let's look at a counterpart to subtraction next.

Negating Tuples

Sometimes you'll want to know what the *opposite* of some vector is. That is to say, given a vector that points from a surface toward a light source, what vector points from the light source back to the surface? (You'll run into this specific case in Chapter 6, *Light and Shading*, on page 75, as well.) Mathematically, you can get it by subtracting the vector from the tuple (0, 0, 0, 0). Go ahead and write a test like the following, to demonstrate this:

features/tuples.feature
```
Scenario: Subtracting a vector from the zero vector
  Given zero ← vector(0, 0, 0)
    And v ← vector(1, -2, 3)
  Then zero - v = vector(-1, 2, -3)
```

But (0, 0, 0, 0) is awkward to think about (it's a vector, but where is it even *pointing*?), and the operation itself is cumbersome to write. You can simplify this by implementing a *negate* operation, which negates each component of the tuple. Add the following test showing the effect of negation on a tuple.

features/tuples.feature
```
Scenario: Negating a tuple
  Given a ← tuple(1, -2, 3, -4)
  Then -a = tuple(-1, 2, -3, 4)
```

That's pretty much how it works: (x, y, z, w) becomes (-x, -y, -z, -w).

 If your language supports operator overloading, negation can be implemented as a unary minus operator (-tuple). Otherwise, a method (tuple.negate()) or a function (negate(tuple)) works fine. In this book, it's assumed that -tuple is the negation operator.

Scalar Multiplication and Division

Now let's say you have some vector and you want to know what point lies 3.5 times farther in that direction. (This will come up in Chapter 5, *Ray-Sphere*

Intersections, on page 57, when you're finding where a ray intersects a sphere.) So you lay that vector end-to-end 3.5 times to see just how far the point is from the start, like in the following illustration.

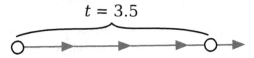

$$t = 3.5$$

It turns out that multiplying the vector by 3.5 does just what you need. The 3.5 here is a *scalar value* because multiplying by it *scales* the vector (changes its length uniformly). To do it, you multiply each component of the tuple by the scalar. Write these tests to demonstrate the effect:

features/tuples.feature
```
Scenario: Multiplying a tuple by a scalar
  Given a ← tuple(1, -2, 3, -4)
  Then a * 3.5 = tuple(3.5, -7, 10.5, -14)

Scenario: Multiplying a tuple by a fraction
  Given a ← tuple(1, -2, 3, -4)
  Then a * 0.5 = tuple(0.5, -1, 1.5, -2)
```

Note that last test, where you multiply the tuple by 0.5. This is essentially the same thing as dividing the tuple by 2, right? You can always implement division with multiplication, but sometimes it's simpler to describe an operation as division. It works like you'd expect—dividing each component of the tuple by the scalar. Add the following test to demonstrate this.

features/tuples.feature
```
Scenario: Dividing a tuple by a scalar
  Given a ← tuple(1, -2, 3, -4)
  Then a / 2 = tuple(0.5, -1, 1.5, -2)
```

That's the last of the familiar arithmetic operators. Next let's look at some new ones that will primarily be useful with vectors.

Magnitude

Remember, at the start of this chapter, when you read that a vector was a value that encoded direction and distance? The distance represented by a vector is called its *magnitude*, or *length*. It's how far you would travel in a straight line if you were to walk from one end of the vector to the other. Add some tests like the following, showing the magnitude of several different vectors.

features/tuples.feature
```
Scenario: Computing the magnitude of vector(1, 0, 0)
  Given v ← vector(1, 0, 0)
  Then magnitude(v) = 1
```

```
Scenario: Computing the magnitude of vector(0, 1, 0)
  Given v ← vector(0, 1, 0)
  Then magnitude(v) = 1

Scenario: Computing the magnitude of vector(0, 0, 1)
  Given v ← vector(0, 0, 1)
  Then magnitude(v) = 1

Scenario: Computing the magnitude of vector(1, 2, 3)
  Given v ← vector(1, 2, 3)
  Then magnitude(v) = √14

Scenario: Computing the magnitude of vector(-1, -2, -3)
  Given v ← vector(-1, -2, -3)
  Then magnitude(v) = √14
```

Pythagoras' theorem taught us how to compute this, with some squares and a square root:

$$\text{magnitude}(v) = \sqrt{v_x^2 + v_y^2 + v_z^2 + v_w^2}$$

Vectors with magnitudes of 1 are called a *unit vectors*, and these will be super handy. You'll use them when computing your view matrix in *Defining a View Transformation*, on page 97, when determining the direction perpendicular to a surface (*Computing the Normal on a Sphere*, on page 77), and even when generating the rays you want to cast into your scene (Chapter 5, *Ray-Sphere Intersections*, on page 57).

You won't always be able to start with a nice, neat, unit vector though. Very often, in fact, you'll be starting with a difference between two points, and you'll need to be able to take that and turn it into a unit vector while preserving its direction.

Normalization to the rescue!

Normalization

Normalization is the process of taking an arbitrary vector and converting it into a unit vector. It will keep your calculations anchored relative to a common scale (the unit vector), which is pretty important. If you were to skip normalizing your ray vectors or your surface normals, your calculations would be scaled differently for every ray you cast, and your scenes would look terrible (if they rendered at all).

Add the following tests to your suite, showing the effect of normalizing a couple of different vectors and also confirming that the length of a normalized vector is 1.

```
features/tuples.feature
Scenario: Normalizing vector(4, 0, 0) gives (1, 0, 0)
  Given v ← vector(4, 0, 0)
  Then normalize(v) = vector(1, 0, 0)

Scenario: Normalizing vector(1, 2, 3)
  Given v ← vector(1, 2, 3)
                            # vector(1/√14,   2/√14,   3/√14)
  Then normalize(v) = approximately vector(0.26726, 0.53452, 0.80178)

Scenario: The magnitude of a normalized vector
  Given v ← vector(1, 2, 3)
  When norm ← normalize(v)
  Then magnitude(norm) = 1
```

You normalize a tuple by dividing each of its components by its magnitude. In pseudocode, it looks something like this:

```
function normalize(v)
  return tuple(v.x / magnitude(v),
               v.y / magnitude(v),
               v.z / magnitude(v),
               v.w / magnitude(v))
end function
```

With that, you can turn any vector (or rather, any vector with a nonzero magnitude) into a unit vector.

Dot Product

When dealing with vectors, a *dot product* (also called a *scalar product*, or *inner product*) is going to turn up when you start intersecting rays with objects, as well as when you compute the shading on a surface. The dot product takes two vectors and returns a scalar value. Add this test to demonstrate the dot product's effect.

```
features/tuples.feature
Scenario: The dot product of two tuples
  Given a ← vector(1, 2, 3)
    And b ← vector(2, 3, 4)
  Then dot(a, b) = 20
```

Given those two vectors, the dot product is computed as the sum of the products of the corresponding components of each vector. Here's pseudocode showing what that looks like:

```
function dot(a, b)
  return a.x * b.x +
         a.y * b.y +
         a.z * b.z +
         a.w * b.w
end function
```

The dot product can feel pretty abstract, but here's one quick way to internalize it: the *smaller* the dot product, the *larger* the angle between the vectors. For example, given two unit vectors, a dot product of 1 means the vectors are identical, and a dot product of -1 means they point in opposite directions. More specifically, and again if the two vectors are unit vectors, the dot product is actually the *cosine* of the angle between them, which fact will come in handy when you get to Chapter 6, *Light and Shading*, on page 75. If you'd like to read more about what the dot product means and how to understand it, I recommend the following article: betterexplained.com/articles/vector-calculus-understanding-the-dot-product.

You certainly don't need any deep understanding of the dot product to implement it, though. (Lucky you!) For now, just make the test pass, and then move on.

Joe asks:
Does the dot product need the w component?

If you've been exposed to dot products before, you might wonder if w belongs in this computation, since the dot product only makes sense on vectors, and all of our vectors will have a w of 0.

The answer is: it depends. I've chosen to include it here because the dot product applies to vectors of any dimension, not just three, and because it preserves a certain symmetry with the other operations. Also, if you happen to use the dot product on points instead of vectors accidentally, keeping the w in the computation might help you identify the bug sooner rather than later!

Cross Product

Okay, last one. The *cross product* is another vector operation, but unlike the dot product, it returns another vector instead of a scalar, which the following test demonstrates. Go ahead and add it to your suite.

```
features/tuples.feature
Scenario: The cross product of two vectors
  Given a ← vector(1, 2, 3)
    And b ← vector(2, 3, 4)
  Then cross(a, b) = vector(-1, 2, -1)
    And cross(b, a) = vector(1, -2, 1)
```

Note that this is specifically testing *vectors*, not *tuples*. This is because the four-dimensional cross product is significantly more complicated than the three-dimensional cross product, and your ray tracer really only needs the three-dimensional version anyway.

Also, note that if you change the order of the operands, you change the direction of the resulting vector. Keep this in mind as you use the cross product: order matters!

In pseudocode, the cross product of two three-dimensional vectors comes together like this:

```
function cross(a, b)
  return vector(a.y * b.z - a.z * b.y,
                a.z * b.x - a.x * b.z,
                a.x * b.y - a.y * b.x)
end function
```

You get a new vector that is perpendicular to both of the original vectors.

What does this mean? Consider the following three mutually perpendicular vectors, X, Y, and Z.

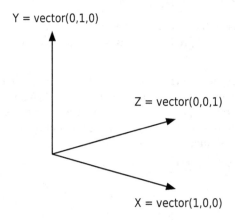

Y = vector(0,1,0)

Z = vector(0,0,1)

X = vector(1,0,0)

If you take the cross product of X and Y, you get Z. Similarly, Y cross Z gets you X, and Z cross X is Y. The results are always perpendicular to the inputs.

Again, order is important here. X cross Y gives you Z, but Y cross X gives you -Z!

You'll use this primarily when working with view transformations (in Chapter 7, *Making a Scene*, on page 91), but it will also pop up when you start rendering triangles (in Chapter 15, *Triangles*, on page 207).

Putting It Together

As far as first steps go, this one wasn't too bad, and it's laid the groundwork for some great things. You've got a working implementation of points and vectors! Those things are going to pop up everywhere. Sadly, you have no ray tracer yet to plug your code into, but you can still have some fun with it.

Try playing with this little program, firing virtual projectiles and seeing how far they go. It'll let you exercise the vector and point routines you've written. Start with the following two data structures:

- A *projectile* has a *position* (a point) and a *velocity* (a vector).
- An *environment* has *gravity* (a vector) and *wind* (a vector).

Then, add a tick(environment, projectile) function which returns a new projectile, representing the given projectile after one unit of time has passed. (The actual units here don't really matter—maybe they're seconds, or milliseconds. Whatever. We'll just call them "ticks.")

In pseudocode, the tick() function should do the following:

```
function tick(env, proj)
  position ← proj.position + proj.velocity
  velocity ← proj.velocity + env.gravity + env.wind
  return projectile(position, velocity)
end function
```

Now, initialize a projectile and an environment. Use whatever values you want, but these might get you started:

```
# projectile starts one unit above the origin.
# velocity is normalized to 1 unit/tick.
p ← projectile(point(0, 1, 0), normalize(vector(1, 1, 0)))

# gravity -0.1 unit/tick, and wind is -0.01 unit/tick.
e ← environment(vector(0, -0.1, 0), vector(-0.01, 0, 0))
```

Then, run tick repeatedly until the projectile's y position is less than or equal to 0. Report the projectile's position after each tick, and the number of ticks it takes for the projectile to hit the ground. Try multiplying the projectile's initial velocity by larger and larger numbers to see how much farther the projectile goes!

Once you've had a chance to play with this virtual cannon a bit, move to the next chapter. You're going to implement the visual side of your ray tracer, the *canvas* onto which everything will eventually be drawn.

## CHAPTER 2

Drawing on a Canvas

Points and vectors may be fundamental to a ray tracer, but without a way to turn them into something visual, most folks won't care. It's a good thing you're about to implement a *canvas*, then, isn't it?

A canvas is a kind of virtual drawing board, which your ray tracer will use to turn your scenes into images you can actually *see*. In this chapter, you're going to create a canvas that supports millions of colors, and which you can subsequently save as an image file.

To get there, we'll talk about colors and how to represent them, as well as some color operations that you'll need to support. Once you've got a handle on that, you'll move on to the canvas itself, and you'll finish up with a small project to revisualize your projectile launcher from the previous chapter.

Let's jump right in.

Representing Colors

Each pixel on your computer monitor is a composite of three colors: red, green, and blue. If you take those three colors and mix them in different quantities, you get just about every other color you can imagine, from red, yellow, and green, to cyan, blue, and purple, and everything in between.

If you let red, green, and blue each be a value between 0 and 1 (with 0 meaning the color is entirely absent, and 1 meaning the color is fully present), then the figure on page 16 shows some possible colors you can get by combining them.

If all components are 1, you get white. If all components are 0, you get black.

And did you catch that? A color is a tuple, just like vectors and points! In fact, when it comes time to make this real, it may make sense to build your

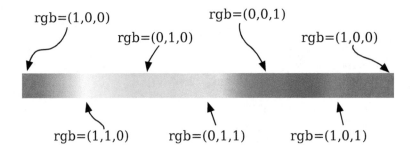

color implementation on top of your tuple implementation, rather than starting from scratch.

One way or another, you're going to need to be able to create a color from a (red, green, blue) tuple. Add the following test, which does just that.

features/tuples.feature
```
Scenario: Colors are (red, green, blue) tuples
  Given c ← color(-0.5, 0.4, 1.7)
  Then c.red = -0.5
    And c.green = 0.4
    And c.blue = 1.7
```

In practice, you'll only use numbers between 0 and 1 for those components, but don't put any constraints on them just yet. If a color is especially bright or dark somewhere in your scene, it may go through multiple transformations before reaching your virtual "eye," dropping it to less than 0 or increasing it to greater than 1 at any point along the way. Limiting the color prematurely can make parts of your scene too bright or dark in the final image.

Once that test is passing, move on. We'll talk about the different operations that your color implementation will need to support.

Implementing Color Operations

Colors, as you'll see, tend to interact with each other. Whether it's a green light reflecting on a yellow surface, or a blue surface viewed through a red glass, or some other combination of transparency and reflection, colors can affect each other. For example, the figure on page 17 shows how different colored panes of glass affect the colors viewed through them.

Fortunately, we can handle all of these combinations with just four operations: adding and subtracting colors, multiplying a color by a scalar, and multiplying a color by another color.

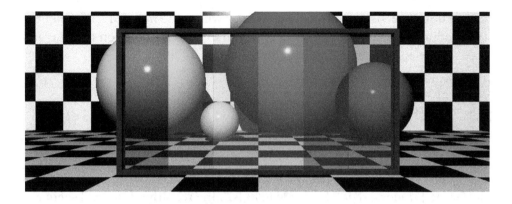

Here's where colors especially show their relationship to vectors and points. Addition, subtraction, and multiplication by a scalar all work exactly like you saw with tuples in Chapter 1, *Tuples, Points, and Vectors*, on page 1. Write the following tests to emphasize this, showing that you expect the same behavior with colors.

```
features/tuples.feature
Scenario: Adding colors
  Given c1 ← color(0.9, 0.6, 0.75)
    And c2 ← color(0.7, 0.1, 0.25)
  Then c1 + c2 = color(1.6, 0.7, 1.0)

Scenario: Subtracting colors
  Given c1 ← color(0.9, 0.6, 0.75)
    And c2 ← color(0.7, 0.1, 0.25)
  Then c1 - c2 = color(0.2, 0.5, 0.5)

Scenario: Multiplying a color by a scalar
  Given c ← color(0.2, 0.3, 0.4)
  Then c * 2 = color(0.4, 0.6, 0.8)
```

The final color operation, multiplying a color by another color, is used to blend two colors together. You'll use it when (for example) you want to know the visible color of a yellow-green surface when illuminated by a reddish-purple light. Implement the following test to show what you expect to happen.

```
features/tuples.feature
Scenario: Multiplying colors
  Given c1 ← color(1, 0.2, 0.4)
    And c2 ← color(0.9, 1, 0.1)
  Then c1 * c2 = color(0.9, 0.2, 0.04)
```

This method of blending two colors works by multiplying corresponding components of each color to form a new color. It's technically called the *Hadamard product* (or *Schur product*), but it doesn't really matter what you call it. It just needs to produce a new color where the new red component is the product of the red components of the other colors, and so on for blue and green. In pseudocode, it looks like this:

```
function hadamard_product(c1, c2)
  r ← c1.red * c2.red
  g ← c1.green * c2.green
  b ← c1.blue * c2.blue
  return color(r, g, b)
end function
```

Consider this test again. It says that if you were to view that yellow-green surface (c2) under a reddish-purple light (c1), the resulting color will seem red (because its red component, 0.9, is largest). The following image compares that yellow-green sphere in white light, versus reddish-purple light, and shows visually what the test is asserting.

That's all you need to do with colors for now. Once those tests are passing, you'll be ready for the next step: a proper image canvas!

Creating a Canvas

A *canvas* is just a rectangular grid of pixels—much like your computer screen. Your implementation will allow its size to be configurable, so you can specify how wide and high the canvas ought to be.

Add the following test to your suite. It demonstrates how a canvas is created and shows every pixel in the canvas should be initialized to black (color(0, 0, 0)).

```
features/canvas.feature
Scenario: Creating a canvas
  Given c ← canvas(10, 20)
  Then c.width = 10
    And c.height = 20
    And every pixel of c is color(0, 0, 0)
```

Pixels are drawn to the canvas by specifying a position and a color. Write the following test, introducing a function called write_pixel(canvas, x, y, color) and showing how it is used.

```
features/canvas.feature
Scenario: Writing pixels to a canvas
  Given c ← canvas(10, 20)
    And red ← color(1, 0, 0)
  When write_pixel(c, 2, 3, red)
  Then pixel_at(c, 2, 3) = red
```

Note that the x and y parameters are assumed to be 0-based in this book. That is to say, x may be anywhere from 0 to width - 1 (inclusive), and y may be anywhere from 0 to height - 1 (inclusive).

You won't need any other methods for writing to your canvas, since your ray tracer will work pixel-by-pixel over the entire scene. Make those tests all pass, and then we can talk about how to save this canvas to disk in a format that will actually be meaningful.

Saving a Canvas

The canvas, by itself, is just an intermediate step. It might represent an image of your scene, but you can't look at it directly. You can't show it to anyone. You can't use it to brag about how awesome your 3D-rendered scene looks, or how amazing your ray tracer is. To do that, you need to be able to take the information in your canvas and write it out to a file, which could then be viewed, emailed, tweeted, Instagrammed, or whatever.

Let's make that happen.

You could choose from a *lot* of different image formats, but you're only going to implement one of them: the Portable Pixmap (PPM) format from the Netpbm project.[1] There are several flavors of the PPM format, but the version you'll implement (called "plain" PPM) is straight text.

 Joe asks:

How do I view a PPM file?

If you use a Mac, you're in luck, because Preview.app (which is part of the OS) can open PPM files. From the finder, just double-click on the PPM file you want to view, or type open my-image.ppm from the command line.

The story is more complicated for Linux and Windows, but not terribly so. There are a lot of tools that you can get for either platform that will open PPM files, but you really can't go wrong with the GNU Image Manipulation Program (GIMP).[a] It's free, it's cross-platform, it's open-source, and it's well-maintained.

———————
a.　www.gimp.org

Every plain PPM file begins with a header consisting of three lines of text. The following figure shows one possible header.

```
P3
80 40
255
```

The first line is the string P3 (which is the identifier, or "magic number," for the flavor of PPM we're using), followed by a new line. The second line consists of two numbers which describe the image's width and height in pixels. The header in the previous figure describes an image that is 80 pixels wide, and 40 tall. The third line (255) specifies the *maximum color value*, which means that each red, green, and blue value will be scaled to lie between 0 and 255, inclusive.

Write the following test. It introduces a function called canvas_to_ppm(canvas) which returns a PPM-formatted string. This test will help ensure that the header is created properly.

features/canvas.feature
```
Scenario: Constructing the PPM header
  Given c ← canvas(5, 3)
  When ppm ← canvas_to_ppm(c)
```

———————
1.　netpbm.sourceforge.net

Then lines 1-3 of ppm are

```
"""
P3
5 3
255
"""
```

Immediately following this header is the pixel data, which contains each pixel represented as three integers: red, green, and blue. Each component should be scaled to between 0 and the maximum color value given in the header (for example, 255), and each value should be separated from its neighbors by a space.

Add the following test to your suite to show that the PPM pixel data is constructed correctly for a canvas where three pixels have been colored. Note that color components that would be greater than 255 are limited (or *clamped*) to 255, and components that would be less than 0 are clamped to 0.

features/canvas.feature
```
Scenario: Constructing the PPM pixel data
  Given c ← canvas(5, 3)
    And c1 ← color(1.5, 0, 0)
    And c2 ← color(0, 0.5, 0)
    And c3 ← color(-0.5, 0, 1)
  When write_pixel(c, 0, 0, c1)
    And write_pixel(c, 2, 1, c2)
    And write_pixel(c, 4, 2, c3)
    And ppm ← canvas_to_ppm(c)
  Then lines 4-6 of ppm are
    """
    255 0 0 0 0 0 0 0 0 0 0 0 0 0 0
    0 0 0 0 0 0 0 128 0 0 0 0 0 0 0
    0 0 0 0 0 0 0 0 0 0 0 0 0 0 255
    """
```

Notice how the first row of pixels comes first, then the second row, and so forth. Further, each row is terminated by a new line.

In addition, no line in a PPM file should be more than 70 characters long. Most image programs tend to accept PPM images with lines longer than that, but it's a good idea to add new lines as needed to keep the lines shorter. (Just be careful to put the new line where a space would have gone, so you don't split a number in half!)

Implement the following test to ensure that pixel data lines do not exceed 70 characters.

features/canvas.feature
```
Scenario: Splitting long lines in PPM files
  Given c ← canvas(10, 2)
  When every pixel of c is set to color(1, 0.8, 0.6)
    And ppm ← canvas_to_ppm(c)
  Then lines 4-7 of ppm are
    """
    255 204 153 255 204 153 255 204 153 255 204 153 255 204 153 255 204
    153 255 204 153 255 204 153 255 204 153 255 204 153
    255 204 153 255 204 153 255 204 153 255 204 153 255 204 153 255 204
    153 255 204 153 255 204 153 255 204 153 255 204 153
    """
```

One more thing. Some image programs (notably ImageMagick[2]) won't process PPM files correctly unless the files are terminated by a newline character. Add the following test to satisfy those picky consumers.

features/canvas.feature
```
Scenario: PPM files are terminated by a newline character
  Given c ← canvas(5, 3)
  When ppm ← canvas_to_ppm(c)
  Then ppm ends with a newline character
```

That's really all there is to PPM files. The next step is to wrap it all up with a bow and do something fun with it! Let's revisit the program you wrote in the previous chapter.

Putting It Together

In the previous chapter, you wrote a program to compute the trajectory of a projectile, using nothing but points and vectors. You've got a new tool, now, though!

For this challenge, you'll once again compute the trajectory of a projectile, just as before, but this time you'll plot its course on your brand-new canvas. After each tick, take the coordinates of the projectile and color the corresponding pixel on the canvas. When the loop finishes, save your canvas to disk and view the result. It ought to look something like the figure on page 23. The pixel sizes have been exaggerated here, plotted as squares instead of single dots, to make them visible in print.

As you tackle this challenge, note a few things:

1. The canvas y coordinate is upside-down compared to your world coordinates. It's zero at the top of your canvas, and increases as you move down.

---

2. www.imagemagick.org

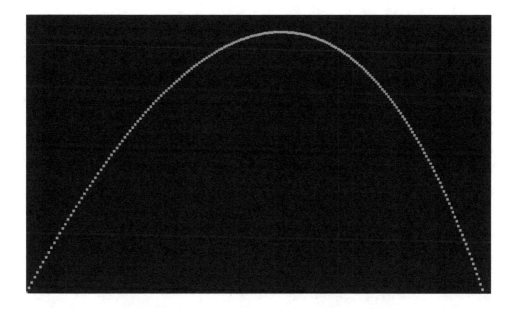

To convert your projectile's coordinates to canvas coordinates, subtract the projectile's y from the canvas's height.

2. It's going to be really, really easy to accidentally plot a point that is outside the bounds of your canvas. Make sure you handle this case, either by having the canvas ignore points outside its bounds or by preventing your program from plotting such points in the first place.

3. Your projectile coordinates will be floating point numbers. The pixels on your canvas, however, are at integer coordinates. Be sure to convert your projectile's x and y coordinates to integers before plotting them.

4. After your loop finishes, be sure to save your canvas to a file! That's the whole point of this exercise, after all.

You may need to experiment a bit to find a canvas size and projectile velocity that complement each other. Initially, you'll probably find that either your projectile barely makes a blip on your canvas, or it'll go streaking off the side at light speed! If it helps, the image above was made with the following settings:

```
start ← point(0, 1, 0)
velocity ← normalize(vector(1, 1.8, 0)) * 11.25
p ← projectile(start, velocity)

gravity ← vector(0, -0.1, 0)
wind ← vector(-0.01, 0, 0)
e ← environment(gravity, wind)

c ← canvas(900, 550)
```

The projectile's velocity was normalized to a unit vector, and then multiplied by 11.25 to increase its magnitude. That, and the velocity vector, and the canvas size, were all determined empirically. Experiment with different starting vectors and speeds and see what happens!

Once you've played with that a bit, move on! We're going to switch back to math mode for the next couple of chapters to build out some more fundamentals that you'll need for your ray tracer.

## CHAPTER 3

Matrices

Hey, look. That shiny red sphere from before has company now. Its friends appear to be a cigar-looking matte blue ovoid, and a squashed green plastic thing that's tipped toward us, as if curious to see who's looking.

Would it surprise you to learn that these are all just spheres? They've been moved around, scaled, and rotated a bit too, but deep down, they're all still perfectly spherical. These transformations are all thanks to a little thing called a *matrix*.

A matrix is a grid of numbers that you can manipulate as a single unit. For example, here's a 2x2 matrix. It has two rows and two columns.

$$\begin{bmatrix} 3 & 1 \\ 2 & 7 \end{bmatrix}$$

And here's a 3x5 matrix, with three rows and five columns:

$$\begin{bmatrix} 9 & 1 & 2 & 0 & 3 \\ 0 & 0 & 2 & 3 & 1 \\ 8 & 7 & 5 & 4 & 6 \end{bmatrix}$$

For your ray tracer, you'll use primarily 4x4 matrices—those with exactly four rows and four columns, like this:

$$\begin{bmatrix} 1 & 2 & 0 & 0 \\ 0 & 1 & 4 & 1 \\ 0 & 1 & 1 & 3 \\ 0 & 0 & 0 & 1 \end{bmatrix}$$

In this chapter, you'll implement a 4x4 matrix data structure and a few general matrix operations. In the chapter after this one, Chapter 4, *Matrix Transformations*, on page 43, you'll build on those operations, adding functionality to make it easier to manipulate points and vectors (and, ultimately, shapes).

Ready? Let's do this!

Creating a Matrix

First things first. You need to be able to describe a new matrix. Write a test like the following, which shows that a matrix is composed of four rows of four floating point numbers each, for a total of sixteen numbers. It should also show how to refer to the elements of the matrix.

```
features/matrices.feature
Scenario: Constructing and inspecting a 4x4 matrix
  Given the following 4x4 matrix M:
    |  1   |  2   |  3   |  4   |
    |  5.5 |  6.5 |  7.5 |  8.5 |
    |  9   | 10   | 11   | 12   |
    | 13.5 | 14.5 | 15.5 | 16.5 |
  Then M[0,0] = 1
    And M[0,3] = 4
    And M[1,0] = 5.5
    And M[1,2] = 7.5
    And M[2,2] = 11
    And M[3,0] = 13.5
    And M[3,2] = 15.5
```

The first thing to notice is when talking about the individual elements of the matrix, we specify the element's *row* first, and then its *column*. For example, element M_{23} is the one at row 2, column 3. Also note in this book, row and column indices will be zero-based, so row 2 is actually the third row.

Later, in *Inverting Matrices*, on page 33, you'll need to be able to instantiate both 2x2 and 3x3 matrices in addition to 4x4 matrices, so take a moment to make sure you can create matrices of those sizes as well. Add the following tests to show that your code supports those dimensions:

features/matrices.feature
```
Scenario: A 2x2 matrix ought to be representable
  Given the following 2x2 matrix M:
    | -3 |  5 |
    |  1 | -2 |
  Then M[0,0] = -3
    And M[0,1] = 5
    And M[1,0] = 1
    And M[1,1] = -2

Scenario: A 3x3 matrix ought to be representable
  Given the following 3x3 matrix M:
    | -3 |  5 |  0 |
    |  1 | -2 | -7 |
    |  0 |  1 |  1 |
  Then M[0,0] = -3
    And M[1,1] = -2
    And M[2,2] = 1
```

 Keep your matrix implementation as simple as possible. Prefer native types wherever you can, and avoid complicated abstractions. Your matrices will be doing a lot of work!

Another critical part of your matrix implementation is *matrix comparison*. You'll be comparing matrices a lot, especially in this chapter and the next, so it's important to get it right. The following two tests are not exhaustive but ought to point you in the right direction. For example, you'll want to make sure that very similar numbers are handled correctly when comparing matrices, as described in *Comparing Floating Point Numbers,* on page 5.

features/matrices.feature
```
Scenario: Matrix equality with identical matrices
  Given the following matrix A:
      | 1 | 2 | 3 | 4 |
      | 5 | 6 | 7 | 8 |
      | 9 | 8 | 7 | 6 |
      | 5 | 4 | 3 | 2 |
    And the following matrix B:
      | 1 | 2 | 3 | 4 |
      | 5 | 6 | 7 | 8 |
      | 9 | 8 | 7 | 6 |
      | 5 | 4 | 3 | 2 |
  Then A = B

Scenario: Matrix equality with different matrices
  Given the following matrix A:
      | 1 | 2 | 3 | 4 |
      | 5 | 6 | 7 | 8 |
      | 9 | 8 | 7 | 6 |
      | 5 | 4 | 3 | 2 |
```

```
    And the following matrix B:
      | 2 | 3 | 4 | 5 |
      | 6 | 7 | 8 | 9 |
      | 8 | 7 | 6 | 5 |
      | 4 | 3 | 2 | 1 |
  Then A != B
```

Once you've got the basic matrix data structure working, linear algebra is your oyster. We're going to do some wild things with matrices, but we'll start small; let's talk about multiplying them together.

Multiplying Matrices

Multiplication is the tool you'll use to perform transformations like scaling, rotation, and translation. It's certainly possible to apply them one at a time, sequentially, but in practice you'll often want to apply several transformations at once. Multiplying them together is how you make that happen, as you'll see when you get to Chapter 4, *Matrix Transformations*, on page 43.

So let's talk about matrix multiplication. It takes two matrices and produces another matrix by multiplying their component elements together in a specific way. You'll see how that works shortly, but start first by writing a test that describes what you expect to happen when you multiply two 4x4 matrices together. Don't worry about 2x2 or 3x3 matrices here; your ray tracer won't need to multiply those at all.

```
features/matrices.feature
Scenario: Multiplying two matrices
  Given the following matrix A:
      | 1 | 2 | 3 | 4 |
      | 5 | 6 | 7 | 8 |
      | 9 | 8 | 7 | 6 |
      | 5 | 4 | 3 | 2 |
    And the following matrix B:
      | -2 | 1 | 2 |  3 |
      |  3 | 2 | 1 | -1 |
      |  4 | 3 | 6 |  5 |
      |  1 | 2 | 7 |  8 |
  Then A * B is the following 4x4 matrix:
      | 20|  22 |  50 |  48 |
      | 44|  54 | 114 | 108 |
      | 40|  58 | 110 | 102 |
      | 16|  26 |  46 |  42 |
```

Let's look at how this is done for a single element of a matrix, going step-by-step to find the product for element C_{10}, highlighted in the figure on page 29.

$$
A \qquad\qquad B \qquad\qquad C
$$

$$
\begin{bmatrix} 1 & 2 & 3 & 4 \\ 2 & 3 & 4 & 5 \\ 3 & 4 & 5 & 6 \\ 4 & 5 & 6 & 7 \end{bmatrix} \times \begin{bmatrix} 0 & 1 & 2 & 4 \\ 1 & 2 & 4 & 8 \\ 2 & 4 & 8 & 16 \\ 4 & 8 & 16 & 32 \end{bmatrix} = \begin{bmatrix} \ \end{bmatrix}
$$

Element C_{10} is in row 1, column 0, so you need to look at row 1 of the A matrix, and column 0 of the B matrix, as shown in the following figure.

$$
A \qquad\qquad B \qquad\qquad C
$$

$$
\begin{bmatrix} 1 & 2 & 3 & 4 \\ 2 & 3 & 4 & 5 \\ 3 & 4 & 5 & 6 \\ 4 & 5 & 6 & 7 \end{bmatrix} \times \begin{bmatrix} 0 & 1 & 2 & 4 \\ 1 & 2 & 4 & 8 \\ 2 & 4 & 8 & 16 \\ 4 & 8 & 16 & 32 \end{bmatrix} = \begin{bmatrix} \ \end{bmatrix}
$$

row 1   column 0   row 1, col 0

Then, you multiply corresponding pairs of elements together (A_{10} and B_{00}, A_{11} and B_{10}, A_{12} and B_{20}, and A_{13} and B_{30}), and add the products. The following figure shows how this comes together.

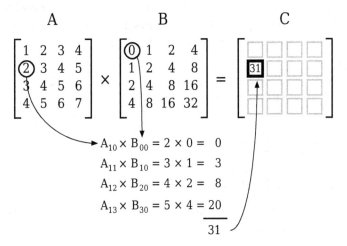

$$
A_{10} \times B_{00} = 2 \times 0 = 0
$$
$$
A_{11} \times B_{10} = 3 \times 1 = 3
$$
$$
A_{12} \times B_{20} = 4 \times 2 = 8
$$
$$
A_{13} \times B_{30} = 5 \times 4 = 20
$$
$$
\overline{31}
$$

The result, here, is 31, and to find the other elements, you perform this same process for each row-column combination of the two matrices.

Stated as an algorithm, the multiplication of two 4x4 matrices looks like this:

1. Let A and B be the matrices to be multiplied, and let M be the result.

2. For every row r in A, and every column c in B:

3. Let $M_{rc} = A_{r0} * B_{0c} + A_{r1} * B_{1c} + A_{r2} * B_{2c} + A_{r3} * B_{3c}$

As pseudocode, the algorithm might look like this:

```
function matrix_multiply(A, B)
  M ← matrix()

  for row ← 0 to 3
    for col ← 0 to 3
      M[row, col] ← A[row, 0] * B[0, col] +
                    A[row, 1] * B[1, col] +
                    A[row, 2] * B[2, col] +
                    A[row, 3] * B[3, col]
    end for
  end for

  return M
end function
```

If this all feels kind of familiar, it might be because you've already implemented something very similar—the dot product of two vectors on page 10. Yes, it's true. Matrix multiplication computes the dot product of every row-column combination in the two matrices! Pretty cool.

Now, we're not done yet. Matrices can actually be multiplied by *tuples*, in addition to other matrices. Multiplying a matrix by a tuple produces another tuple. Start with a test again, like the following, to express what you expect to happen when multiplying a matrix and a tuple.

features/matrices.feature
```
Scenario: A matrix multiplied by a tuple
  Given the following matrix A:
      | 1 | 2 | 3 | 4 |
      | 2 | 4 | 4 | 2 |
      | 8 | 6 | 4 | 1 |
      | 0 | 0 | 0 | 1 |
    And b ← tuple(1, 2, 3, 1)
  Then A * b = tuple(18, 24, 33, 1)
```

How does it work? The trick begins by treating the tuple as a really skinny (one column!) matrix, like this:

$$(1, 2, 3, 1) \Rightarrow \begin{bmatrix} 1 \\ 2 \\ 3 \\ 1 \end{bmatrix}$$

Four rows. One column.

It comes together just as it did when multiplying two 4x4 matrices together, but now you're only dealing with a single column in the second "matrix." The following figure illustrates this, highlighting the row and column used when computing the value of c_{10}.

$$
\begin{array}{ccc}
\text{A} & \text{b} & \text{c} \\
\begin{bmatrix} 1 & 2 & 3 & 4 \\ 2 & 4 & 4 & 2 \\ 8 & 6 & 4 & 1 \\ 0 & 0 & 0 & 1 \end{bmatrix} \times & \begin{bmatrix} 1 \\ 2 \\ 3 \\ 1 \end{bmatrix} = & \begin{bmatrix} \square \\ 24 \\ \square \\ \square \end{bmatrix} \\
\text{row 1} & \text{column 0} & \begin{array}{c} \text{row 1,} \\ \text{col 0} \end{array}
\end{array}
$$

To compute the value of c_{10}, you consider only row 1 of matrix A, and column 0 (the *only* column!) of tuple b. If you think of that row of the matrix as a tuple, then the answer is found by taking the dot product of that row and the other tuple:

$$2 \times 1 + 4 \times 2 + 4 \times 3 + 2 \times 1 = 24$$

The other elements of c are computed similarly. It really is the exact same algorithm used for multiplying two matrices, with the sole difference being the number of columns in the second "matrix."

 If you're feeling uncomfortable with how much magic there is in these algorithms, check out "An Intuitive Guide to Linear Algebra"[1] on BetterExplained.com. It does a good job of making sense of this stuff!

Pause here to make the tests pass that you've written so far. Once you have them working, carry on! We're going to look at a very special matrix, and we'll use multiplication to understand some of what makes it so special.

The Identity Matrix

You know that you can multiply any number by 1 and get the original number. The number 1 is called the *multiplicative identity* for that reason. Well, the *identity matrix* is like the number 1, but for matrices. If you multiply any matrix or tuple by the identity matrix, you get back the matrix or tuple you started with.

---

1. betterexplained.com/articles/linear-algebra-guide

This may sound utterly pointless right now, but consider this: if multiplying by the identity matrix just returns the original value, it means you can use it as the default transformation for any object in your scene. You don't need any special cases to tell the difference between a shape with a transformation and a shape without. This is, in fact, exactly what you'll use it for when you get to Chapter 5, *Ray-Sphere Intersections*, on page 57.

Add the following tests to illustrate the (non-)effect of multiplying by the identity matrix.

features/matrices.feature
```
Scenario: Multiplying a matrix by the identity matrix
  Given the following matrix A:
    | 0 | 1 |  2 |  4 |
    | 1 | 2 |  4 |  8 |
    | 2 | 4 |  8 | 16 |
    | 4 | 8 | 16 | 32 |
  Then A * identity_matrix = A

Scenario: Multiplying the identity matrix by a tuple
  Given a ← tuple(1, 2, 3, 4)
  Then identity_matrix * a = a
```

The identity matrix is all zeros, except for those elements along the diagonal, which are each set to 1:

$$identity = \begin{bmatrix} 1 & 0 & 0 & 0 \\ 0 & 1 & 0 & 0 \\ 0 & 0 & 1 & 0 \\ 0 & 0 & 0 & 1 \end{bmatrix}$$

Again, you only need to worry about the 4x4 identity matrix for your ray tracer. Next up, let's look at another matrix operation.

Transposing Matrices

Matrix transposition will come in handy when you get to Chapter 6, *Light and Shading*, on page 75. You'll use it when translating certain vectors (called *normal* vectors) between object space and world space. This may sound like science fiction, but is crucial to shading your objects correctly.

When you transpose a matrix, you turn its rows into columns and its columns into rows:

$$transpose \begin{bmatrix} 0 & 9 & 3 & 0 \\ 9 & 8 & 0 & 8 \\ 1 & 8 & 5 & 3 \\ 0 & 0 & 5 & 8 \end{bmatrix} = \begin{bmatrix} 0 & 9 & 1 & 0 \\ 9 & 8 & 8 & 0 \\ 3 & 0 & 5 & 5 \\ 0 & 8 & 3 & 8 \end{bmatrix}$$

Transposing a matrix turns the first row into the first column, the second row into the second column, and so forth. Here's a test that demonstrates this.

```
features/matrices.feature
Scenario: Transposing a matrix
  Given the following matrix A:
    | 0 | 9 | 3 | 0 |
    | 9 | 8 | 0 | 8 |
    | 1 | 8 | 5 | 3 |
    | 0 | 0 | 5 | 8 |
  Then transpose(A) is the following matrix:
    | 0 | 9 | 1 | 0 |
    | 9 | 8 | 8 | 0 |
    | 3 | 0 | 5 | 5 |
    | 0 | 8 | 3 | 8 |
```

And interestingly, the transpose of the identity matrix always gives you the identity matrix. Implement the following test to show that this is true.

```
features/matrices.feature
Scenario: Transposing the identity matrix
  Given A ← transpose(identity_matrix)
  Then A = identity_matrix
```

See? Good, clean fun. Make those tests pass, and then move on. It's time to talk about *matrix inversion*.

Inverting Matrices

If you multiply 5 by 4, you get 20. If you later decide to undo that operation, you can multiply 20 by the *inverse* of 4 (or $\frac{1}{4}$) and get 5 again.

That's pretty much the idea for matrices, too. If you multiply some matrix A by another matrix B, producing C, you can multiply C by the inverse of B to get A again. You'll use this approach a *lot*, starting in Chapter 5, *Ray-Sphere Intersections*, on page 57, because inverting matrices is the key to transforming and deforming shapes in a ray tracer.

Inverting matrices is a bit more complicated than inverting numbers, though. You'll employ a method known as *cofactor expansion*. If that sounds intimidating, take heart! We'll approach it nice and slow, one step at a time. Starting with routines to compute the determinant of a 2x2 matrix, we'll move incrementally through arcane-sounding things like submatrices, minors, and cofactors, and then come back to determinants again. Finally, we'll wrap up this chapter with the algorithm for matrix inversion itself.

Let's begin with the *determinant*.

Determining Determinants

The *determinant* is a number that is derived from the elements of a matrix. The name comes from the use of matrices to solve systems of equations, where it's used to *determine* whether or not the system has a solution. If the determinant is zero, then the corresponding system of equations has no solution.

You won't be using matrices to solve equations here, though. For you, the determinant is just one of the pieces that you'll use to compute the inverse of a matrix.

We'll start small, building the algorithm from the bottom up. Here's where those 2x2 matrices come in handy, because inverting larger matrices begins by finding the determinants of 2x2 matrices. Add the following test to your suite, to show that your code can do just that.

features/matrices.feature
```
Scenario: Calculating the determinant of a 2x2 matrix
  Given the following 2x2 matrix A:
    |  1 | 5 |
    | -3 | 2 |
  Then determinant(A) = 17
```

It works like this:

$$\text{determinant} \begin{bmatrix} a & b \\ c & d \end{bmatrix} = ad - bc$$

Isn't that lovely? That's all the magic you need to find the determinant of a 2x2 matrix! That right there is the seed for everything else involved in inverting matrices.

You need a few more tools before you can find the determinant of a larger matrix, though. Be patient! Make that new test pass, and then read on. The next concept you need to implement is that of *submatrices*, which will be used to help reduce larger matrices to sizes that you know how to work with.

Spotting Submatrices

A *submatrix* is what is left when you delete a single row and column from a matrix. Because you're always removing one row and one column, it effectively reduces the size of the matrix by one. The submatrix of a 4x4 matrix is 3x3, and the submatrix of a 3x3 matrix is 2x2. And guess what? You know how to find the determinant of 2x2 matrices! Submatrices are the very tools you'll use to divide and conquer those larger beasts.

Add the following two tests that show what you get when extracting a submatrix from a matrix. They introduce a new function, submatrix(matrix, row, column), which returns a copy of the given matrix with the given row and column removed.

```
features/matrices.feature
Scenario: A submatrix of a 3x3 matrix is a 2x2 matrix
  Given the following 3x3 matrix A:
    |  1 | 5 |  0 |
    | -3 | 2 |  7 |
    |  0 | 6 | -3 |
  Then submatrix(A, 0, 2) is the following 2x2 matrix:
    | -3 | 2 |
    |  0 | 6 |

Scenario: A submatrix of a 4x4 matrix is a 3x3 matrix
  Given the following 4x4 matrix A:
    | -6 |  1 |  1 | 6 |
    | -8 |  5 |  8 | 6 |
    | -1 |  0 |  8 | 2 |
    | -7 |  1 | -1 | 1 |
  Then submatrix(A, 2, 1) is the following 3x3 matrix:
    | -6 |  1 | 6 |
    | -8 |  8 | 6 |
    | -7 | -1 | 1 |
```

There's no magic there, and, really, no math. Didn't I tell you we were going to take this nice and slow? Go ahead and make those tests pass. Next up are *minors*.

Manipulating Minors

Okay, so you're now acquainted with *determinants* and *submatrices*. This is perfect, because now you have all the tools you need to compute the *minors* of a 3x3 matrix. (Not quite 4x4 yet, but you're getting closer!)

The *minor* of an element at row i and column j is the *determinant* of the *submatrix* at (i,j). Implement the following test, which introduces a new function, minor(matrix, row, column).

```
features/matrices.feature
Scenario: Calculating a minor of a 3x3 matrix
  Given the following 3x3 matrix A:
    | 3 |  5 |  0 |
    | 2 | -1 | -7 |
    | 6 | -1 |  5 |
    And B ← submatrix(A, 1, 0)
  Then determinant(B) = 25
    And minor(A, 1, 0) = 25
```

See that? You find the submatrix at the given location, and then compute the determinant of that submatrix. The answer is the minor. (You have to admit: "minor" is easier to say than "determinant of the submatrix.")

Make that test pass, and then we'll look at the last concept we need to start putting this matrix inversion puzzle together.

Computing Cofactors

Cofactors are the last tool you'll need to compute the determinants of larger matrices. They're minors that have (possibly) had their sign changed. Add the following test to demonstrate what's expected from the cofactor. It introduces a new function, cofactor(matrix, row, column).

features/matrices.feature
```
Scenario: Calculating a cofactor of a 3x3 matrix
  Given the following 3x3 matrix A:
      |  3 |  5 |  0 |
      |  2 | -1 | -7 |
      |  6 | -1 |  5 |
  Then minor(A, 0, 0) = -12
    And cofactor(A, 0, 0) = -12
    And minor(A, 1, 0) = 25
    And cofactor(A, 1, 0) = -25
```

So how's that work? Well, first you compute the minor at the given row and column. Then you consider that row and column to determine whether or not to negate the result. The following figure is helpful:

$$\begin{bmatrix} + & - & + \\ - & + & - \\ + & - & + \end{bmatrix}$$

If the row and column identifies a spot with a +, then the minor's sign doesn't change. If the row and column identifies a spot with a -, then you negate the minor.

Of course, you can do this without looking at a figure, too: if row + column is an odd number, then you negate the minor. Otherwise, you just return the minor as is. Make that test pass and then read on!

Determining Determinants of Larger Matrices

Now that you have those three ideas ready—determinants, minors, and cofactors—you can finally implement the determinant of 3x3 and 4x4 matrices. (In fact, the idea generalizes to arbitrarily large matrices, too, but for your purposes here, you don't need to go any higher than 4x4.)

First, set the stage by writing the following two tests, showing the determinant and some of the cofactors of a 3x3 and a 4x4 matrix. (Why the cofactors? Sit tight. All will be clear shortly!)

features/matrices.feature
```
Scenario: Calculating the determinant of a 3x3 matrix
  Given the following 3x3 matrix A:
    |  1 |  2 |  6 |
    | -5 |  8 | -4 |
    |  2 |  6 |  4 |
  Then cofactor(A, 0, 0) = 56
    And cofactor(A, 0, 1) = 12
    And cofactor(A, 0, 2) = -46
    And determinant(A) = -196

Scenario: Calculating the determinant of a 4x4 matrix
  Given the following 4x4 matrix A:
    | -2 | -8 |  3 |  5 |
    | -3 |  1 |  7 |  3 |
    |  1 |  2 | -9 |  6 |
    | -6 |  7 |  7 | -9 |
  Then cofactor(A, 0, 0) = 690
    And cofactor(A, 0, 1) = 447
    And cofactor(A, 0, 2) = 210
    And cofactor(A, 0, 3) = 51
    And determinant(A) = -4071
```

Those tests shouldn't be passing yet. Let's fix that.

Finding the determinant of matrices larger than 2x2 works recursively. Consider the 3x3 matrix from the previous tests.

$$\begin{bmatrix} 1 & 2 & 6 \\ -5 & 8 & -4 \\ 2 & 6 & 4 \end{bmatrix}$$

To find the determinant, look at any one of the rows or columns. It really doesn't matter which, so let's just choose the first row.

$$\begin{bmatrix} 1 & 2 & 6 \\ \cdot & \cdot & \cdot \\ \cdot & \cdot & \cdot \end{bmatrix}$$

Then, for each of those elements, you'll multiply the element by its cofactor, and add the products together.

$$1 \cdot 56 + 2 \cdot 12 + 6 \cdot -46 = -196$$

And that's the determinant! The magical thing is that it doesn't matter which row or column you choose. *It just works.*

And it works for 4x4 matrices, too. Here, consider the matrix from the test you wrote:

$$\begin{bmatrix} -2 & -8 & 3 & 5 \\ -3 & 1 & 7 & 3 \\ 1 & 2 & -9 & 6 \\ -6 & 7 & 7 & -9 \end{bmatrix}$$

Once again, you only need to look at a single row or column, so let's choose the first row.

$$\begin{bmatrix} -2 & -8 & 3 & 5 \\ \cdot & \cdot & \cdot & \cdot \\ \cdot & \cdot & \cdot & \cdot \\ \cdot & \cdot & \cdot & \cdot \end{bmatrix}$$

Then, multiply each element by its cofactor, and add the results.

$$-2 \cdot 690 + -8 \cdot 447 + 3 \cdot 210 + 5 \cdot 51 = -4071$$

Voilà! The determinant!

There's no denying that it's a lot to process, though. To give you a leg up, here's a bit of pseudocode for that algorithm:

```
function determinant(M)
  det ← 0

  if M.size = 2
    det ← M[0, 0] * M[1, 1] - M[0, 1] * M[1, 0]

  else
    for column ← 0 to M.size - 1
      det ← det + M[0, column] * cofactor(M, 0, column)
    end for
  end if

  return det
end function
```

Go ahead and make those tests pass. You're on the home stretch now. With a fully functional determinant, you're ready to tackle *inversion*.

Implementing Inversion

Okay, you're to the culmination of this whole process now. Here's where it all comes together! Remember, inversion is the operation that allows you to reverse the effect of multiplying by a matrix. It'll be crucial to the transformation of shapes in your ray tracer, allowing you to move shapes around, make them bigger or smaller, rotate them, and more. It's no overstatement to say that without inversion, there's no point in building anything else!

Now, one of the tricky things about matrix inversion is that not every matrix is invertible. Before you dive headlong into inverting matrices, you ought to first be able to identify whether such a task is even possible!

Add the following tests to show that your code can tell invertible matrices from noninvertible ones.

features/matrices.feature

```
Scenario: Testing an invertible matrix for invertibility
  Given the following 4x4 matrix A:
    |  6 |  4 |  4 |  4 |
    |  5 |  5 |  7 |  6 |
    |  4 | -9 |  3 | -7 |
    |  9 |  1 |  7 | -6 |
  Then determinant(A) = -2120
    And A is invertible

Scenario: Testing a noninvertible matrix for invertibility
  Given the following 4x4 matrix A:
    | -4 |  2 | -2 | -3 |
    |  9 |  6 |  2 |  6 |
    |  0 | -5 |  1 | -5 |
    |  0 |  0 |  0 |  0 |
  Then determinant(A) = 0
    And A is not invertible
```

And just as the tests suggest, the determinant is the key. If the determinant is ever 0, the matrix is not invertible. Anything else is okay.

Once that's working, add the following test. It exercises a new function called inverse(matrix), which produces the inverse of the given matrix.

features/matrices.feature

```
Scenario: Calculating the inverse of a matrix
  Given the following 4x4 matrix A:
      | -5 |  2 |  6 | -8 |
      |  1 | -5 |  1 |  8 |
      |  7 |  7 | -6 | -7 |
      |  1 | -3 |  7 |  4 |
    And B ← inverse(A)
  Then determinant(A) = 532
    And cofactor(A, 2, 3) = -160
    And B[3,2] = -160/532
    And cofactor(A, 3, 2) = 105
    And B[2,3] = 105/532
    And B is the following 4x4 matrix:
      |  0.21805 |  0.45113 |  0.24060 | -0.04511 |
      | -0.80827 | -1.45677 | -0.44361 |  0.52068 |
      | -0.07895 | -0.22368 | -0.05263 |  0.19737 |
      | -0.52256 | -0.81391 | -0.30075 |  0.30639 |
```

It's no accident that the test also calculates some cofactors and determinants—it all relates to the algorithm for inversion itself. That algorithm consists of several steps, starting with the construction of a *matrix of cofactors.* That is, you create a matrix that consists of the cofactors of each of the original elements:

$$\begin{bmatrix} -5 & 2 & 6 & -8 \\ 1 & -5 & 1 & 8 \\ 7 & 7 & -6 & -7 \\ 1 & -3 & 7 & 4 \end{bmatrix} \Rightarrow \begin{bmatrix} 116 & -430 & -42 & -278 \\ 240 & -775 & -119 & -433 \\ 128 & -236 & -28 & -160 \\ -24 & 277 & 105 & 163 \end{bmatrix}$$

Then, transpose that cofactor matrix:

$$\begin{bmatrix} 116 & -430 & -42 & -278 \\ 240 & -775 & -119 & -433 \\ 128 & -236 & -28 & -160 \\ -24 & 277 & 105 & 163 \end{bmatrix} \Rightarrow \begin{bmatrix} 116 & 240 & 128 & -24 \\ -430 & -775 & -236 & 277 \\ -42 & -119 & -28 & 105 \\ -278 & -433 & -160 & 163 \end{bmatrix}$$

Finally, divide each of the resulting elements by the determinant of the original matrix.

$$\begin{bmatrix} 116 & 240 & 128 & -24 \\ -430 & -775 & -236 & 277 \\ -42 & -119 & -28 & 105 \\ -278 & -433 & -160 & 163 \end{bmatrix} \div 532 \Rightarrow \begin{bmatrix} 0.21805 & 0.45113 & 0.24060 & -0.04511 \\ -0.80827 & -1.45677 & -0.44361 & 0.52068 \\ -0.07895 & -0.22368 & -0.05263 & 0.19737 \\ -0.52256 & -0.81391 & -0.30075 & 0.30639 \end{bmatrix}$$

Whew! And that's the inverse. What a ride!

While it's certainly possible to implement this by doing exactly what the preceding examples suggest (finding the matrix of cofactors, and then transposing it, and so forth) you can actually do it a bit more efficiently by combining the operations. Here's some pseudocode demonstrating what I mean:

```
function inverse(M)
  fail if M is not invertible

  M2 ← new matrix of same size as M

  for row ← 0 to M.size - 1
    for col ← 0 to M.size - 1
      c ← cofactor(M, row, col)

      # note that "col, row" here, instead of "row, col",
      # accomplishes the transpose operation!
      M2[col, row] ← c / determinant(M)
    end for
  end for

  return M2
end function
```

It's important that this all be correct. Any bugs in this code will cause you no end of headaches down the road. Add the following two tests to give a little more coverage for your matrix routines.

features/matrices.feature
```
Scenario: Calculating the inverse of another matrix
  Given the following 4x4 matrix A:
    |  8 | -5 |  9 |  2 |
    |  7 |  5 |  6 |  1 |
    | -6 |  0 |  9 |  6 |
    | -3 |  0 | -9 | -4 |
  Then inverse(A) is the following 4x4 matrix:
    | -0.15385 | -0.15385 | -0.28205 | -0.53846 |
    | -0.07692 |  0.12308 |  0.02564 |  0.03077 |
    |  0.35897 |  0.35897 |  0.43590 |  0.92308 |
    | -0.69231 | -0.69231 | -0.76923 | -1.92308 |

Scenario: Calculating the inverse of a third matrix
  Given the following 4x4 matrix A:
    |  9 |  3 |  0 |  9 |
    | -5 | -2 | -6 | -3 |
    | -4 |  9 |  6 |  4 |
    | -7 |  6 |  6 |  2 |
  Then inverse(A) is the following 4x4 matrix:
    | -0.04074 | -0.07778 |  0.14444 | -0.22222 |
    | -0.07778 |  0.03333 |  0.36667 | -0.33333 |
    | -0.02901 | -0.14630 | -0.10926 |  0.12963 |
    |  0.17778 |  0.06667 | -0.26667 |  0.33333 |
```

One last thing to note about the inverse: at the beginning of this section, you read that "if you multiply some matrix A by another matrix B, producing C, you can multiply C by the inverse of B to get A again." Well, we can't let such a statement slide by unproven! Add one more test to show that the inverse does, in truth, behave as described.

features/matrices.feature
```
Scenario: Multiplying a product by its inverse
  Given the following 4x4 matrix A:
    |  3 | -9 |  7 |  3 |
    |  3 | -8 |  2 | -9 |
    | -4 |  4 |  4 |  1 |
    | -6 |  5 | -1 |  1 |
  And the following 4x4 matrix B:
    |  8 |  2 |  2 |  2 |
    |  3 | -1 |  7 |  0 |
    |  7 |  0 |  5 |  4 |
    |  6 | -2 |  0 |  5 |
  And C ← A * B
  Then C * inverse(B) = A
```

Make sure all of your tests are passing now. Once everything's green, take a deep breath and give yourself a solid pat on the back. You just implemented one of the pillars of linear algebra—with tests, even!

Putting It Together

You now have 4x4 matrices with support for multiplication, transposition, and inversion. Not bad!

Sadly, there's not a lot related to ray tracing that you can do with those routines just yet, but you'll take care of *that* little problem in the next chapter, Chapter 4, *Matrix Transformations*, on page 43. However, there's always room for a bit of experimentation. Before moving on, take a few minutes to explore a little more.

1. What happens when you invert the identity matrix?

2. What do you get when you multiply a matrix by its inverse?

3. Is there any difference between the *inverse* of the *transpose* of a matrix, and the *transpose* of the *inverse*?

4. Remember how multiplying the identity matrix by a tuple gives you the tuple, unchanged? Now, try changing any single element of the identity matrix to a different number, and then multiplying it by a tuple. What happens to the tuple?

When you're ready, turn the page! In the next chapter you'll use your matrices to implement *transformations*, entities that will help you position and orient the objects in your scenes.

## CHAPTER 4

Matrix Transformations

Awesomesauce! You're about to take the foundation of matrix operations you implemented in the previous chapter and start doing some practical things, like *transformations*, which your ray tracer will (eventually) use to move and deform objects. Consider the following scene.

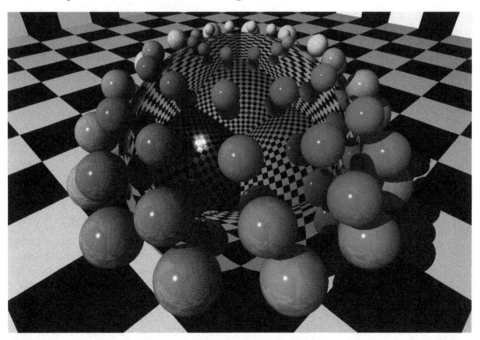

Your ray tracer won't be able to render those reflections until Chapter 11, *Reflection and Refraction*, on page 141, but the scene itself is not really too complicated—a few colored spheres, some checkered planes. The relevant bit here, though, is how each of those spheres is sized and positioned. Without transformations, you'd have to explicitly describe each sphere's radius and location, which would be tedious (in a decidedly trigonometric sense) to get correct. Perhaps surprisingly, this would also increase the complexity of your ray tracer, as you'll see in Chapter 5, *Ray-Sphere Intersections*, on page 57.

With transformations, though, you add each of those smaller spheres to the scene at the origin, and then apply a series of transformations to them: scaling, translation, and a couple of rotations. No hairy math or tedious computations involved!

Best of all, these transformations use the matrix operations you just polished off. We'll take a look at how to construct a matrix to represent each of these transformations, as well as how to chain several of them together as a single matrix.

Ready? Let's start with translation.

Translation

Translation is a transformation that moves a point, like so.

It changes the coordinates of the point by adding to or subtracting from them. For example, if the point had an x coordinate of 3, and you moved it 4 units in x, it would wind up with an x coordinate of 7.

 Joe asks:
Can't we just use vectors to translate points?

Well, yes, as a matter of fact, we can. You saw in *Tuples, Points, and Vectors* how to add a vector to a point and thus translate the point in the direction of the vector. This works well.

The problem with it is that it can only do translation—we can't use the same operation (that is, adding a vector) and get rotation, or scaling, or shearing. What we want is a single operation that can produce any of these transformations and concatenate them in arbitrary order.

Matrix multiplication happens to be just such a tool.

The workhorse here will be a new translation(x,y,z) function which should return a 4x4 translation matrix. Implement the following test to show it in action. Don't worry about making these next few tests pass yet, though; I'll show you the secret sauce shortly.

features/transformations.feature
```
Scenario: Multiplying by a translation matrix
  Given transform ← translation(5, -3, 2)
    And p ← point(-3, 4, 5)
  Then transform * p = point(2, 1, 7)
```

Further, if you take the inverse of a translation matrix, you get another translation matrix that moves points in reverse. Add the following test to your suite to demonstrate this.

features/transformations.feature
```
Scenario: Multiplying by the inverse of a translation matrix
  Given transform ← translation(5, -3, 2)
    And inv ← inverse(transform)
    And p ← point(-3, 4, 5)
  Then inv * p = point(-8, 7, 3)
```

Now let's throw a wrench into things: multiplying a translation matrix by a *vector* should not change the vector! Remember, a vector is just an arrow. Moving it around in space does not change the direction it points. Add the following test to show that vectors are not changed by translation:

features/transformations.feature
```
Scenario: Translation does not affect vectors
  Given transform ← translation(5, -3, 2)
    And v ← vector(-3, 4, 5)
  Then transform * v = v
```

You might wonder how you're going to pull that off. A matrix that affects points but not vectors? Can it really be so?

Gather round!

In *Tuples, Points, and Vectors*, you read that the difference between a point and a vector was just that a vector had a 0 in its w component. This is where that feature pays dividends. It turns out that the way a translation matrix is constructed makes it so that a 0 in the w component of a tuple will cause the translation to be ignored.

Let's look at this mysterious (spoiler: not really mysterious) translation matrix and see just how it is structured. Start with an identity matrix t, and then add the desired x, y, and z values to (respectively) the t_{03}, t_{13}, and t_{23} elements, as shown in the following figure.

$$\text{translation}(x, y, z) = \begin{bmatrix} 1 & 0 & 0 & x \\ 0 & 1 & 0 & y \\ 0 & 0 & 1 & z \\ 0 & 0 & 0 & 1 \end{bmatrix}$$

You will find that, when multiplied by a vector, the 0 in w causes those translation values to disappear, like magic. With a point, though, the 1 in w has the desired effect, and causes the point to move.

Slick!

So that's translation. Make those tests pass, and we'll look at *scaling* next.

Scaling

Where translation moves a point by adding to it, *scaling* moves it by multiplication. When applied to an object centered at the origin, this transformation scales all points on the object, effectively making it larger (if the scale value is greater than 1) or smaller (if the scale value is less than 1), as shown in the figure.

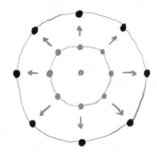

You'll need a new function, called scaling(x,y,z), that returns a 4x4 translation matrix. Add the following test to demonstrate how it's used to scale a point.

features/transformations.feature
```
Scenario: A scaling matrix applied to a point
  Given transform ← scaling(2, 3, 4)
    And p ← point(-4, 6, 8)
  Then transform * p = point(-8, 18, 32)
```

Now, unlike translation, scaling applies to vectors as well, changing their length. Add the following test to show how vectors are affected by scaling.

features/transformations.feature
```
Scenario: A scaling matrix applied to a vector
  Given transform ← scaling(2, 3, 4)
    And v ← vector(-4, 6, 8)
  Then transform * v = vector(-8, 18, 32)
```

And as you might expect, multiplying a tuple by the inverse of a scaling matrix will scale the tuple in the opposite way (shrinking instead of growing, or vice versa). Add the following test to show that this is so.

features/transformations.feature
```
Scenario: Multiplying by the inverse of a scaling matrix
  Given transform ← scaling(2, 3, 4)
    And inv ← inverse(transform)
    And v ← vector(-4, 6, 8)
  Then inv * v = vector(-2, 2, 2)
```

To construct a scaling matrix, take an identity matrix t and change the values at t_{00}, t_{11}, and t_{22} to be (respectively) the x, y, and z scaling values.

$$\text{scaling}(\boldsymbol{x}, \boldsymbol{y}, \boldsymbol{z}) = \begin{bmatrix} \boldsymbol{x} & 0 & 0 & 0 \\ 0 & \boldsymbol{y} & 0 & 0 \\ 0 & 0 & \boldsymbol{z} & 0 \\ 0 & 0 & 0 & 1 \end{bmatrix}$$

While we're on the subject of scaling, let's take a moment and discuss its near cousin: *reflection*. Reflection is a transformation that takes a point and *reflects* it—moving it to the other side of an axis. It can be useful when you have an object in your scene that you want to flip (or mirror) in some direction. Maybe the model is leaning the wrong way, facing the wrong direction. Maybe it's a face that's looking to the right when you want it looking to the left. Rather than breaking out a 3D modeler and editing the model, you can simply reflect the model across the appropriate axis.

Reflection is essentially the same thing as scaling by a negative value. Implement the following test, which shows how a point can be reflected across the x axis by scaling the x component by -1.

features/transformations.feature
```
Scenario: Reflection is scaling by a negative value
  Given transform ← scaling(-1, 1, 1)
    And p ← point(2, 3, 4)
  Then transform * p = point(-2, 3, 4)
```

Just like that, the point was moved from the positive side of the x axis, to the negative.

Make your tests pass, and then let's move on to rotation.

Rotation

Multiplying a tuple by a *rotation* matrix will rotate that tuple around an axis. This can get complicated if you're trying to rotate around an arbitrary line, so we're not going to take that route. We're only going to deal with the simplest rotations here—rotating around the x, y, and z axes.

Trigonometric Functions

 Rotation matrices depend on the *sine* and *cosine* functions from trigonometry. Don't worry about dredging your high school math memories, though. Check your implementation language for a Math namespace, where you will usually find the functions named sin and cos.

The rotation will appear to be clockwise around the corresponding axis when viewed along that axis, toward the negative end. So, if you're rotating around the x axis, it will rotate as depicted in the following figure.

Another way to describe this is to say that rotations in your ray tracer will obey the *left-hand rule*, which harks back to *Left-Handed vs. Right-Handed Coordinates*, on page 3: if you point the thumb of your left hand in the direction of the axis of rotation, then the rotation itself will follow the direction of your remaining fingers as you curl them toward the palm of your hand.

Each of the three axes requires a different matrix to implement the rotation, so we'll look at them each in turn. Angles will be given in radians, so if your math library prefers other units (like degrees), you'll need to adapt accordingly.

> **Joe asks:**
> ## What are radians?
>
> A full circle (360 degrees) consists of 2π radians, which means a half circle (180 degrees) is π radians, and a quarter circle (90 degrees) is $\frac{\pi}{2}$ radians. If you're not used to thinking in terms of radians, it may be helpful to write a function to convert them from degrees. The formula looks like this:
>
> $$\mathrm{radians}(deg) = \frac{deg}{180}\pi$$

Rotation Around the X Axis

This first rotation matrix rotates a tuple some number of radians around the x axis, and will be created by introducing a new rotation_x(radians) function. Prove it works by adding the following test, which shows off rotating a point around the x axis.

features/transformations.feature
```
Scenario: Rotating a point around the x axis
  Given p ← point(0, 1, 0)
    And half_quarter ← rotation_x(π / 4)
    And full_quarter ← rotation_x(π / 2)
  Then half_quarter * p = point(0, √2/2, √2/2)
    And full_quarter * p = point(0, 0, 1)
```

Visually, the test performs the following two rotations:

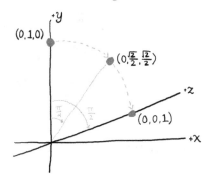

Next, add another test showing that the inverse of this rotation matrix simply rotates in the opposite direction.

features/transformations.feature

```
Scenario: The inverse of an x-rotation rotates in the opposite direction
  Given p ← point(0, 1, 0)
    And half_quarter ← rotation_x(π / 4)
    And inv ← inverse(half_quarter)
  Then inv * p = point(0, √2/2, -√2/2)
```

The transformation matrix for rotating r radians around the x axis is constructed like this:

$$\text{rotation}_x(r) = \begin{bmatrix} 1 & 0 & 0 & 0 \\ 0 & \cos r & -\sin r & 0 \\ 0 & \sin r & \cos r & 0 \\ 0 & 0 & 0 & 1 \end{bmatrix}$$

Very nice. Now, on to the next axis.

Rotation Around the Y Axis

The y axis rotation works just like the x axis rotation, only changing the axis. Add the following test to demonstrate the difference.

features/transformations.feature

```
Scenario: Rotating a point around the y axis
  Given p ← point(0, 0, 1)
    And half_quarter ← rotation_y(π / 4)
    And full_quarter ← rotation_y(π / 2)
  Then half_quarter * p = point(√2/2, 0, √2/2)
    And full_quarter * p = point(1, 0, 0)
```

Again, visually, that rotation looks like this:

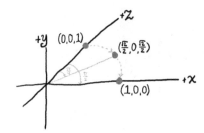

The transformation matrix for rotating r radians around the y axis is constructed like this:

$$\text{rotation}_y(r) = \begin{bmatrix} \cos r & 0 & \sin r & 0 \\ 0 & 1 & 0 & 0 \\ -\sin r & 0 & \cos r & 0 \\ 0 & 0 & 0 & 1 \end{bmatrix}$$

Just so. One more axis to go!

Rotation Around the Z Axis

And last, but not least: the z axis rotation. Show that it works just like the other rotations, by implementing the following test.

features/transformations.feature
```
Scenario: Rotating a point around the z axis
  Given p ← point(0, 1, 0)
    And half_quarter ← rotation_z(π / 4)
    And full_quarter ← rotation_z(π / 2)
  Then half_quarter * p = point(-√2/2, √2/2, 0)
    And full_quarter * p = point(-1, 0, 0)
```

And here's the corresponding visualization:

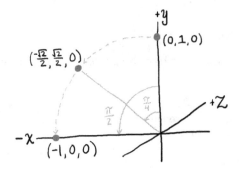

This rotation may seem backward, but break out the left-hand rule and check it out. Point your left thumb along the positive z axis, and then curl your fingers. They curl toward the negative x axis, just as illustrated!

Finally, the transformation matrix itself is this:

$$\text{rotation}_z(r) = \begin{bmatrix} \cos r & -\sin r & 0 & 0 \\ \sin r & \cos r & 0 & 0 \\ 0 & 0 & 1 & 0 \\ 0 & 0 & 0 & 1 \end{bmatrix}$$

That takes care of rotating a point or vector around any of our three primary axes. Make those tests pass, and then move on. We're going to look at one more transformation.

Shearing

A *shearing* (or *skew*) transformation has the effect of making straight lines slanted. It's probably the most (visually) complex transformation that we'll implement, though the implementation is no more complicated than any of the others.

When applied to a tuple, a shearing transformation changes each component of the tuple in proportion to the other two components. So the x component changes in proportion to y and z, y changes in proportion to x and z, and z changes in proportion to x and y.

The following illustration shows how this works in two dimensions. Specifically, note how differently the same transformation affects each point in x as the y component changes.

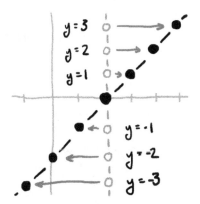

This is what "changing in proportion" means: the farther the y coordinate is from zero, the more the x value changes.

In three dimensions each component may be affected by either of the other two components, so there are a total of six parameters that may be used to define the shear transformation:

- x in proportion to y
- x in proportion to z
- y in proportion to x
- y in proportion to z
- z in proportion to x
- z in proportion to y

Write the following tests, demonstrating how a point is affected by each of these parameters. In each, notice how the coordinate being moved moves by the amount of the other coordinate. For instance, in this first test x is initially 2, but moving x in proportion to y adds 1 times y (or 3) to x (2) and produces a new x of 5.

features/transformations.feature
```
Scenario: A shearing transformation moves x in proportion to y
  Given transform ← shearing(1, 0, 0, 0, 0, 0)
    And p ← point(2, 3, 4)
  Then transform * p = point(5, 3, 4)
```

The remaining tests work similarly, adding the two components together to get the new component value.

features/transformations.feature
```
Scenario: A shearing transformation moves x in proportion to z
  Given transform ← shearing(0, 1, 0, 0, 0, 0)
    And p ← point(2, 3, 4)
  Then transform * p = point(6, 3, 4)

Scenario: A shearing transformation moves y in proportion to x
  Given transform ← shearing(0, 0, 1, 0, 0, 0)
    And p ← point(2, 3, 4)
  Then transform * p = point(2, 5, 4)

Scenario: A shearing transformation moves y in proportion to z
  Given transform ← shearing(0, 0, 0, 1, 0, 0)
    And p ← point(2, 3, 4)
  Then transform * p = point(2, 7, 4)

Scenario: A shearing transformation moves z in proportion to x
  Given transform ← shearing(0, 0, 0, 0, 1, 0)
    And p ← point(2, 3, 4)
  Then transform * p = point(2, 3, 6)
```

```
Scenario: A shearing transformation moves z in proportion to y
  Given transform ← shearing(0, 0, 0, 0, 0, 1)
    And p ← point(2, 3, 4)
  Then transform * p = point(2, 3, 7)
```

The transformation matrix for a shear transformation is given in the following figure, where (for instance) x_y means "x moved in proportion to y," and represents the amount by which to multiply y before adding it to x.

$$\text{shearing}(x_y, x_z, y_x, y_z, z_x, z_y) = \begin{bmatrix} 1 & x_y & x_z & 0 \\ y_x & 1 & y_z & 0 \\ z_x & z_y & 1 & 0 \\ 0 & 0 & 0 & 1 \end{bmatrix}$$

That's the last of the transformation matrices that we'll cover here. Take some time now to make sure your tests are all passing before moving on. Once you're ready, let's talk about how you can combine these matrices to create more complex transformations.

Chaining Transformations

As you've seen, you can create transformation matrices to translate, scale, rotate, and skew. But what if you want to do more than one at a time?

It's a completely reasonable expectation. Let's say that you are (eventually) going to render a teapot. The model you're rendering is at the origin and is small relative to the rest of the scene. The model is also tipped on its side. You'd like to rotate it so it's right-side up, scale it to a reasonable size, and then translate it so it's sitting on a table, instead of the floor.

You could apply each transformation in sequence, like this:

```
# rotate the teapot to be right-side up
A ← rotation_x(π / 2)
teapot ← A * teapot

# next, make the teapot 5x larger
B ← scaling(5, 5, 5)
teapot ← B * teapot

# finally, move the teapot onto a table
C ← translation(10, 5, 7)
teapot ← C * teapot
```

But that's just the same as this:

```
A ← rotation_x(π / 2)
B ← scaling(5, 5, 5)
C ← translation(10, 5, 7)

teapot ← C * (B * (A * teapot))
```

Or, since matrix multiplication is associative:

```
teapot ← (C * B * A) * teapot
```

Note that the order of the multiplications is important! Matrix multiplication is associative, but *not* commutative. When it comes to matrices, A × B is not guaranteed to be the same as B × A.

So, if you want a single matrix that rotates, and then scales, and then translates, you can multiply the translation matrix by the scaling matrix, and then by the rotation matrix. That is to say, you must concatenate the transformations in *reverse order* to have them applied in the order you want! Add the following tests to demonstrate this (particularly counterintuitive) result.

features/transformations.feature
```
Scenario: Individual transformations are applied in sequence
  Given p ← point(1, 0, 1)
    And A ← rotation_x(π / 2)
    And B ← scaling(5, 5, 5)
    And C ← translation(10, 5, 7)
  # apply rotation first
  When p2 ← A * p
  Then p2 = point(1, -1, 0)
  # then apply scaling
  When p3 ← B * p2
  Then p3 = point(5, -5, 0)
  # then apply translation
  When p4 ← C * p3
  Then p4 = point(15, 0, 7)

Scenario: Chained transformations must be applied in reverse order
  Given p ← point(1, 0, 1)
    And A ← rotation_x(π / 2)
    And B ← scaling(5, 5, 5)
    And C ← translation(10, 5, 7)
  When T ← C * B * A
  Then T * p = point(15, 0, 7)
```

Awesome! You now have vectors and points, and matrix transformations. This is a fantastic foundation for the rest of your ray tracer! Let's find something to do with those pieces before moving on.

Putting It Together

Here's a program for you to write. Picture an analog clock. There are (typically) twelve positions around the edge, representing the hours. Got it? Okay. Your

Fluent APIs

Depending on your implementation language, you may be able to present a more intuitive interface for concatenating transformation matrices. A *fluent API*, for instance, could let you declare your transformations in a natural order like this:

```
transform ← identity().
            rotate_x(π / 2).
            scale(5, 5, 5).
            translate(10, 5, 7)
```

The call to identity() returns the identity matrix, and rotate_x(π/2) is then invoked on it. This multiplies the corresponding rotation matrix by the caller, "rotation" times "identity," effectively flipping the order of operations around. Each subsequent call in this chain multiplies its matrix by the result of the previous call, eventually turning the whole chain "inside out."

challenge is to write a program that uses a rotation matrix to compute the positions of those hours on the clock face, and draw a pixel onto a canvas for each of them. The result ought to look something like this:

Here are four hints to get you started. (Feel free to stop reading now if you want to see if you can make it work with no hints at all!)

Hint #1

First, assume the clock is centered at the origin, point(0,0,0). Let the origin be in the middle of your canvas.

Hint #2

Next, choose an axis to orient the clock. If, for example, it's oriented along the y axis and you're looking at it face-on, then you're looking toward the negative end of the y axis. The following figure shows this orientation.

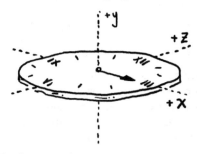

This means twelve o'clock is on the +z axis at point(0,0,1), and three o'clock is on the +x axis at point(1,0,0).

Hint #3

Now, rotate the twelve o'clock point around the y axis to find the other hour positions. There are 2π radians in a circle, so each hour is rotated $^{2\pi}/_{12}$ (or $^{\pi}/_{6}$) radians. In pseudocode, then, it would look something like this:

```
# compute y-axis rotation for hour #3
r ← rotation_y(3 * π/6)

# given: position of twelve o'clock
twelve ← point(0,0,1)

# compute position of three o'clock by rotating twelve o'clock
three ← r * twelve
```

In this case, you should find that three o'clock is at point(1,0,0).

Hint #4

Decide how large the clock is to be drawn on your canvas. For example, if your canvas is square, you might let the clock's radius be $^{3}/_{8}$ the canvas's width.

For each point that you compute, multiply the x and z components by this radius, and then move them to the center of your canvas by adding the coordinates of the center point. Let x be the x coordinate of the pixel, and z be the y coordinate.

Don't forget to save your canvas as a PPM file when you're done!

Once you've got that nailed down, move on. It's time to start intersecting rays and spheres!

## CHAPTER 5

Ray-Sphere Intersections

Awesome news! You're all done with the foundational work, and now you get to start on the meat of an actual ray tracer. From here on out, each chapter will culminate in something concrete, something *visual*, which will add to your growing store of eye candy.

For this chapter, that visual bit won't be particularly impressive. It'll just be a humble filled circle drawn to your canvas, like this:

Primitive? Undoubtedly! But you'll draw it by exercising the most basic muscle in the body of a ray tracer: ray casting.

Ray casting is the process of creating a *ray*, or line, and finding the intersections of that ray with the objects in a scene. We'll cover all of that in this chapter, using material from the previous chapters as we go.

Let's do this!

Creating Rays

Each ray created by your ray tracer will have a starting point called the *origin*, and a vector called the *direction* which says where it points. Write the following test, showing how you create a ray and what its primary attributes should be:

```
features/rays.feature
Scenario: Creating and querying a ray
  Given origin ← point(1, 2, 3)
    And direction ← vector(4, 5, 6)
  When r ← ray(origin, direction)
  Then r.origin = origin
    And r.direction = direction
```

Armed with a ray's origin and direction, you can find points that lie any distance t along the ray. Why t? Blame the mathematicians! It stands for *time*, which only makes sense once you think of the ray's *direction vector* as its *speed*. For example, if the ray moves one unit every second, then the following figure from *Scalar Multiplication and Division*, on page 7, shows how far the ray travels in 3.5 seconds.

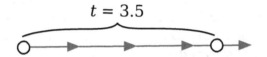

Perform the following test, which introduces a new function called position(ray, t). This function should compute the point at the given distance t along the ray.

```
features/rays.feature
Scenario: Computing a point from a distance
  Given r ← ray(point(2, 3, 4), vector(1, 0, 0))
  Then position(r, 0) = point(2, 3, 4)
    And position(r, 1) = point(3, 3, 4)
    And position(r, -1) = point(1, 3, 4)
    And position(r, 2.5) = point(4.5, 3, 4)
```

To find the position, you multiply the ray's direction by t to find the total distance traveled, and then add that to the ray's origin. In pseudocode, it looks like this:

```
function position(ray, t)
  return ray.origin + ray.direction * t
end function
```

You'll make good use of this in Chapter 6, *Light and Shading*, on page 75, when you start turning intersections into actual surface information. It's part of the process of computing realistic shading for your scenes.

Make sure your tests are passing before moving on. In the next section we'll look at intersecting those rays with spheres.

Intersecting Rays with Spheres

We're going to make your life as simple as possible by assuming every sphere's origin (its center point) is situated at the world origin (that's point(0, 0, 0)). We'll also assume that these are all *unit spheres*, with radii of 1.

If you were to cast a ray through the center of one of these spheres, you would see the ray intersect in two places, like this:

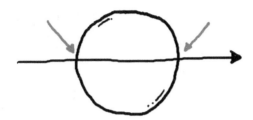

More specifically, if the ray originates at (0, 0, -5), and passes directly through the origin, it should intersect the sphere at (0, 0, -1) and (0, 0, 1), 4 and 6 units (respectively) away from the ray's origin, like the following figure shows.

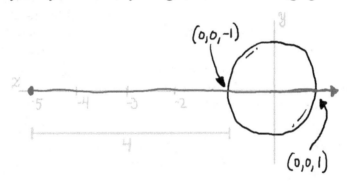

Add the following test to demonstrate this. It introduces two new functions: sphere(), which returns a new sphere object, and intersect(sphere, ray), which returns the collection of t values where the ray intersects the sphere.

```
features/spheres.feature
Scenario: A ray intersects a sphere at two points
  Given r ← ray(point(0, 0, -5), vector(0, 0, 1))
    And s ← sphere()
  When xs ← intersect(s, r)
  Then xs.count = 2
    And xs[0] = 4.0
    And xs[1] = 6.0
```

The sphere() function should return a unique value each time it is invoked. Depending on your programming language, you might need to pass something unique (an integer, or a string) to the function as the new sphere's id. You'll add some attributes to the sphere later in this chapter (when you start incorporating matrix transformations), but for now it has no associated data. Just make sure that no two invocations of sphere() return the same value.

Now, if you move your ray's starting point 1 unit in the positive y direction, the ray will be *tangent* to the sphere. It will intersect at one point, just glancing off the edge, like this:

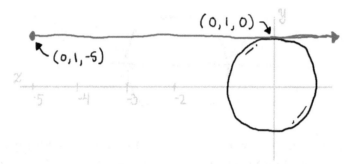

Implement the following test, which corresponds to this scenario. It should instantiate a ray 1 unit farther in the y direction, and intersect it with the same unit sphere. Even though it truly intersects at only a single point, for simplicity's sake you'll have your code return *two* intersections, with the same point at each. (This will help later when determining object overlaps, in Chapter 16, *Constructive Solid Geometry (CSG)*, on page 227.) Assert that both intersections are at the same point.

```
features/spheres.feature
Scenario: A ray intersects a sphere at a tangent
  Given r ← ray(point(0, 1, -5), vector(0, 0, 1))
    And s ← sphere()
  When xs ← intersect(s, r)
  Then xs.count = 2
    And xs[0] = 5.0
    And xs[1] = 5.0
```

Now move your ray's starting point just a bit more along the positive y direction. The ray should miss the sphere entirely, passing above the sphere and not intersecting it at all. Write the following test to show that this is true.

```
features/spheres.feature
Scenario: A ray misses a sphere
  Given r ← ray(point(0, 2, -5), vector(0, 0, 1))
    And s ← sphere()
  When xs ← intersect(s, r)
  Then xs.count = 0
```

Before making these tests pass, there are a few edge cases to consider. For example, what happens if your ray originates inside the sphere? Well, there should be one intersection in front of the ray, and another behind it, as the following figure illustrates.

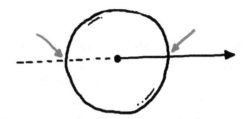

Yes, the ray actually extends *behind* the starting point, but let's not get distracted by definitions! Go ahead and write the following test, showing that when the ray starts at the center of a sphere, the first intersection is behind the ray's origin, and the second is in front of it.

```
features/spheres.feature
Scenario: A ray originates inside a sphere
  Given r ← ray(point(0, 0, 0), vector(0, 0, 1))
    And s ← sphere()
  When xs ← intersect(s, r)
  Then xs.count = 2
    And xs[0] = -1.0
    And xs[1] = 1.0
```

Lastly, if the sphere is completely behind the ray, you should still see two intersections—both with a negative t value. The following figure shows what this looks like.

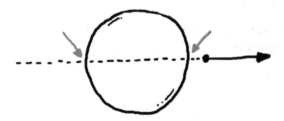

The following test shows that this is so, with both intersections occurring behind the ray's origin.

```
features/spheres.feature
Scenario: A sphere is behind a ray
  Given r ← ray(point(0, 0, 5), vector(0, 0, 1))
    And s ← sphere()
  When xs ← intersect(s, r)
  Then xs.count = 2
    And xs[0] = -6.0
    And xs[1] = -4.0
```

Let's take a look now at what needs to happen to make these tests pass. To compute the intersection of a ray and a sphere you'll need those routines you've implemented up to this point, including tuple arithmetic, the dot product, and even (later in this chapter) matrix inversion and transformations. It's a good thing you've already got those working, isn't it?

The math behind intersecting a ray and a sphere is really quite elegant, but for the sake of brevity we'll skip the derivations and jump straight to the implementation. If you really want to dig into the math, you'll find plenty of resources online. Check out the "Line-sphere intersection" article on Wikipedia,[1] the "Ray-Sphere Intersection" tutorial at Lighthouse3d,[2] or the "Ray-Sphere Intersection" post from Scratchapixel's series on "A Minimal Ray-Tracer."[3]

Begin the algorithm by computing the *discriminant*—a number that tells you whether the ray intersects the sphere at all. In pseudocode, the calculations look like this:

```
# the vector from the sphere's center, to the ray origin
# remember: the sphere is centered at the world origin
sphere_to_ray ← ray.origin - point(0, 0, 0)

a ← dot(ray.direction, ray.direction)
b ← 2 * dot(ray.direction, sphere_to_ray)
c ← dot(sphere_to_ray, sphere_to_ray) - 1

discriminant ← b² - 4 * a * c
```

That discriminant value is the key. If it's negative, then the ray misses and no intersections occur between the sphere and the ray.

```
if discriminant < 0 then
  return ()
end if
```

---

1. en.wikipedia.org/wiki/Line-sphere_intersection
2. www.lighthouse3d.com/tutorials/maths/ray-sphere-intersection
3. www.scratchapixel.com/lessons/3d-basic-rendering/minimal-ray-tracer-rendering-simple-shapes/ray-sphere-intersection

Otherwise, you'll see either one (for rays that hit the sphere at a perfect tangent) or two intersections, but your function should always return two in either case. For the tangent case, both intersections will have the same t value, as mentioned earlier. Also, make sure the intersections are returned in increasing order, to make it easier to determine which intersections are significant, later.

```
t1 ← (-b - √(discriminant)) / (2 * a)
t2 ← (-b + √(discriminant)) / (2 * a)

return (t1, t2)
```

At this point, your tests should all be passing. Yay! Pat yourself on the back, and exult in the fact you've implemented the heart of an actual ray tracer!

This is only part of the solution, though. Your ray tracer will eventually need to know more than the t values at each intersection. Let's look at how to keep track of that additional information next.

Tracking Intersections

Currently, your intersect function returns a set of t values, but imagine for a moment a beautifully complex scene, full of spheres, cubes, cylinders, cones and dozens of creative combinations. You cast your ray into that scene and get back a double handful of intersections. You now know where the intersections occurred (thanks to the t values), but you have no idea how to draw them. What object was intersected at that point? What color is it? What are its material properties? Should there be a reflection or not? You just don't know.

With the addition of one more property, you'll have the foundation of what you need to answer those questions. You're going to create a new data structure, called an *intersection*, which will (for now) aggregate two things:

1. The t value of the intersection, and

2. The object that was intersected.

You'll add additional properties in later chapters, but these will suffice for now. Go ahead and add the following test to show both how to create an intersection and how its properties are accessed.

features/intersections.feature
```
Scenario: An intersection encapsulates t and object
  Given s ← sphere()
  When i ← intersection(3.5, s)
  Then i.t = 3.5
    And i.object = s
```

You'll also need a way to aggregate these intersection objects so you can work with multiple intersections at once. (Consider your sphere intersection routine, which can return zero, one, or two intersections.) Write the following test, which introduces a new function called intersections(i1, i2, ...). This should return a new collection of the given intersection objects.

features/intersections.feature
```
Scenario: Aggregating intersections
  Given s ← sphere()
    And i1 ← intersection(1, s)
    And i2 ← intersection(2, s)
  When xs ← intersections(i1, i2)
  Then xs.count = 2
    And xs[0].t = 1
    And xs[1].t = 2
```

This list of intersections could just be an array primitive in your implementation language, but note that you'll be adding a function shortly (in *Identifying Hits*, on page 64) that operates on these lists of intersections.

Now it's time to break some code! Modify your existing tests so that they assume your intersect function returns a list of these intersection records, instead of bare t values. Also, add the following test, which will show that the object property is being set by intersect.

features/spheres.feature
```
Scenario: Intersect sets the object on the intersection
  Given r ← ray(point(0, 0, -5), vector(0, 0, 1))
    And s ← sphere()
  When xs ← intersect(s, r)
  Then xs.count = 2
    And xs[0].object = s
    And xs[1].object = s
```

Make your tests pass again by modifying your intersect function so it creates a record for each intersection, instead of returning the t values directly. All you need now is to be able to decide which of all those intersections you actually care about, which introduces the hit.

Identifying Hits

When rendering your scene, you'll need to be able to identify which one of all the intersections is actually visible from the ray's origin. Some may be behind the ray, and others may be hidden behind (or *occluded by*) other objects. For the sake of discussion, we'll call the visible intersection the *hit*. This is really the only intersection that matters for most things.

The hit will never be behind the ray's origin, since that's effectively behind the camera, so you can ignore all intersections with negative t values when determining the hit. In fact, the hit will always be the intersection with the lowest nonnegative t value.

> \|//
> ᷓᷟ   **Joe asks:**
> # Why do I have to keep all the intersections?
>
> You just read that you can ignore all intersections with negative t values when determining the hit. So why keep them around at all? Wouldn't it be easier to just not return them from the intersect() function in the first place?
>
> Certainly. It's a fair optimization, right up until you get to Chapter 11, *Reflection and Refraction*, on page 141. At that point, these seemingly irrelevant intersections suddenly become important! They'll be used to help determine which shapes contain other shapes. This will be also useful in Chapter 16, *Constructive Solid Geometry (CSG)*, on page 227, to inform how to render collections of objects related by boolean operations.
>
> So, hang onto those negative t values for now! Your future self will thank you.

Write the following tests, which introduce a function called hit(intersections). This function returns the hit from a collection of intersection records. Writing these tests will show how hit should behave in a few different situations.

features/intersections.feature
```
Scenario: The hit, when all intersections have positive t
  Given s ← sphere()
    And i1 ← intersection(1, s)
    And i2 ← intersection(2, s)
    And xs ← intersections(i2, i1)
  When i ← hit(xs)
  Then i = i1

Scenario: The hit, when some intersections have negative t
  Given s ← sphere()
    And i1 ← intersection(-1, s)
    And i2 ← intersection(1, s)
    And xs ← intersections(i2, i1)
  When i ← hit(xs)
  Then i = i2

Scenario: The hit, when all intersections have negative t
  Given s ← sphere()
    And i1 ← intersection(-2, s)
    And i2 ← intersection(-1, s)
    And xs ← intersections(i2, i1)
  When i ← hit(xs)
  Then i is nothing
```

```
Scenario: The hit is always the lowest nonnegative intersection
  Given s ← sphere()
  And i1 ← intersection(5, s)
  And i2 ← intersection(7, s)
  And i3 ← intersection(-3, s)
  And i4 ← intersection(2, s)
  And xs ← intersections(i1, i2, i3, i4)
When i ← hit(xs)
Then i = i4
```

Don't let that last test trip you up! The intersections are intentionally given in random order; it's up to your intersections() function to maintain a sorted list or, at the very least, sort the list on demand. This will be important down the road when you have more complicated scenes with multiple objects. It won't be feasible for each shape to manually preserve the sort order of that intersection list.

That rounds out your suite of intersection-related functionality. Make those tests all pass, and then let's take a look at how to move, resize, rotate, and deform your spheres.

Transforming Rays and Spheres

A unit sphere fixed at the origin is (at best) barely useful. You certainly couldn't have more than one, which makes it hard to make any kind of scene out of them. What you want is to be able to transform this sphere—scale it larger or smaller, move it around, and maybe (if one side were textured differently) rotate it a bit.

If you allow moving the sphere, though, your beautiful ray-sphere intersection algorithm has to change, because it assumes the sphere is always at the origin and always has a radius of 1. It would be lovely if you could keep that assumption, while still allowing spheres to be resized and repositioned. It would make your implementation so much cleaner and simpler.

Well, let's consider this. You *say* you want to move the sphere, but what you *really* want, fundamentally, is for the distance between the sphere and the ray's origin to increase or decrease, or the relationship between the ray's direction and the sphere's position to change, like the two pictures shown on page 67.

In the one on the left, the ray's origin and the sphere are separated by 2 units. In the one on the right, they've moved further apart. But contemplate this for a moment: *did the sphere move, or the ray?* Does it even matter? Regardless

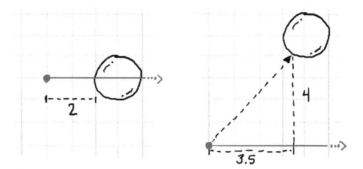

of which one moved, the distance between them increased, right? So, here's a crazy idea. What if, instead of moving the sphere, *you move the ray?*

(I know. It's pretty wild.)

Want to translate your sphere away from the ray? That's just the same as translating the *ray* away from the *sphere*, in the opposite direction, as the following figures show.

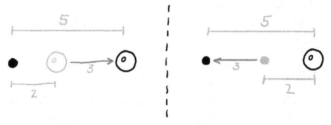

In the figure on the left, the sphere is moved away from the dot (perhaps the origin of a ray). On the right, the dot is moved away from the sphere. In both cases, the sphere and the dot wind up 5 units apart.

But what about scaling? What if you want to make your sphere bigger? It turns out that this is just the same as *shrinking the distance* between the ray and the sphere. It's an inverse relationship. You scale the ray by the *inverse* of how you were wanting to scale the sphere, as in the following figure:

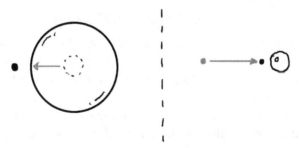

Okay, but what about rotation? Surely it can't be that simple for something like rotation? Oh, but it can! Consider the following figure. On the left, you see that rotating an object exposes a different side of that object to the ray. On the right, the same result is accomplished by rotating the *ray* around the *object*.

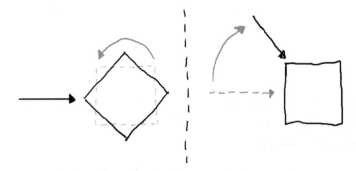

If you want to rotate your sphere, you rotate the ray by the *inverse* of the rotation you wanted to apply to the sphere.

In other words: whatever transformation you want to apply to the sphere, apply the *inverse* of that transformation to the ray, instead. Crazy, right? But it works!

World Space vs. Object Space

Another way to think about transformation matrices is to think of them as converting points between two different coordinate systems. At the scene level, everything is in *world space* coordinates, relative to the overall world. But at the object level, everything is in *object space* coordinates, relative to the object itself.

Multiplying a point in object space by a transformation matrix converts that point to world space—scaling it, translating, rotating it, or whatever. Multiplying a point in world space by the *inverse* of the transformation matrix converts that point back to object space.

Want to intersect a ray in world space with a sphere in object space? Just convert the ray's origin and direction to that same object space, and you're golden.

So, first, make sure your ray is transformable. Add the following tests to your suite, introducing a transform(ray, matrix) function which applies the given transformation matrix to the given ray, and returns a new ray with transformed origin and direction. Make sure it returns a new ray, rather than modifying the ray in place! You need to keep the original, untransformed ray, so that you can use it to calculate locations in world space later.

features/rays.feature

```
Scenario: Translating a ray
  Given r ← ray(point(1, 2, 3), vector(0, 1, 0))
    And m ← translation(3, 4, 5)
  When r2 ← transform(r, m)
  Then r2.origin = point(4, 6, 8)
    And r2.direction = vector(0, 1, 0)

Scenario: Scaling a ray
  Given r ← ray(point(1, 2, 3), vector(0, 1, 0))
    And m ← scaling(2, 3, 4)
  When r2 ← transform(r, m)
  Then r2.origin = point(2, 6, 12)
    And r2.direction = vector(0, 3, 0)
```

Notice how, in the second test, the ray's direction vector is left unnormalized. This is intentional, and important! Transforming a ray has the effect of (potentially) stretching or shrinking its direction vector. You have to leave that vector with its new length, so that when the t value is eventually computed, it represents an intersection at the correct distance (in world space!) from the ray's origin.

Pause here and make those tests pass by implementing the transform(ray, matrix) function.

Once your rays can be transformed, the next step is to allow a transformation to be assigned to a sphere. Implement the following tests to demonstrate both that a sphere has a default transformation and that its transformation can be assigned.

features/spheres.feature

```
Scenario: A sphere's default transformation
  Given s ← sphere()
  Then s.transform = identity_matrix

Scenario: Changing a sphere's transformation
  Given s ← sphere()
    And t ← translation(2, 3, 4)
  When set_transform(s, t)
  Then s.transform = t
```

Finally, make it so that your intersect function transforms the ray before doing the calculation. Add the following tests to illustrate two possible scenarios.

features/spheres.feature

```
Scenario: Intersecting a scaled sphere with a ray
  Given r ← ray(point(0, 0, -5), vector(0, 0, 1))
    And s ← sphere()
  When set_transform(s, scaling(2, 2, 2))
    And xs ← intersect(s, r)
```

```
    Then xs.count = 2
      And xs[0].t = 3
      And xs[1].t = 7
Scenario: Intersecting a translated sphere with a ray
  Given r ← ray(point(0, 0, -5), vector(0, 0, 1))
    And s ← sphere()
  When set_transform(s, translation(5, 0, 0))
    And xs ← intersect(s, r)
  Then xs.count = 0
```

Now go and make those tests pass. You'll need to make sure the ray passed to intersect is transformed by the inverse of the sphere's transformation matrix. In pseudocode, it means adding a line at the top of the function, like this:

```
function intersect(sphere, ray)
  ray2 ← transform(ray, inverse(sphere.transform))

  # ...
end function
```

Make sure you use the new ray in the function's other calculations, as well.

Once everything is working, pat yourself on the back! Isn't it beautiful? You get to keep your lovely unit sphere, and still deform it in all kinds of ways. You can turn it into an ellipsoid by scaling it nonuniformly, skew it with a shear transformation, and translate it wherever you want in a scene—all by applying the inverse of the transformation to the ray.

It's magical!

You still can't render a 3D scene, but you're closer than you were. In fact, you're getting really close. It's time to put some of these concepts together into something concrete, and show just how close you are.

Putting It Together

Your final task in this chapter is to write a program that casts rays at a sphere and draws the picture to a canvas. Any ray that hits the sphere should result in a colored pixel (red, for example), and any miss should be drawn in black. The result will be a silhouette of the sphere—not three-dimensional, but definitely round!

Here are a few hints to help you along. Stop reading at any time if you feel like you've got a handle on the solution!

Hint #1

Think as if you're trying to cast the shadow of your object onto some wall behind it, as in the following figure.

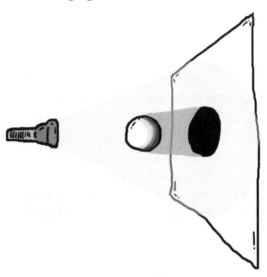

You cast each ray from some starting point toward some point on the wall that corresponds to a position on your canvas. If the ray intersects the sphere, a shadow is cast, which you'll mark with a colored pixel.

Hint #2

Figure out how far your ray's origin is from the sphere. Also, decide where your wall will be. Moving the ray origin closer to the sphere will make the sphere in the drawing larger. Moving it farther away will make the sphere smaller. Moving the wall will do similarly. For the sake of a place to start, try these values:

```
# start the ray at z = -5
ray_origin ← point(0, 0, -5)

# put the wall at z = 10
wall_z ← 10
```

Then decide how large your wall needs to be. Because you're using unit spheres, the maximum y value for the sphere is going to be 1. With that, you can extrapolate between the ray origin and the wall to see how large the wall should be, as shown in the figure on page 72.

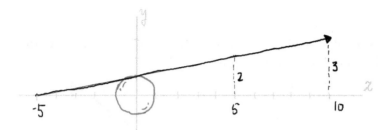

So, with the wall at z = 10, it needs to be at least 6 units across in order to capture the sphere's entire shadow. Give yourself a bit of margin, and call it 7. (Just assume the wall is a square.)

```
wall_size ← 7.0
```

Hint #3

Decide how large you want your canvas to be (in pixels). A canvas 100 pixels on a side is probably good for starting with. (Larger images will take exponentially longer to render.)

```
canvas_pixels ← 100
```

Once you know how many pixels fit along each side of the wall, you can divide the wall size by the number of pixels to get the size of a single pixel (in world space units).

```
pixel_size ← wall_size / canvas_pixels
```

Then, assume you're looking directly at the center of the sphere. Half of the wall will be to the left of that, and half to the right. Compute that size.

```
half ← wall_size / 2
```

Since the wall is centered around the origin (because the sphere is at the origin), this means that this half variable describes the minimum and maximum x and y coordinates of your wall.

Hint #4

Now that you know the origin of every ray, the dimensions of your canvas, and the size of your wall, you can compute, cast, and intersect rays. The following is one possible way to approach it, in pseudocode:

```
canvas ← canvas(canvas_pixels, canvas_pixels)
color ← color(1, 0, 0) # red
shape ← sphere()

# for each row of pixels in the canvas
for y ← 0 to canvas_pixels - 1
```

```
➤      # compute the world y coordinate (top = +half, bottom = -half)
➤      world_y ← half - pixel_size * y

       # for each pixel in the row
       for x ← 0 to canvas_pixels - 1

         # compute the world x coordinate (left = -half, right = half)
         world_x ← -half + pixel_size * x

         # describe the point on the wall that the ray will target
         position ← point(world_x, world_y, wall_z)

         r ← ray(ray_origin, normalize(position - ray_origin))
         xs ← intersect(shape, r)

         if hit(xs) is defined
           write_pixel(canvas, x, y, color)
         end if

       end for

     end for
```

Don't forget to save the canvas to a file at the end!

Note the highlighted lines, where the world y coordinate is calculated. In world space, the y coordinate increases as you go up, and decreases as you go down. But on the canvas, the top is at y = 0, and y increases as you go *down*. Thus, to render the circle correctly, you have to flip the y coordinate, which is accomplished by subtracting it from its maximum value (the top of the wall, or half).

If all goes well, you should see a circle, much like the following:

Congratulations! This is the silhouette of your sphere, drawn to your canvas one ray at a time.

Once you've got that much working, try deforming the sphere with some transformations and see what happens. Here are some ideas:

```
# shrink it along the y axis
shape.transform ← scaling(1, 0.5, 1)

# shrink it along the x axis
shape.transform ← scaling(0.5, 1, 1)

# shrink it, and rotate it!
shape.transform ← rotation_z(pi / 4) * scaling(0.5, 1, 1)

# shrink it, and skew it!
shape.transform ← shearing(1, 0, 0, 0, 0, 0) * scaling(0.5, 1, 1)
```

When you've had about as much fun as you can stand with this, move on. A silhouette is effective, but you can do much better. In the next chapter, you'll add lighting and shading to make that sphere look three-dimensional!

## CHAPTER 6

Light and Shading

Hot diggity! You are unstoppable. You just drew the silhouette of a three-dimensional sphere with nothing but some code and math! That's, like, level-10 wizard stuff.

Still—sad, but true!—the results are not quite what most people think of as "3D rendered." Time to fix that.

In this chapter, you'll implement a model to simulate the reflection of light from a surface, which will finally allow you to draw that sphere and make it look three dimensional. In fact, by the end of the chapter, you'll have rendered an image very much like this one:

To do this, you'll add a source of light, and then implement a shading algorithm to approximate how brightly that light illuminates the surfaces it shines on. It might sound complicated, but it's not. The truth is that most ray tracers favor approximations over physically accurate simulations, so that to shade any point, you only need to know four vectors. These are illustrated in the figure on page 76.

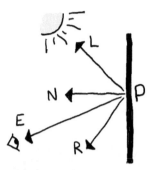

If P is where your ray intersects an object, these four vectors are defined as:

- E is the *eye vector*, pointing from P to the origin of the ray (usually, where the eye exists that is looking at the scene).

- L is the *light vector*, pointing from P to the position of the light source.

- N is the *surface normal*, a vector that is perpendicular to the surface at P.

- R is the *reflection vector*, pointing in the direction that incoming light would bounce, or reflect.

You already have the tools to compute the first two vectors:

- To find E, you can negate the ray's direction vector, turning it around to point back at its origin.

- To find L, you subtract P from the position of the light source, giving you the vector pointing toward the light.

The surface normal and reflection vector, though...those are new. Before you can use those, we need to pause and talk about how to compute them.

Surface Normals

A *surface normal* (or just *normal*) is a vector that points perpendicular to a surface at a given point. Consider a table, as shown in the following figure.

A flat surface like a table will have the same normal at every point on its surface, as shown by the vectors labeled N. If the table is level, the normals will be the same as "up," but even if we tilt the table, they'll still be perpendicular to the table's surface, like the following figure shows.

Things get a little trickier when we start talking about nonplanar surfaces (those that aren't uniformly flat). Take the planetoid in the following figure for example.

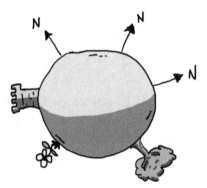

The three normal vectors certainly aren't all pointing the same direction! But each is perpendicular to the surface of the sphere at the point where it lives.

Let's look at how to actually compute those normal vectors.

Computing the Normal on a Sphere

Start by writing the following tests to demonstrate computing the normal at various points on a sphere. Introduce a new function, normal_at(sphere, point), which will return the normal on the given sphere, at the given point. You may assume that the point will always be on the surface of the sphere.

features/spheres.feature
```
Scenario: The normal on a sphere at a point on the x axis
  Given s ← sphere()
  When n ← normal_at(s, point(1, 0, 0))
  Then n = vector(1, 0, 0)

Scenario: The normal on a sphere at a point on the y axis
  Given s ← sphere()
  When n ← normal_at(s, point(0, 1, 0))
  Then n = vector(0, 1, 0)

Scenario: The normal on a sphere at a point on the z axis
  Given s ← sphere()
  When n ← normal_at(s, point(0, 0, 1))
  Then n = vector(0, 0, 1)

Scenario: The normal on a sphere at a nonaxial point
  Given s ← sphere()
  When n ← normal_at(s, point(√3/3, √3/3, √3/3))
  Then n = vector(√3/3, √3/3, √3/3)
```

One other feature of these normal vectors is hiding in plain sight: they're *normalized*. Add the following test to your suite, which shows that a surface normal should always be normalized.

features/spheres.feature
```
Scenario: The normal is a normalized vector
  Given s ← sphere()
  When n ← normal_at(s, point(√3/3, √3/3, √3/3))
  Then n = normalize(n)
```

Now, let's make those tests pass by implementing that normal_at() function. To understand how it will work its magic, take a look at the unit circle in the following figure. It's centered on the origin, and a point (presumably a point of intersection) has been highlighted on its circumference.

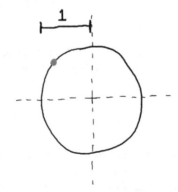

Let's say you want to find the normal at that highlighted point. Draw an arrow from the origin of the circle to that point, as in the following figure.

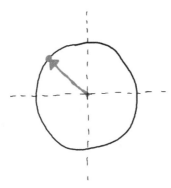

It turns out that this arrow—this vector!—is perpendicular to the surface of the circle at the point where it intersects. It's the normal! Algorithmically speaking, you find the normal by taking the point in question and subtracting the origin of the sphere ((0,0,0) in your case). Here it is in pseudocode:

```
function normal_at(sphere, p)
  return normalize(p - point(0, 0, 0))
end function
```

(Note that, because this is a unit sphere, the vector will be normalized by default for any point on its surface, so it's not strictly necessary to explicitly normalize it here.)

If only that were all there were to it! Sadly, the sphere's transformation matrix is going to throw a (small) wrench into how the normal is computed. Let's take a look at what needs to happen for the normal calculation to compensate for a transformation matrix.

Transforming Normals

Imagine you have a sphere that has been translated some distance from the world origin. If you were to naively apply the algorithm above to find the normal at almost any point on that sphere, you'd find that it no longer works correctly. The figure on page 80 shows how it goes wrong in this case. On the left, the normal for a sphere at the origin is computed. On the right, the normal is computed for a sphere that has been moved away from the origin.

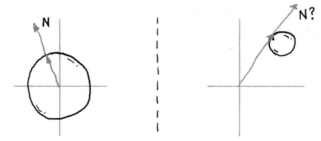

The "normal" on the right is not remotely normalized, and is not even pointing in the correct direction. Why? The problem is that your most basic assumption has been broken: the sphere's origin is no longer at the world origin.

Write the following tests to show what *ought* to happen. They demonstrate computing the normal first on a translated sphere and then on a scaled and rotated sphere.

features/spheres.feature
```
Scenario: Computing the normal on a translated sphere
  Given s ← sphere()
    And set_transform(s, translation(0, 1, 0))
  When n ← normal_at(s, point(0, 1.70711, -0.70711))
  Then n = vector(0, 0.70711, -0.70711)

Scenario: Computing the normal on a transformed sphere
  Given s ← sphere()
    And m ← scaling(1, 0.5, 1) * rotation_z(π/5)
    And set_transform(s, m)
  When n ← normal_at(s, point(0, √2/2, -√2/2))
  Then n = vector(0, 0.97014, -0.24254)
```

These won't pass yet, but you'll turn them green in just a moment.

Remember back when we talked about *World Space vs. Object Space*, on page 68? It turns out that this distinction between world and object space is part of the solution to this conundrum, too. You have a point in world space, and you want to know the normal on the corresponding surface in object space. What to do? Well, first you have to convert the point from world space to object space by multiplying the point by the inverse of the transformation matrix, thus:

```
object_point ← inverse(transform) * world_point
```

With that point now in object space, you can compute the normal as before, because in object space, the sphere's origin is at the world's origin. However! The normal vector you get will *also* be in object space...and to draw anything useful with it you're going to need to convert it back to world space somehow.

Now, if the normal were a *point* you could transform it by multiplying it by the transformation matrix. After all, that's what the transformation matrix does: it transforms points from object space to world space. And in truth, this *almost* works here, too. Consider the following two images of a squashed sphere, which has been scaled smaller in y. The normal vectors of the one on the left have been multiplied by the transformation matrix. The one on the right is how the sphere is *supposed* to look.

The one on the left definitely looks...off. It's as if someone took a picture of a regular, untransformed sphere, and squashed *that*, rather than squashing the sphere itself. What's the difference?

It all comes down to how the normal vectors are being transformed. The following illustration shows what happens. The sphere is scaled in y, squashing it vertically, and the normals are multiplied by the transformation matrix.

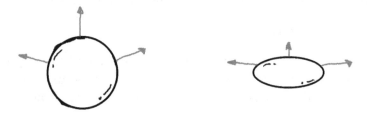

As you can see, multiplying by the transformation matrix doesn't preserve one of the fundamental properties of normal vectors in this case: the normal is not necessarily going to be perpendicular to the surface after being transformed!

So how do you go about keeping the normals perpendicular to their surface? The answer is to multiply the normal by the *inverse transpose matrix* instead. So you take your transformation matrix, invert it, and then transpose the result. *This* is what you need to multiply the normal by.

```
world_normal ← transpose(inverse(transform)) * object_normal
```

Be aware of two additional things here:

1. Technically, you should be finding submatrix(transform, 3, 3) (from *Spotting Sub-matrices*, on page 34) first, and multiplying by the inverse and transpose of *that*. Otherwise, if your transform includes any kind of translation, then multiplying by its transpose will wind up mucking with the w coordinate in your vector, which will wreak all kinds of havoc in later computations. But if you don't mind a bit of a hack, you can avoid all that by just setting world_normal.w to 0 after multiplying by the 4x4 inverse transpose matrix.

2. The inverse transpose matrix may change the length of your vector, so if you feed it a vector of length 1 (a normalized vector), you may not get a normalized vector out! It's best to be safe, and always normalize the result.

In pseudocode, then, your normal_at() function should look something like the following.

```
function normal_at(sphere, world_point)
  object_point ← inverse(sphere.transform) * world_point
  object_normal ← object_point - point(0, 0, 0)
  world_normal ← transpose(inverse(sphere.transform)) * object_normal
  world_normal.w ← 0
  return normalize(world_normal)
end function
```

Go ahead and pause here while you get things working to this point. Once your tests are all green, let's talk about how to compute the *reflection vector*.

Reflecting Vectors

Imagine bouncing a ball to your dog. You toss the ball to the ground at a point halfway between the two of you, the ball bounces up, and your dog (if she is well trained) catches it, like the following figure illustrates.

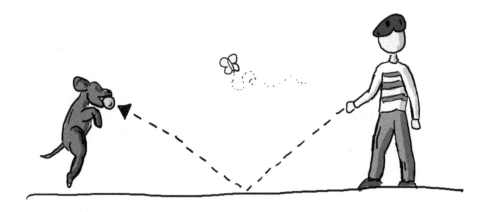

The ball's velocity is *reflected* around the normal at the point where it hits the ground. That is to say, it keeps moving forward, but instead of falling as it does so, now it is rising. Anyone that has ever played with a ball will know intuitively what that means. We all know from experience which direction the ball is likely to bounce.

Write the following two tests to reinforce that intuition. You'll introduce a function called reflect(in, normal), which returns the result of reflecting the in vector around the normal vector.

This first test shows the case where a vector approaches a normal at a 45° angle, moving at equal speed in both x and y. It should emerge at a 45° angle, with its y component reversed.

```
features/tuples.feature
Scenario: Reflecting a vector approaching at 45°
  Given v ← vector(1, -1, 0)
    And n ← vector(0, 1, 0)
  When r ← reflect(v, n)
  Then r = vector(1, 1, 0)
```

This should work regardless of the orientation of the normal vector. For instance, if the ground were slanted at 45°, and the ball were to fall straight down onto it, it ought to bounce away horizontally, as the following test demonstrates.

```
features/tuples.feature
Scenario: Reflecting a vector off a slanted surface
  Given v ← vector(0, -1, 0)
    And n ← vector(√2/2, √2/2, 0)
  When r ← reflect(v, n)
  Then r = vector(1, 0, 0)
```

As you might expect, mathematics is the magic that makes this work. Given two vectors in and normal, the following pseudocode is the incantation that you need.

```
function reflect(in, normal)
  return in - normal * 2 * dot(in, normal)
end function
```

Go ahead and make your tests all pass. Once you're ready, it's time to start shading things!

The Phong Reflection Model

Many different algorithms can simulate the reflection of light, but the one you'll implement here is called the *Phong reflection model* (named for Bui

Tuong Phong, the researcher who developed it). It simulates the interaction between three different types of lighting:

- *Ambient reflection* is background lighting, or light reflected from other objects in the environment. The Phong model treats this as a constant, coloring all points on the surface equally.

- *Diffuse reflection* is light reflected from a matte surface. It depends only on the angle between the light source and the surface normal.

- *Specular reflection* is the reflection of the light source itself and results in what is called a *specular highlight*—the bright spot on a curved surface. It depends only on the angle between the reflection vector and the eye vector and is controlled by a parameter that we'll call *shininess*. The higher the shininess, the smaller and tighter the specular highlight.

The following illustration shows the effects of each of these attributes. The first sphere is rendered using only ambient reflection, the second sphere uses only diffuse reflection, and the third sphere uses only specular reflection. The last sphere combines all three.

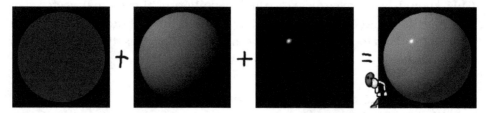

As you can see, by themselves they don't do a whole lot. But when you combine them, you get something with a lot more potential!

The first thing you're going to need for this is a light source. You're going to implement what is called a *point light*—a light source with no size, existing at a single point in space. It is also defined by its *intensity*, or how bright it is. This intensity also describes the color of the light source.

Add the following test to demonstrate the attributes of a point light.

features/lights.feature
```
Scenario: A point light has a position and intensity
  Given intensity ← color(1, 1, 1)
    And position ← point(0, 0, 0)
  When light ← point_light(position, intensity)
  Then light.position = position
    And light.intensity = intensity
```

The next thing you need is a structure called material that encapsulates not just the surface color, but also the four new attributes from the Phong reflection model: ambient, diffuse, specular, and shininess. Each should accept a nonnegative floating point number. For ambient, diffuse, and specular, the typical values are between 0 and 1. For shininess, values between 10 (very large highlight) and 200 (very small highlight) seem to work best, though there is no actual upper bound.

Add the following test, which introduces a material() function and shows the default values of each of the material's attributes.

```
features/materials.feature
Scenario: The default material
  Given m ← material()
  Then m.color = color(1, 1, 1)
    And m.ambient = 0.1
    And m.diffuse = 0.9
    And m.specular = 0.9
    And m.shininess = 200.0
```

Next, add a material property to your sphere, along with the following tests. These show how that property is used and what its default value should be.

```
features/spheres.feature
Scenario: A sphere has a default material
  Given s ← sphere()
  When m ← s.material
  Then m = material()

Scenario: A sphere may be assigned a material
  Given s ← sphere()
    And m ← material()
    And m.ambient ← 1
  When s.material ← m
  Then s.material = m
```

Make your tests pass by implementing the point light, the material() function, and the sphere's material property. Once you've got that, we'll bring it all together with one more function: lighting().

This lighting() function is what will shade your objects so that they appear three-dimensional. It expects five arguments: the material itself, the point being illuminated, the light source, and the eye and normal vectors from the Phong reflection model. While the function is not especially complicated by itself, several cases for the tests to consider will make sure everything checks out. Begin by writing the following series of tests, which will move the eye and light source around to exercise the lighting function in different configurations.

You can assume that each of these tests shares the following setup:

features/materials.feature
```
Background:
  Given m ← material()
    And position ← point(0, 0, 0)
```

For the first test, the eye is positioned directly between the light and the surface, with the normal pointing at the eye, like this:

In this case, you expect ambient, diffuse, and specular to all be at full strength. This means that the total intensity should be 0.1 (the ambient value) + 0.9 (the diffuse value) + 0.9 (the specular value), or 1.9.

features/materials.feature
```
Scenario: Lighting with the eye between the light and the surface
  Given eyev ← vector(0, 0, -1)
    And normalv ← vector(0, 0, -1)
    And light ← point_light(point(0, 0, -10), color(1, 1, 1))
  When result ← lighting(m, light, position, eyev, normalv)
  Then result = color(1.9, 1.9, 1.9)
```

In this next test, the surface and the light remain the same as before, but you'll move the eye to a point 45° off of the normal, as shown in the next illustration.

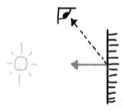

Here, the ambient and diffuse components should be unchanged (because the angle between the light and normal vectors will not have changed), but the specular value should have fallen off to (effectively) 0. Thus, the intensity should be 0.1 + 0.9 + 0, or 1.0.

features/materials.feature
```
Scenario: Lighting with the eye between light and surface, eye offset 45°
  Given eyev ← vector(0, √2/2, -√2/2)
    And normalv ← vector(0, 0, -1)
    And light ← point_light(point(0, 0, -10), color(1, 1, 1))
  When result ← lighting(m, light, position, eyev, normalv)
  Then result = color(1.0, 1.0, 1.0)
```

Next, the eye is back to being directly opposite the surface, but the light is moved to a position 45° off of the normal. The following figure shows how this looks.

Because the angle between the light and normal vectors has changed, the diffuse component becomes $0.9 \times \frac{\sqrt{2}}{2}$. The specular component again falls off to 0, so the total intensity should be $0.1 + 0.9 \times \frac{\sqrt{2}}{2} + 0$, or approximately 0.7364.

features/materials.feature
```
Scenario: Lighting with eye opposite surface, light offset 45°
  Given eyev ← vector(0, 0, -1)
    And normalv ← vector(0, 0, -1)
    And light ← point_light(point(0, 10, -10), color(1, 1, 1))
  When result ← lighting(m, light, position, eyev, normalv)
  Then result = color(0.7364, 0.7364, 0.7364)
```

For this next test, the light and normal vectors are the same as the previous test, but you'll move the eye directly into the path of the reflection vector, like this:

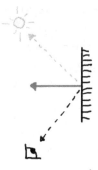

This should cause the specular component to be at full strength, with ambient and diffuse the same as the previous test. The total intensity should therefore be $0.1 + 0.9 \times \frac{\sqrt{2}}{2} + 0.9$, or approximately 1.6364.

features/materials.feature
```
Scenario: Lighting with eye in the path of the reflection vector
  Given eyev ← vector(0, -√2/2, -√2/2)
    And normalv ← vector(0, 0, -1)
    And light ← point_light(point(0, 10, -10), color(1, 1, 1))
  When result ← lighting(m, light, position, eyev, normalv)
  Then result = color(1.6364, 1.6364, 1.6364)
```

For the final test, you move the light behind the surface, like this:

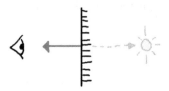

As the light no longer illuminates the surface, the diffuse and specular components go to 0. The total intensity should thus be the same as the ambient component, or 0.1.

features/materials.feature

```
Scenario: Lighting with the light behind the surface
  Given eyev ← vector(0, 0, -1)
    And normalv ← vector(0, 0, -1)
    And light ← point_light(point(0, 0, 10), color(1, 1, 1))
  When result ← lighting(m, light, position, eyev, normalv)
  Then result = color(0.1, 0.1, 0.1)
```

So, those are the tests! Make them pass now by implementing the lighting() function. In a nutshell, it will add together the material's ambient, diffuse, and specular components, weighted by the angles between the different vectors. In (annotated) pseudocode, it looks something like this:

```
function lighting(material, light, point, eyev, normalv)
  # combine the surface color with the light's color/intensity
  effective_color ← material.color * light.intensity

  # find the direction to the light source
  lightv ← normalize(light.position - point)

  # compute the ambient contribution
  ambient ← effective_color * material.ambient

  # light_dot_normal represents the cosine of the angle between the
  # light vector and the normal vector. A negative number means the
  # light is on the other side of the surface.
  light_dot_normal ← dot(lightv, normalv)
  if light_dot_normal < 0
    diffuse ← black
    specular ← black

  else
    # compute the diffuse contribution
    diffuse ← effective_color * material.diffuse * light_dot_normal

    # reflect_dot_eye represents the cosine of the angle between the
    # reflection vector and the eye vector. A negative number means the
    # light reflects away from the eye.
    reflectv ← reflect(-lightv, normalv)
    reflect_dot_eye ← dot(reflectv, eyev)
```

```
    if reflect_dot_eye <= 0
      specular ← black
    else
      # compute the specular contribution
      factor ← pow(reflect_dot_eye, material.shininess)
      specular ← light.intensity * material.specular * factor
    end if
  end if

  # Add the three contributions together to get the final shading
  return ambient + diffuse + specular
end function
```

Go ahead and make those tests all pass. Once they're all green, you can be confident your shading routines are working as they should, and you can move on to the final part of this chapter: rendering a sphere with realistic lighting!

Putting It Together

Okay. Take a look at the program you wrote at the end of the previous chapter, the one where you drew the silhouette of a sphere on a canvas. It's time to revisit that and turn the silhouette into a full-on 3D rendering. Make the following changes to that program:

1. Assign a material to your sphere. The following material will give you a sphere that looks like the illustrations in this chapter.

   ```
   sphere.material ← material()
   sphere.material.color ← color(1, 0.2, 1)
   ```

2. Add a light source. Here's one possible configuration, with a white light behind, above and to the left of the eye:

   ```
   light_position ← point(-10, 10, -10)
   light_color    ← color(1, 1, 1)
   light          ← point_light(light_position, light_color)
   ```

3. In the loop where you cast your rays, make sure you're normalizing the ray direction. It didn't matter before, but it does now! Also, once you've got an intersection, find the normal vector at the hit (the closest intersection), and calculate the eye vector.

   ```
   point  ← position(ray, hit.t)
   normal ← normal_at(hit.object, point)
   eye    ← -ray.direction
   ```

4. Finally, calculate the color with your lighting() function before applying it to the canvas.

   ```
   color ← lighting(hit.object.material, light, point, eye, normal)
   ```

The result, once you're done, should look something like the following figure.

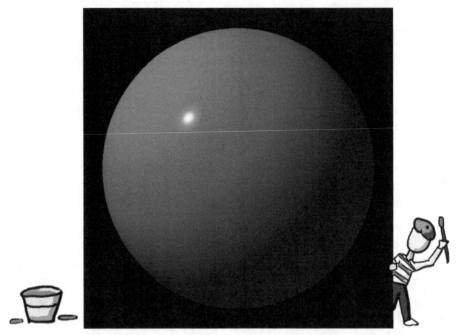

From there, experiment with different transformations of the sphere. Squash it, rotate it, scale it. Try different colors, and different material parameters. What happens when you increase the ambient value? What if the diffuse and specular are both low? What happens when you move the light source, or change its intensity?

Once you've had all the fun you can stand with that, go ahead and turn the page. Next up, it's cameras and worlds, which will set the stage for more complex scenes!

## CHAPTER 7

Making a Scene

Think about this for a second. You've written a program from scratch, with tests, that draws a three-dimensional object by simulating the behavior of light. That's *awesome*.

And it's still only the beginning! More complex scenes are just around the corner. By the end of this chapter you'll be creating worlds with multiple objects and using a virtual camera to capture views of those objects from different viewpoints. Just a few more pages and you'll be rendering images like those in Pierre's gallery, here:

To get there, you'll first implement a *world*—a collection of all objects in a scene—as well as routines for intersecting that world with a ray and computing the colors for intersections. Then you'll build a new matrix transformation, called the *view transformation*, which you'll use to orient the view. Lastly, you'll implement the *camera*, which encapsulates the view and provides an interface for rendering the world onto a canvas.

Ready? Go!

Building a World

The first step is to implement the world object. Think of how much work it was to render a single sphere, and then multiply that by dozens of objects. You begin to see what you gain by having something that will keep track of all of those things for you.

Initially, a world is empty, containing no objects and no light source. Write a test like the following, demonstrating a world() function that returns just such a data structure.

features/world.feature
```
Scenario: Creating a world
  Given w ← world()
  Then w contains no objects
    And w has no light source
```

Some of the tests you'll write in this chapter assume a default world exists with a light source at (-10, 10, -10). This world contains two concentric spheres, where the outermost is a unit sphere and the innermost has a radius of 0.5. Both lie at the origin. Add the following test to ensure that this default world is configured correctly.

features/world.feature
```
Scenario: The default world
  Given light ← point_light(point(-10, 10, -10), color(1, 1, 1))
    And s1 ← sphere() with:
      | material.color    | (0.8, 1.0, 0.6)      |
      | material.diffuse  | 0.7                  |
      | material.specular | 0.2                  |
    And s2 ← sphere() with:
      | transform | scaling(0.5, 0.5, 0.5) |
  When w ← default_world()
  Then w.light = light
    And w contains s1
    And w contains s2
```

Using that default world, write a test describing the behavior of a new intersect_world(world, ray) function, which accepts a world and a ray, and returns the intersections. In this case, since the ray passes through the origin (where both spheres are centered) it should intersect each sphere twice, for a total of four intersections.

features/world.feature
```
Scenario: Intersect a world with a ray
  Given w ← default_world()
    And r ← ray(point(0, 0, -5), vector(0, 0, 1))
  When xs ← intersect_world(w, r)
```

```
Then xs.count = 4
  And xs[0].t = 4
  And xs[1].t = 4.5
  And xs[2].t = 5.5
  And xs[3].t = 6
```

Make that test pass. The intersect_world() function should iterate over all of the objects that have been added to the world, intersecting each of them with the ray, and aggregating the intersections into a single collection. Note that for the test to pass, intersect_world() must return the intersections in sorted order.

> **Joe asks:**
> ## Why do I have to sort the intersections?
>
> All you're doing with the intersections at this point is finding the hit, or the intersection with the minimum positive t value. The list doesn't need to be sorted just to accomplish that, but sorting the intersections has a few benefits. The first is that it simplifies the tests, since it allows you to depend on the order of the returned intersections. The second is that when you get to Chapter 11, *Reflection and Refraction*, on page 141, and Chapter 16, *Constructive Solid Geometry (CSG)*, on page 227, you'll need to be able to iterate over the intersections in ascending order, and having that list already sorted will save you some effort.

Once your suite is passing again, it's time to figure out the shading for the nearest intersection (the "hit," from *Identifying Hits*, on page 64). To help with this, you'll introduce a new function, called prepare_computations(intersection, ray), which will return a new data structure encapsulating some precomputed information relating to the intersection. This will help you in later chapters (like Chapter 11, *Reflection and Refraction*, on page 141) by making it easier to reuse these computations in different calculations.

Write the following test, showing that prepare_computations() precomputes the point (in world space) where the intersection occurred, the eye vector (pointing back toward the eye, or camera), and the normal vector.

features/intersections.feature
```
Scenario: Precomputing the state of an intersection
  Given r ← ray(point(0, 0, -5), vector(0, 0, 1))
    And shape ← sphere()
    And i ← intersection(4, shape)
  When comps ← prepare_computations(i, r)
  Then comps.t = i.t
    And comps.object = i.object
    And comps.point = point(0, 0, -1)
    And comps.eyev = vector(0, 0, -1)
    And comps.normalv = vector(0, 0, -1)
```

The implementation should look familiar, using functions you've already written and used elsewhere. In pseudocode, it'll look something like this:

```
function prepare_computations(intersection, ray)
  # instantiate a data structure for storing some precomputed values
  comps ← new computations data structure

  # copy the intersection's properties, for convenience
  comps.t       ← intersection.t
  comps.object  ← intersection.object

  # precompute some useful values
  comps.point   ← position(ray, comps.t)
  comps.eyev    ← -ray.direction
  comps.normalv ← normal_at(comps.object, comps.point)

  return comps
end function
```

One other case that prepare_computations() should handle for this chapter is where the hit occurs on the *inside* of a shape. Consider the following illustration, where the ray originates inside of a sphere.

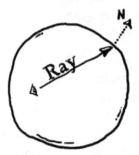

In this case, the surface normal (as currently computed) points *away* from the eye. But if the normal is pointing away from the eye, the shading algorithm from the previous chapter will color the surface far darker than it ought to be. What to do?

Add the following two tests, which show that prepare_computations() sets a fourth attribute, inside, which will be true if the hit occurs inside the object, and false otherwise. Notice, too, that the normal is inverted when the intersection is inside an object, so that the surface may be illuminated properly.

```
features/intersections.feature
Scenario: The hit, when an intersection occurs on the outside
  Given r ← ray(point(0, 0, -5), vector(0, 0, 1))
    And shape ← sphere()
    And i ← intersection(4, shape)
  When comps ← prepare_computations(i, r)
  Then comps.inside = false
```

```
Scenario: The hit, when an intersection occurs on the inside
  Given r ← ray(point(0, 0, 0), vector(0, 0, 1))
    And shape ← sphere()
    And i ← intersection(1, shape)
  When comps ← prepare_computations(i, r)
  Then comps.point = point(0, 0, 1)
    And comps.eyev = vector(0, 0, -1)
    And comps.inside = true
      # normal would have been (0, 0, 1), but is inverted!
    And comps.normalv = vector(0, 0, -1)
```

So, how can you know—mathematically—if the normal points away from the eye vector? Take the dot product of the two vectors, and if the result is negative, they're pointing in (roughly) opposite directions.

```
if dot(comps.normalv, comps.eyev) < 0
  comps.inside ← true
  comps.normalv ← -comps.normalv
else
  comps.inside ← false
end if
```

Once those tests are passing, you can move on to implementing the actual shading logic. Write the following two tests which call a new function, shade_hit(world, comps). The function ought to return the color at the intersection encapsulated by comps, in the given world.

features/world.feature
```
Scenario: Shading an intersection
  Given w ← default_world()
    And r ← ray(point(0, 0, -5), vector(0, 0, 1))
    And shape ← the first object in w
    And i ← intersection(4, shape)
  When comps ← prepare_computations(i, r)
    And c ← shade_hit(w, comps)
  Then c = color(0.38066, 0.47583, 0.2855)

Scenario: Shading an intersection from the inside
  Given w ← default_world()
    And w.light ← point_light(point(0, 0.25, 0), color(1, 1, 1))
    And r ← ray(point(0, 0, 0), vector(0, 0, 1))
    And shape ← the second object in w
    And i ← intersection(0.5, shape)
  When comps ← prepare_computations(i, r)
    And c ← shade_hit(w, comps)
  Then c = color(0.90498, 0.90498, 0.90498)
```

To pass both of these tests, your shade_hit() function needs to call the lighting() (from *The Phong Reflection Model*, on page 83) function with the intersected object's material and the prepared computations.

In pseudocode, it should come together something like this:

```
function shade_hit(world, comps)
  return lighting(comps.object.material,
                  world.light,
                  comps.point, comps.eyev, comps.normalv)
end function
```

Supporting Multiple Light Sources

The world object described here supports only a single light source, but it's not terribly difficult to support more than one. You would need to make sure your shade_hit() function iterates over all of the light sources, calling lighting() for each one and adding the colors together.

Be warned, though: adding multiple light sources will slow your renderer down, especially when you get to Chapter 8, *Shadows*, on page 109. But if you have CPU cycles to burn, having more than one light can make some neat effects possible, like overlapping shadows.

Now, for convenience's sake, tie up the intersect(), prepare_computations(), and shade_hit() functions with a bow and call the resulting function color_at(world, ray). It will intersect the world with the given ray and then return the color at the resulting intersection.

Add the following tests to demonstrate three important cases. The first test shows that when the ray fails to intersect anything, the color that is returned should be black.

```
features/world.feature
Scenario: The color when a ray misses
  Given w ← default_world()
    And r ← ray(point(0, 0, -5), vector(0, 1, 0))
  When c ← color_at(w, r)
  Then c = color(0, 0, 0)
```

This second test shows that the shading should be computed appropriately when the ray intersects an object—in this case, the outermost sphere in the default world.

```
features/world.feature
Scenario: The color when a ray hits
  Given w ← default_world()
    And r ← ray(point(0, 0, -5), vector(0, 0, 1))
  When c ← color_at(w, r)
  Then c = color(0.38066, 0.47583, 0.2855)
```

The third test shows that we expect color_at() to use the hit when computing the color. Here, we put the ray inside the outer sphere, but outside the inner sphere, and pointing at the inner sphere. We expect the hit to be on the inner sphere, and thus return its color.

features/world.feature
```
Scenario: The color with an intersection behind the ray
  Given w ← default_world()
    And outer ← the first object in w
    And outer.material.ambient ← 1
    And inner ← the second object in w
    And inner.material.ambient ← 1
    And r ← ray(point(0, 0, 0.75), vector(0, 0, -1))
  When c ← color_at(w, r)
  Then c = inner.material.color
```

Your color_at() function should do the following:

1. Call intersect_world to find the intersections of the given ray with the given world.

2. Find the hit from the resulting intersections.

3. Return the color black if there is no such intersection.

4. Otherwise, precompute the necessary values with prepare_computations.

5. Finally, call shade_hit to find the color at the hit.

That's all that's needed—for now!—for the world. Make your tests pass. Once everything is green, we'll start talking about how to actually make pictures from these worlds you're constructing. The first step is a matrix called the *view transformation*.

Defining a View Transformation

Right now, all of your rendered images have been painted on a fixed "screen" that you've cast rays at. This works, as you've seen, but it's very difficult to move that screen around. Suppose you wanted to render a picture from some point above and to the right of an object. How would you orient the screen so you could still look at that object?

This is what a *view transformation* will do for you. It's a transformation matrix—like scaling, rotation, and translation—that orients the world relative to your eye, thus allowing you to line everything up and get exactly the shot that you need.

Now, although the transformation actually orients the *world*, it's often far easier to imagine that it moves the *eye*. Moving a camera around is more intuitive than moving the world around in front of the camera! For that reason, in this section you'll introduce a new function, called view_transform(from, to, up), which pretends the eye moves instead of the world. You specify where you want the eye to be in the scene (the from parameter), the point in the scene at which you want to look (the to parameter), and a vector indicating which direction is up. The function then returns to you the corresponding transformation matrix.

Start by writing a test using this new function to describe the world's *default orientation*. The default orientation is the matrix you get if your view parameters (from, to, and up) don't require anything to be scaled, rotated, or translated. In other words, the default orientation is the identity matrix! The following test demonstrates this and shows that the orientation looks from the origin along the z axis in the negative direction, with up in the positive y direction.

features/transformations.feature
```
Scenario: The transformation matrix for the default orientation
  Given from ← point(0, 0, 0)
    And to ← point(0, 0, -1)
    And up ← vector(0, 1, 0)
  When t ← view_transform(from, to, up)
  Then t = identity_matrix
```

This means that turning around and looking in the *positive* z direction is like looking in a mirror: front and back are swapped, and left and right are swapped. The view transformation in this case should be exactly the same as reflecting across the z (front-to-back) and x (left-to-right) axes. As you saw in *Scaling*, on page 46, reflection is the same as scaling by a negative value, so you would expect the view transformation here to be the same as scaling by (-1, 1, -1), which is just what the following test demonstrates.

features/transformations.feature
```
Scenario: A view transformation matrix looking in positive z direction
  Given from ← point(0, 0, 0)
    And to ← point(0, 0, 1)
    And up ← vector(0, 1, 0)
  When t ← view_transform(from, to, up)
  Then t = scaling(-1, 1, -1)
```

Next, add the following test, which shows that the view transformation really does move the *world* and not the *eye*. The test positions the eye at a point 8 units along the z axis, and points the eye back at the origin.

features/transformations.feature

```
Scenario: The view transformation moves the world
  Given from ← point(0, 0, 8)
    And to ← point(0, 0, 0)
    And up ← vector(0, 1, 0)
  When t ← view_transform(from, to, up)
  Then t = translation(0, 0, -8)
```

As you can see, the resulting translation moves everything *backward* 8 units along the z axis, effectively pushing the world away from an eye positioned at the origin! Wild.

Write one more test for the view transformation, this time looking in some arbitrary direction. It should produce a matrix that is a combination of shearing, scaling, and translation.

features/transformations.feature

```
Scenario: An arbitrary view transformation
  Given from ← point(1, 3, 2)
    And to ← point(4, -2, 8)
    And up ← vector(1, 1, 0)
  When t ← view_transform(from, to, up)
  Then t is the following 4x4 matrix:
      | -0.50709 | 0.50709 |  0.67612 | -2.36643 |
      |  0.76772 | 0.60609 |  0.12122 | -2.82843 |
      | -0.35857 | 0.59761 | -0.71714 |  0.00000 |
      |  0.00000 | 0.00000 |  0.00000 |  1.00000 |
```

Note that the up vector doesn't need to be normalized. In fact, it doesn't even need to be exactly perpendicular to the viewing direction. As you'll see shortly, the view_transform() function will tidy that up vector, so you only have to point vaguely in the direction you want. Isn't that convenient?

So, how does this black magic work? Given three inputs, from, to, and up, the algorithm goes like this:

1. Compute the forward vector by subtracting from from to. Normalize the result.

2. Compute the left vector by taking the cross product of forward and the normalized up vector.

3. Compute the true_up vector by taking the cross product of left and forward. This allows your original up vector to be only approximately up, which makes framing scenes a lot easier, since you don't need to personally break out a calculator to figure out the precise upward direction.

4. With these left, true_up, and forward vectors, you can now construct a matrix that represents the orientation transformation:

$$orientation = \begin{bmatrix} left_x & left_y & left_z & 0 \\ true\_up_x & true\_up_y & true\_up_z & 0 \\ -forward_x & -forward_y & -forward_z & 0 \\ 0 & 0 & 0 & 1 \end{bmatrix}$$

5. All that's left is to append a translation to that transformation to move the scene into place before orienting it. Multiply orientation by translation(-from.x, -from.y, -from.z), and you're golden!

Described as pseudocode, your view_transform() function might look like this:

```
function view_transform(from, to, up)
  forward ← normalize(to - from)
  upn ← normalize(up)
  left ← cross(forward, upn)
  true_up ← cross(left, forward)

  orientation ← matrix( left.x,      left.y,      left.z,      0,
                        true_up.x,   true_up.y,   true_up.z,   0,
                        -forward.x,  -forward.y,  -forward.z,  0,
                        0,           0,           0,           1)

  return orientation * translation(-from.x, -from.y, -from.z)
end function
```

Once you've implemented that and made your tests pass, read on! You're ready to plug this view transformation into a virtual camera, giving you a simpler way to look at your scenes.

Implementing a Camera

Just like a real camera, your virtual camera will let you "take pictures" of your scene. You can move it around, zoom in and out, and even rotate the camera upside down if that's the shot you want. The camera is defined by the following four attributes:

- hsize is the horizontal size (in pixels) of the canvas that the picture will be rendered to.

- vsize is the canvas's vertical size (in pixels).

- field_of_view is an angle that describes how much the camera can see. When the field of view is small, the view will be "zoomed in," magnifying a smaller area of the scene.

- transform is a matrix describing how the world should be oriented relative to the camera. This is usually a view transformation like you implemented in the previous section.

Write the following test, showing how a camera is constructed using a new camera(hsize, vsize, field_of_view) function. It also shows that the default transform for a camera is the identity matrix.

features/camera.feature
```
Scenario: Constructing a camera
  Given hsize ← 160
    And vsize ← 120
    And field_of_view ← π/2
  When c ← camera(hsize, vsize, field_of_view)
  Then c.hsize = 160
    And c.vsize = 120
    And c.field_of_view = π/2
    And c.transform = identity_matrix
```

One of the primary responsibilities of the camera is to map the three-dimensional scene onto a two-dimensional canvas. To do this, you'll make the camera do just what you've done in previous exercises and place the canvas somewhere in the scene so that rays can be projected through it. But contrary to what you've done before, the camera's canvas will always be exactly one unit in front of the camera. As you'll see shortly, this makes the math a bit cleaner.

The first step is to make sure the camera knows the size (in world-space units) of the pixels on the canvas. Add the following two tests to show that the pixel size is calculated correctly for a canvas with a horizontal aspect (hsize > vsize), and one with a vertical aspect (vsize > hsize).

features/camera.feature
```
Scenario: The pixel size for a horizontal canvas
  Given c ← camera(200, 125, π/2)
  Then c.pixel_size = 0.01

Scenario: The pixel size for a vertical canvas
  Given c ← camera(125, 200, π/2)
  Then c.pixel_size = 0.01
```

The algorithm for computing this value goes like this:

1. You know the canvas is one unit away, and you know the angle of the field of view. By cutting the field of view in half, you create a right triangle, as shown in the figure on page 102.

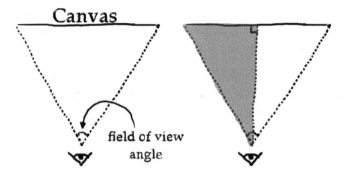

The width of that half of the canvas, then, can be computed by taking the tangent of half of the field of view. Call that value half_view, as in the following formula.

$$half\_view = \tan \frac{field\_of\_view}{2}$$

2. The *aspect ratio* is the ratio of the horizontal size of the canvas, to its vertical size. Compute that with the following formula.

$$aspect = \frac{hsize}{vsize}$$

3. Now, if the horizontal size is greater than or equal to the vertical size (aspect ≥ 1), then half_view is half the width of the canvas, and $^{half\_view}/_{aspect}$ is half the canvas's height.

   If the vertical size is greater than the horizontal size (aspect < 1), then half_view is instead half the *height* of the canvas, and half the canvas's *width* is half_view × aspect.

   Call these two values half_width and half_height, respectively.

   (Hang on to these half_width and half_height variables, by the way. You'll need them again soon ...)

4. Finally, compute the size of a single pixel on the canvas by dividing the full width the canvas (half_width × 2) by the horizontal size (in pixels) of the canvas (hsize). Call this pixel_size.

   (Note that the assumption here is that the pixels are square, so you don't actually need to compute the vertical size of the pixel—it's going to be the same as the horizontal size.)

In pseudocode, it should look something like this:

```
half_view ← tan(camera.field_of_view / 2)
aspect ← camera.hsize / camera.vsize
```

```
if aspect >= 1 then
  camera.half_width ← half_view
  camera.half_height ← half_view / aspect
else
  camera.half_width ← half_view * aspect
  camera.half_height ← half_view
end if

camera.pixel_size ← (camera.half_width * 2) / camera.hsize
```

You'll use the pixel_size and those half_width and half_height values you computed to create rays that can pass through any given pixel on the canvas. Implement the following three tests to ensure this works. These introduce a new function, ray_for_pixel(camera, x, y), which returns a new ray that starts at the camera and passes through the indicated (x, y) pixel on the canvas. The first two tests use an untransformed camera to cast rays through the center and corner of the canvas, and the third tries a ray with a camera that has been translated and rotated.

features/camera.feature
```
Scenario: Constructing a ray through the center of the canvas
  Given c ← camera(201, 101, π/2)
  When r ← ray_for_pixel(c, 100, 50)
  Then r.origin = point(0, 0, 0)
    And r.direction = vector(0, 0, -1)

Scenario: Constructing a ray through a corner of the canvas
  Given c ← camera(201, 101, π/2)
  When r ← ray_for_pixel(c, 0, 0)
  Then r.origin = point(0, 0, 0)
    And r.direction = vector(0.66519, 0.33259, -0.66851)

Scenario: Constructing a ray when the camera is transformed
  Given c ← camera(201, 101, π/2)
  When c.transform ← rotation_y(π/4) * translation(0, -2, 5)
    And r ← ray_for_pixel(c, 100, 50)
  Then r.origin = point(0, 2, -5)
    And r.direction = vector(√2/2, 0, -√2/2)
```

The Camera Transform vs. the World

Note that in the last test, the ray's origin winds up at (0, 2, -5), despite the camera's transformation including a translation of (0, -2, 5). That's not a typo! Remember that the camera's transformation describes how the *world* is moved relative to the *camera*. Further, you're transforming everything by the *inverse* of that transformation, so moving the world (0, -2, 5) is effectively the same as moving the ray's origin in the opposite direction: (0, 2, -5).

Now, make those tests pass. The ray_for_pixel() function must compute the world coordinates at the *center* of the given pixel, and then construct a ray that passes through that point. Assuming two inputs, px (the x position of the pixel) and py (the y position of the pixel), the pseudocode for the algorithm looks like this:

```
function ray_for_pixel(camera, px, py)
  # the offset from the edge of the canvas to the pixel's center
  xoffset ← (px + 0.5) * camera.pixel_size
  yoffset ← (py + 0.5) * camera.pixel_size

  # the untransformed coordinates of the pixel in world space.
  # (remember that the camera looks toward -z, so +x is to the *left*.)
  world_x ← camera.half_width - xoffset
  world_y ← camera.half_height - yoffset

  # using the camera matrix, transform the canvas point and the origin,
  # and then compute the ray's direction vector.
  # (remember that the canvas is at z=-1)
  pixel ← inverse(camera.transform) * point(world_x, world_y, -1)
  origin ← inverse(camera.transform) * point(0, 0, 0)
  direction ← normalize(pixel - origin)

  return ray(origin, direction)
end function
```

Okay, one more function and you'll be finished with the camera. The last bit to implement is the render(camera, world) function, which uses the camera to render an image of the given world.

Add the following test to your suite. It's a nonrigorous demonstration of how the render() function ought to work. It renders the default world with a camera and then makes sure that the pixel in the very middle of the resulting canvas is the expected color.

```
features/camera.feature
Scenario: Rendering a world with a camera
  Given w ← default_world()
    And c ← camera(11, 11, π/2)
    And from ← point(0, 0, -5)
    And to ← point(0, 0, 0)
    And up ← vector(0, 1, 0)
    And c.transform ← view_transform(from, to, up)
  When image ← render(c, w)
  Then pixel_at(image, 5, 5) = color(0.38066, 0.47583, 0.2855)
```

You'll probably find that the implementation of this function looks a lot like code you've already written. When you rendered an image at the end of Chapter 5, *Ray-Sphere Intersections*, on page 57, you created a canvas and cast a ray through each of its pixels, coloring the pixels with the colors of the corresponding intersections. That's exactly what this function will do, except instead of computing the location of each pixel, you'll let your new ray_for_pixel() function do the work.

In pseudocode, it looks like this:

```
function render(camera, world)
  image ← canvas(camera.hsize, camera.vsize)

  for y ← 0 to camera.vsize - 1
    for x ← 0 to camera.hsize - 1
      ray ← ray_for_pixel(camera, x, y)
      color ← color_at(world, ray)
      write_pixel(image, x, y, color)
    end for
  end for

  return image
end function
```

Go ahead and make sure all of your tests are passing. Once everything works, let's wrap up this chapter with a small project that uses your new world and camera code.

Putting It Together

Look back at the program you wrote at the end of the previous chapter. It's time to clean that up, taking advantage of the world and camera that you've just written and adding a few more spheres to make the scene more interesting.

Here's one example of what you might build:

This was constructed from six spheres, arranged as follows:

1. The floor is an extremely flattened sphere with a matte texture.

```
floor ← sphere()
floor.transform ← scaling(10, 0.01, 10)
floor.material ← material()
floor.material.color ← color(1, 0.9, 0.9)
floor.material.specular ← 0
```

2. The wall on the left has the same scale and color as the floor, but is also rotated and translated into place.

```
left_wall ← sphere()
left_wall.transform ← translation(0, 0, 5) *
                      rotation_y(-π/4) * rotation_x(π/2) *
                      scaling(10, 0.01, 10)
left_wall.material ← floor.material
```

Note the order in which the transformations are multiplied: the wall needs to be scaled, then rotated in x, then rotated in y, and lastly translated, so the transformations are multiplied in the *reverse order!*

3. The wall on the right is identical to the left wall, but is rotated the opposite direction in y.

```
right_wall ← sphere()
right_wall.transform ← translation(0, 0, 5) *
                       rotation_y(π/4) * rotation_x(π/2) *
                       scaling(10, 0.01, 10)
right_wall.material ← floor.material
```

4. The large sphere in the middle is a unit sphere, translated upward slightly and colored green.

```
middle ← sphere()
middle.transform ← translation(-0.5, 1, 0.5)
middle.material ← material()
middle.material.color ← color(0.1, 1, 0.5)
middle.material.diffuse ← 0.7
middle.material.specular ← 0.3
```

5. The smaller green sphere on the right is scaled in half.

```
right ← sphere()
right.transform ← translation(1.5, 0.5, -0.5) * scaling(0.5, 0.5, 0.5)
right.material ← material()
right.material.color ← color(0.5, 1, 0.1)
right.material.diffuse ← 0.7
right.material.specular ← 0.3
```

6. The smallest sphere is scaled by a third, before being translated.

```
left ← sphere()
left.transform ← translation(-1.5, 0.33, -0.75) * scaling(0.33, 0.33, 0.33)
left.material ← material()
left.material.color ← color(1, 0.8, 0.1)
left.material.diffuse ← 0.7
left.material.specular ← 0.3
```

The light source is white, shining from above and to the left:

```
world.light_source ← point_light(point(-10, 10, -10), color(1, 1, 1))
```

And the camera is configured like so:

```
camera ← camera(100, 50, π/3)
camera.transform ← view_transform(point(0, 1.5, -5),
                                  point(0, 1, 0),
                                  vector(0, 1, 0))

# render the result to a canvas.
canvas ← render(camera, world)
```

Experiment with other colors and material properties. Try deforming the spheres with scaling, rotation, and shearing transforms. Add more spheres. Move the camera around, try different fields of view, and see what happens when you change the direction of the up vector!

 You'll probably find that your renderer is *slow*, so stick with smaller resolutions while experimenting. Save the high-resolution renders for final versions of your scene, when you've got everything arranged and lit just how you want it, and can afford to wait ten or fifteen minutes (or more!) for your program to slog through a million pixels or so.

Once you're done playing with that, though, turn the page. You're about to add support for shadows to your renderer, which will do wonders for the realism of your scenes.

## CHAPTER 8

Shadows

Your ray tracer is really starting to come together. Just look at it! You've got spheres, realistic shading, a powerful camera, and a world that supports scenes with many objects.

It's a pity those objects don't cast shadows, though. Shadows add a delightful dash of realism to a scene. Check out the following figure which shows the same scene both with and without shadows:

Your brain uses those shadows as cues for depth perception. Without shadows, the image looks artificial and shallow, and that will never do.

Thus, the time has come to add shadows, and the best part is that you've already written most of the infrastructure to support this. The first step is to adjust your lighting() function to handle the case where a point is in shadow. Then you'll implement a new method for determining whether a point is in shadow or not, and last you'll tie those pieces together so your ray tracer actually renders the shadows.

Let's dig into it!

Lighting in Shadows

Given some point, you can know that it lies in shadow if there is another object sitting between it and the light source, as shown in the following figure.

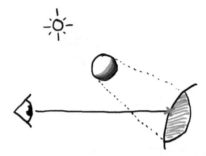

The light source is unable to contribute anything to that point. Take a moment and recall how your lighting() function works, from *The Phong Reflection Model*, on page 83. The diffuse component relies on the vector to the light source, and the specular component depends on the reflection vector. Since both components have a dependency on the light source, the lighting() function should ignore them when the point is in shadow and use only the ambient component.

Add the following test to the others you wrote for the lighting() function. It's identical to the one titled "Lighting with the eye between the light and the surface" on page 86, where the specular and diffuse components were both at their maximum values, but this time you're going to pass a new argument to the lighting() function indicating that the point is in shadow. It should cause the diffuse and specular components to be ignored, resulting in the ambient value alone contributing to the lighting.

(Recall that the m and position variables being passed to the lighting() function are defined in the "Background" block on page 86.)

features/materials.feature
```
Scenario: Lighting with the surface in shadow
  Given eyev ← vector(0, 0, -1)
    And normalv ← vector(0, 0, -1)
    And light ← point_light(point(0, 0, -10), color(1, 1, 1))
    And in_shadow ← true
  When result ← lighting(m, light, position, eyev, normalv, in_shadow)
  Then result = color(0.1, 0.1, 0.1)
```

You may need to fix your other tests to accommodate the addition of that new parameter. Go ahead and address that, and then make this new test pass as well by making your lighting() function ignore the specular and diffuse components when in_shadow is true.

Once things are all passing again, let's teach your ray tracer how to tell when a point is in shadow.

Testing for Shadows

A ray tracer computes shadows by casting a ray, called a *shadow ray*, from each point of intersection toward the light source. If something intersects that shadow ray between the point and the light source, then the point is considered to be in shadow. You're going to write a new function, is_shadowed(world, point), which will do just this.

Implement the following four tests, which demonstrate four different scenarios. Each assumes the existence of the default world that was defined in *Building a World*, on page 92.

In the first test, the world is set up like the following figure.

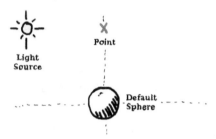

Nothing at all lies along the line connecting the point and the light source, and the point should therefore not be in shadow.

features/world.feature
```
Scenario: There is no shadow when nothing is collinear with point and light
  Given w ← default_world()
    And p ← point(0, 10, 0)
  Then is_shadowed(w, p) is false
```

In the second test, the point is placed on the far side of the default world's spheres, putting them between it and the light source, like this:

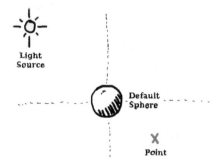

The point should be in the shadow cast by the spheres.

features/world.feature
```
Scenario: The shadow when an object is between the point and the light
  Given w ← default_world()
    And p ← point(10, -10, 10)
  Then is_shadowed(w, p) is true
```

The next test positions the point so the light lies between it and the spheres.

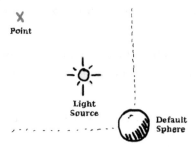

Once again, the point should not be in shadow, because nothing lies between the point and the light.

features/world.feature
```
Scenario: There is no shadow when an object is behind the light
  Given w ← default_world()
    And p ← point(-20, 20, -20)
  Then is_shadowed(w, p) is false
```

The last test is similar, but it positions the point to lie between the light and the spheres, like this:

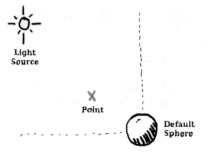

And again, even in this configuration nothing lies between the light and the point, so the point is still not shadowed.

features/world.feature
```
Scenario: There is no shadow when an object is behind the point
  Given w ← default_world()
    And p ← point(-2, 2, -2)
  Then is_shadowed(w, p) is false
```

The algorithm for is_shadowed() goes like this:

1. Measure the distance from point to the light source by subtracting point from the light position, and taking the magnitude of the resulting vector. Call this distance.

2. Create a ray from point toward the light source by normalizing the vector from step 1.

3. Intersect the world with that ray.

4. Check to see if there was a hit, and if so, whether t is less than distance. If so, the hit lies between the point and the light source, and the point is in shadow.

In pseudocode it might look like this:

```
function is_shadowed(world, point)
  v ← world.light.position - point
  distance ← magnitude(v)
  direction ← normalize(v)

  r ← ray(point, direction)
  intersections ← intersect_world(world, r)

  h ← hit(intersections)
  if h is present and h.t < distance
    return true
  else
    return false
  end if
end function
```

Recall from *Identifying Hits*, on page 64, that the hit() function returns the intersection with the lowest *nonnegative* t value. Thus, the hit's t will never be negative, so you don't need to worry about checking for intersections that occur behind the point.

Implement that function, make those tests pass, and then move on. Just one more thing needs changing to actually render those shadows!

Rendering Shadows

The final bit to actually render the shadows requires a small change to your shade_hit() function from *Building a World*, on page 92. You need to check whether the point is in shadow or not, and then pass that state to your lighting() function.

Add the following test to those that you wrote for the shade_hit() function. To demonstrate the case where some object is shadowing the point of intersection, it creates a world and two spheres, and positions a light so that the second sphere is in the shadow of the first. Then, a ray and an intersection are created such that the point of intersection is in the shadow. The shade_hit() function should return only the ambient color of the second sphere in this case.

```
features/world.feature
Scenario: shade_hit() is given an intersection in shadow
  Given w ← world()
    And w.light ← point_light(point(0, 0, -10), color(1, 1, 1))
    And s1 ← sphere()
    And s1 is added to w
    And s2 ← sphere() with:
      | transform | translation(0, 0, 10) |
    And s2 is added to w
    And r ← ray(point(0, 0, 5), vector(0, 0, 1))
    And i ← intersection(4, s2)
  When comps ← prepare_computations(i, r)
    And c ← shade_hit(w, comps)
  Then c = color(0.1, 0.1, 0.1)
```

Now, making this test pass may seem to be merely a matter of taking the point of intersection and sending it directly to the is_shadowed() function. But if you do this, you're liable to wind up with a rendered picture that looks like it's been attacked by fleas, as in the following figure.

This effect is called *acne*, and it happens because computers cannot represent floating point numbers very precisely. In general they do okay, but because of rounding errors, it will be impossible to say *exactly* where a ray intersects a surface. The answer you get will be close—generally within a tiny margin of error—but that wiggle is sometimes *just enough* to cause the calculated point of intersection to lie *beneath* the actual surface of the sphere.

As a result, the shadow ray intersects the sphere itself, causing the sphere to cast a shadow on its own point of intersection. This is obviously not ideal.

The solution is to adjust the point just slightly in the direction of the normal, before you test for shadows. This will bump it above the surface and prevent self-shadowing.

Add the following test, which sets up a sphere and an intersection such that the intersection occurs at z=0. After calling the prepare_computations() function you wrote in Chapter 7, *Making a Scene*, on page 91, there should be a new attribute, over_point, which will be almost identical to point, with the z component slightly less than z=0.

```
features/intersections.feature
Scenario: The hit should offset the point
  Given r ← ray(point(0, 0, -5), vector(0, 0, 1))
    And shape ← sphere() with:
      | transform | translation(0, 0, 1) |
    And i ← intersection(5, shape)
  When comps ← prepare_computations(i, r)
  Then comps.over_point.z < -EPSILON/2
    And comps.point.z > comps.over_point.z
```

Note that the test compares the over_point's z component to half of -EPSILON to make sure the point has been adjusted in the correct direction.

In pseudocode, your prepare_computations() function will need to do something like this:

```
# after computing and (if appropriate) negating
# the normal vector...
comps.over_point ← comps.point + comps.normalv * EPSILON
```

EPSILON is the tiny number discussed in *Comparing Floating Point Numbers*, on page 5, and is used here to bump the point just a bit in the direction of the normal.

Next, modify your shade_hit() function so that it invokes is_shadowed() with the hit's newly offset over_point attribute, and then call the lighting() function (again with over_point) with the result. It'll look like this in pseudocode:

```
function shade_hit(world, comps)
  shadowed ← is_shadowed(world, comps.over_point)

  return lighting(comps.object.material,
                  world.light,
                  comps.over_point, comps.eyev, comps.normalv,
                  shadowed)
end function
```

Go ahead and make that change to your shade_hit() function and make sure your tests are all passing. Once they are, it'll be time to wrap this chapter up and render some shadows!

Putting It Together

Your code is written. Your tests are passing. It's time to see how these shadows look in practice.

Start with the program you wrote at the end of the last chapter. If you set it up to duplicate the scene in the book, you should see each of those colored spheres casting shadows now! If you designed your own scene, you may or may not need to move things around so that shadows are being cast on other objects; make the changes necessary until you can demonstrate that shadows are truly being rendered.

Then, start playing! Deform your spheres and watch the shadows deform accordingly. Simulate an eclipse by positioning a smaller sphere between a larger one and the light source. If you're feeling particularly ambitious, see if you can make some shadow puppets by deforming and translating spheres!

Once you've wrung all the fun you can out of casting shadows, move on! It's time to add another graphics primitive to join your spheres: the plane.

## CHAPTER 9

Planes

You've been able to accomplish quite a bit so far using nothing but spheres as graphic primitives, which is pretty amazing. The world consists of a lot more than just spheres, though—even cleverly transformed spheres. In this chapter you'll add a new graphics primitive—the plane—which will be perfect for modeling floors, walls, and backgrounds.

The biggest initial hurdle will probably be refactoring your code to support different types of graphics primitives. We'll begin the chapter by talking about how you might go about this refactoring, and identify the functionality that all primitives will have in common. Once the common functionality has been factored out and you've got your test suite updated, we'll move on to the actual implementation of planes.

First, refactoring!

Refactoring Shapes

You may or may not have used an object-oriented programming language thus far to build your ray tracer. Honestly, it really doesn't matter! But since we need some kind of common vocabulary to describe the upcoming refactoring, let's just agree to use terms like "classes," "objects," "parents," and "inheritance." Translate these concepts into your own environments accordingly.

The goal of this next step is to take your Sphere implementation, identify the functionality that will be common to all shapes, and refactor those bits into an abstract parent that all other shapes will inherit from. Once the common bits have been moved into the abstract parent, you'll simplify your Sphere implementation by inheriting it from that parent.

So, what will all shapes have in common? Here's a list that you can start with:

- All shapes have a transformation matrix. Unless explicitly set, this will be the identity matrix as described in Chapter 5, *Ray-Sphere Intersections*, on page 57.

- All shapes have a material, which should default to the one described in *The Phong Reflection Model*, on page 83.

- When intersecting the shape with a ray, all shapes need to first convert the ray into object space, transforming it by the inverse of the shape's transformation matrix.

- When computing the normal vector, all shapes need to first convert the point to object space, multiplying it by the inverse of the shape's transformation matrix. Then, after computing the normal they must transform it by the inverse of the transpose of the transformation matrix, and then normalize the resulting vector before returning it.

Later chapters, like Chapter 14, *Groups*, on page 193, and Chapter 16, *Constructive Solid Geometry (CSG)*, on page 227, will add to that list, but those four items are all you need to worry about for now.

Begin by writing some tests that describe what this refactoring should look like when it's done. Because this will depend heavily on your programming language and how you've architected things so far, consider the following tests to be guidelines—ideas for how to build your own tests.

Each of the following tests assumes there is a function called test_shape(), which exists solely to demonstrate the abstract behaviors of the Shape class. As Shape itself is abstract, the test_shape() function instantiates and returns a special subclass of Shape we'll call TestShape, which implements just enough behavior to be concrete. (We'll talk about what that means, specifically, in a moment.)

First, write a couple of tests that show that a shape has a default transformation and that the transformation is assignable. These replace the tests named "A sphere's default transformation" and "Changing a sphere's default transformation" (from the sphere scenarios on page 69) and are essentially identical to them, merely calling test_shape() instead of sphere().

features/shapes.feature
```
Scenario: The default transformation
  Given s ← test_shape()
  Then s.transform = identity_matrix

Scenario: Assigning a transformation
  Given s ← test_shape()
  When set_transform(s, translation(2, 3, 4))
  Then s.transform = translation(2, 3, 4)
```

Add a couple more tests now, showing that a shape has a default material and that the material may be assigned as well. These replace the tests named "A sphere has a default material" and "A sphere may be assigned a material" (from the sphere scenarios on page 85).

features/shapes.feature
```
Scenario: The default material
  Given s ← test_shape()
  When m ← s.material
  Then m = material()

Scenario: Assigning a material
  Given s ← test_shape()
    And m ← material()
    And m.ambient ← 1
  When s.material ← m
  Then s.material = m
```

Next, test the behavior of the intersect(ray, shape) function, which is now *abstract*, meaning it relies on a separate concrete implementation to flesh out the behavior and actually perform the intersection. All you really need to check here, though, is that the ray is transformed before being passed on to the concrete implementation.

One possible way to implement this (and which the following tests assume) is to declare a local_intersect(shape, local_ray) function for each concrete subclass of Shape. The abstract intersect() function transforms the ray and then calls local_intersect() with that transformed ray, returning the resulting collection of intersections. The following pseudocode shows how it might look:

```
function intersect(shape, ray)
  local_ray ← transform(ray, inverse(shape.transform))
  return local_intersect(shape, local_ray)
end function
```

For the purposes of these tests, you really don't care whether any intersections occur or not, since the test shape has no real existence. All you need to know is whether the local_ray parameter to local_intersect() has been transformed appropriately. One way to do this is to have the test shape's implementation of local_intersect() assign local_ray to a variable somewhere (perhaps as an instance variable, or a global variable), which your tests can then inspect.

The following two tests assume the existence of a new property on the test shape, saved_ray, which the test shape's local_intersect() function should set to the ray parameter. These tests are both based on (and replace) the tests called "Intersecting a scaled sphere with a ray" and "Intersecting a translated sphere with a ray" (from the sphere scenarios on page 69).

```
features/shapes.feature
Scenario: Intersecting a scaled shape with a ray
  Given r ← ray(point(0, 0, -5), vector(0, 0, 1))
    And s ← test_shape()
  When set_transform(s, scaling(2, 2, 2))
    And xs ← intersect(s, r)
  Then s.saved_ray.origin = point(0, 0, -2.5)
    And s.saved_ray.direction = vector(0, 0, 0.5)

Scenario: Intersecting a translated shape with a ray
  Given r ← ray(point(0, 0, -5), vector(0, 0, 1))
    And s ← test_shape()
  When set_transform(s, translation(5, 0, 0))
    And xs ← intersect(s, r)
  Then s.saved_ray.origin = point(-5, 0, -5)
    And s.saved_ray.direction = vector(0, 0, 1)
```

The last bit of common logic is in the normal_at(sphere, point) function, from *Computing the Normal on a Sphere*, on page 77. The goal here is to make it so that individual concrete shapes don't have to worry about transforming points or normals—all they have to do is compute the normal itself.

Borrowing the same strategy as was presented for the intersect() function, you might consider creating a local_normal_at(shape, local_point) function for each concrete subclass, which accepts a point in local (object) space, and returns the normal in the same space. The normal_at(shape, point) becomes generalized, so that it transforms the point, invokes the appropriate local_normal_at() function, transforms the resulting normal, and returns it. In pseudocode, it might look like this:

```
function normal_at(shape, point)
  local_point  ← inverse(shape.transform) * point
  local_normal ← local_normal_at(shape, local_point)
  world_normal ← transpose(inverse(shape.transform)) * local_normal
  world_normal.w ← 0

  return normalize(world_normal)
end function
```

The following two tests replace the ones called "Computing the normal on a translated sphere" and "Computing the normal on a transformed sphere" (from the sphere scenarios on page 80). These demonstrate that translation doesn't affect the normal but that scaling and rotation do. For the test shape's local_normal_at() function, make it convert the point in question to a vector:

$$\text{local\_normal\_at}(p) = \text{vector}(p_x, p_y, p_z)$$

This will be enough for you to test that the behavior is correct.

features/shapes.feature
```
Scenario: Computing the normal on a translated shape
  Given s ← test_shape()
  When set_transform(s, translation(0, 1, 0))
    And n ← normal_at(s, point(0, 1.70711, -0.70711))
  Then n = vector(0, 0.70711, -0.70711)

Scenario: Computing the normal on a transformed shape
  Given s ← test_shape()
    And m ← scaling(1, 0.5, 1) * rotation_z(π/5)
  When set_transform(s, m)
    And n ← normal_at(s, point(0, √2/2, -√2/2))
  Then n = vector(0, 0.97014, -0.24254)
```

That's the last of the common behavior that needs to be shuffled around! All that's left to finish the refactoring is to tidy up your sphere implementation so that it uses this new shape abstraction.

The following checklist may help you here:

1. If possible, consider writing a test to check that a Sphere is a Shape. This tells you in one stroke that every sphere will have the common behaviors of all shapes.

2. Remove the transformation and material tests from your sphere suite. Those are now being checked in the tests belonging to the abstract parent class.

3. Change your sphere's existing intersect() tests to invoke the sphere's local_intersect() instead. You don't need to test the intersect() function, because you've already demonstrated that intersect() calls local_intersect() and that the ray is appropriately transformed.

4. Similarly, change your sphere's existing normal_at() tests so that they call local_normal_at().

5. Write your sphere's local_intersect() and local_normal_at() functions.

You'll probably find that you get to remove quite a bit of code from your sphere tests and from the sphere implementation itself. This is a cause for celebration! Once your tests are all passing, you should totally take a moment to do a little victory dance. Or buy yourself some ice cream. Whichever makes you happiest.

Regardless of how you celebrate, once you're ready, read on! It's time to use this refactored foundation to describe a plane.

Implementing a Plane

A *plane* is a perfectly flat surface that extends infinitely in two dimensions. For simplicity, your ray tracer will implement a plane in xz—that is, extending infinitely far in both x and z dimensions, passing through the origin. Using transformation matrices, though, you'll be able to rotate and translate your planes into any orientation you like.

Because a plane has no curvature, its normal vector is constant everywhere—it doesn't change. Every single point on the plane has the same normal: vector(0, 1, 0). This means that implementing the local_normal_at() function for the plane is rather uninteresting! Add the following test to check the expected normal vector for a few arbitrary points on the plane. It assumes that the plane() function returns a new plane.

features/planes.feature
```
Scenario: The normal of a plane is constant everywhere
  Given p ← plane()
  When n1 ← local_normal_at(p, point(0, 0, 0))
    And n2 ← local_normal_at(p, point(10, 0, -10))
    And n3 ← local_normal_at(p, point(-5, 0, 150))
  Then n1 = vector(0, 1, 0)
    And n2 = vector(0, 1, 0)
    And n3 = vector(0, 1, 0)
```

The logic to intersect a ray with a plane is the only other bit that needs implementing, and it has four cases to consider:

1. The ray is parallel to the plane, and will thus never intersect it.

2. The ray is *coplanar* with the plane, which is to say that the ray's origin is on the plane, and the ray's direction is parallel to the plane. You're viewing the plane edge-on. In this case, every point on the ray intersects the plane, resulting in an infinite number of intersections. That's unwieldy! But since a plane is infinitely thin, it's invisible when viewed like this, so we'll assume the ray misses in this case.

3. The ray origin is above the plane.

4. The ray origin is below the plane.

Test the first two cases by writing the following two tests. Each sets up a plane and a ray with a direction parallel to the plane. In both cases, local_intersect() should return an empty set of intersections.

```
features/planes.feature
Scenario: Intersect with a ray parallel to the plane
  Given p ← plane()
    And r ← ray(point(0, 10, 0), vector(0, 0, 1))
  When xs ← local_intersect(p, r)
  Then xs is empty

Scenario: Intersect with a coplanar ray
  Given p ← plane()
    And r ← ray(point(0, 0, 0), vector(0, 0, 1))
  When xs ← local_intersect(p, r)
  Then xs is empty
```

To know if a ray is parallel to the plane, you need to note that the plane is in xz—it has no slope in y at all. Thus, if your ray's direction vector also has no slope in y (its y component is 0), it is parallel to the plane. In practice, you'll want to treat any tiny number as 0 for this comparison, as the following pseudocode shows (using EPSILON as the threshold for "tiny number"):

```
function local_intersect(plane, ray)
  if abs(ray.direction.y) < EPSILON
    return () # empty set -- no intersections
  end if

  # remaining intersection logic goes here
end function
```

Implement the next two tests to flesh out the behavior of the local_intersect() function, specifically testing the remaining intersection logic. The first checks the case of a ray intersecting a plane from above, and the second checks an intersection from below.

```
features/planes.feature
Scenario: A ray intersecting a plane from above
  Given p ← plane()
    And r ← ray(point(0, 1, 0), vector(0, -1, 0))
  When xs ← local_intersect(p, r)
  Then xs.count = 1
    And xs[0].t = 1
    And xs[0].object = p

Scenario: A ray intersecting a plane from below
  Given p ← plane()
    And r ← ray(point(0, -1, 0), vector(0, 1, 0))
  When xs ← local_intersect(p, r)
  Then xs.count = 1
    And xs[0].t = 1
    And xs[0].object = p
```

To make these pass, you'll need to implement the following formula for computing the intersection of a ray with a plane. Note that this formula only works if the plane is as described above—in xz, with the normal pointing in the positive y direction.

$$t = \frac{-origin_y}{direction_y}$$

The variable origin is the ray's origin, and direction is the ray's direction vector. The following pseudocode shows how the complete local_intersect() function might look.

```
function local_intersect(ray, plane)
  if abs(ray.direction.y) < EPSILON
    return () # empty set -- no intersections
  end if

  t ← -ray.origin.y / ray.direction.y
  return ( intersection(t, plane) )
end function
```

Go ahead and make your tests pass, now. Once you've got things stable again, wrap it up with the following short project to test your newest graphic primitive.

Putting It Together

Write a small scene consisting of a single plane as the floor, and a sphere or two sitting atop it. For example, here are the same three spheres from the previous chapters, sitting on a plane:

Other things you might try:

- Add a wall as a backdrop by rotating it $\pi/2$ radians around the x axis and translating it a few units in the positive z direction.

- Make a hexagonal-shaped room by carefully rotating and translating planes, and then position the camera from above, looking down, so you can see the geometry in action.

- Add a ceiling by translating another plane vertically, in y. (Be careful to position your light source below the ceiling!)

- Instead of displaying an entire sphere atop the plane, translate the sphere so it is partially embedded in the plane.

See what else you can come up with! Once you're done experimenting, read on. Next, you're going to see how to decorate these planes and spheres with geometric patterns of colors, which will make your scenes even more interesting.

## CHAPTER 10

Patterns

Your ray tracer is really coming together now. Planes and spheres, shading, ray-traced shadows—yeah, seriously. This is some lovely stuff.

It gets even better, though! In this next chapter, you're going to add yet more lickable eye candy in the form of patterns, like this:

Yeah! Instead of rendering an entire shape with the same boring color, you're going to implement geometric rules that define how any given point in space ought to be colored. We'll cover four of these patterns: stripes, gradients, rings, and checkers. Then you'll be set loose to experiment and invent a few of your own!

Here we go.

Making a Striped Pattern

A *pattern* is a function that accepts a point in space and returns a color. For example, consider the following stripe pattern:

As the x coordinate changes, the pattern alternates between the two colors. The other two dimensions, y and z, have no effect on it. In other words, the function looks like this:

$$\text{color}(point, c_a, c_b) = \begin{cases} c_a, & \text{if floor}(point_x) \bmod 2 = 0 \\ c_b, & \text{otherwise} \end{cases}$$

That is to say, if the x coordinate is between 0 and 1, return the first color. If between 1 and 2, return the second, and so forth, alternating between the two.

Add this pattern in your program. To do so, you'll create a data structure that encapsulates the colors used by the pattern, as well as a function that will choose the appropriate color for some point.

To begin, most of the tests in this chapter will assume the existence of the following two color constants, black and white:

```
features/patterns.feature
Background:
  Given black ← color(0, 0, 0)
    And white ← color(1, 1, 1)
```

With those defined, you can write the following test introducing a new function, stripe_pattern(a, b), which returns a pattern instance encapsulating the two colors a and b.

```
features/patterns.feature
Scenario: Creating a stripe pattern
  Given pattern ← stripe_pattern(white, black)
  Then pattern.a = white
    And pattern.b = black
```

Now, write a couple of tests for another new function, stripe_at(pattern, point), which should return the appropriate color for the given pattern and point.

features/patterns.feature

```
Scenario: A stripe pattern is constant in y
  Given pattern ← stripe_pattern(white, black)
  Then stripe_at(pattern, point(0, 0, 0)) = white
    And stripe_at(pattern, point(0, 1, 0)) = white
    And stripe_at(pattern, point(0, 2, 0)) = white

Scenario: A stripe pattern is constant in z
  Given pattern ← stripe_pattern(white, black)
  Then stripe_at(pattern, point(0, 0, 0)) = white
    And stripe_at(pattern, point(0, 0, 1)) = white
    And stripe_at(pattern, point(0, 0, 2)) = white

Scenario: A stripe pattern alternates in x
  Given pattern ← stripe_pattern(white, black)
  Then stripe_at(pattern, point(0, 0, 0)) = white
    And stripe_at(pattern, point(0.9, 0, 0)) = white
    And stripe_at(pattern, point(1, 0, 0)) = black
    And stripe_at(pattern, point(-0.1, 0, 0)) = black
    And stripe_at(pattern, point(-1, 0, 0)) = black
    And stripe_at(pattern, point(-1.1, 0, 0)) = white
```

Make those two tests pass by implementing the stripe_pattern() and stripe_at() functions. Remember: stripe_pattern() returns a new instance of the data structure, and stripe_at() implements the function that chooses the color at a given point. Once these tests are passing, read on!

The next step is to add this stripe pattern to your material. Start by writing another test to show that the lighting() function (from *The Phong Reflection Model*, on page 83) returns the color from the pattern.

features/materials.feature

```
Scenario: Lighting with a pattern applied
  Given m.pattern ← stripe_pattern(color(1, 1, 1), color(0, 0, 0))
    And m.ambient ← 1
    And m.diffuse ← 0
    And m.specular ← 0
    And eyev ← vector(0, 0, -1)
    And normalv ← vector(0, 0, -1)
    And light ← point_light(point(0, 0, -10), color(1, 1, 1))
  When c1 ← lighting(m, light, point(0.9, 0, 0), eyev, normalv, false)
    And c2 ← lighting(m, light, point(1.1, 0, 0), eyev, normalv, false)
  Then c1 = color(1, 1, 1)
    And c2 = color(0, 0, 0)
```

Note that the test uses a material with only ambient illumination. This is a handy trick for making sure the lighting() function returns an easily predictable color, since the color won't be affected by angles, normals, or lights.

Make this test pass by modifying your lighting() function, adding some code to get the color from the pattern (via stripe_at()) if the material has a pattern set. In pseudocode, your change might look something like this:

```
function lighting(material, light, point, eyev, normalv, in_shadow)
  if material has a pattern
    color ← stripe_at(material.pattern, point)
  else
    color ← material.color
  end if

  # then, compute the lighting as usual, using `color`
  # instead of `material.color`

  # ...
end function
```

With that change, your test suite should be passing again. Yay! What is more, you can now (kind of) render a scene containing a striped texture. Give it a try, but don't be disappointed if it doesn't behave entirely as expected yet...

Whenever you're ready, read on. We'll talk about how to transform patterns next, which is how you'll finally whip this feature into shape.

Transforming Patterns

Right now, your stripes implementation has one small problem. If you've played around with it at all, you may have seen it: the stripes are completely fixed, frozen in place. It's as if you were to shine a flashlight on your scene, with a stripe filter over the bulb. You'd find that every object that has a stripe pattern is covered with stripes of exactly the same size and orientation, regardless of how the objects themselves are arranged, as in this scene:

Because the point being passed to the stripe_at() function is in *world space*, the patterns completely ignore the transformations of the objects to which they are applied.

This is unfortunate, because we expect a pattern to move when its object moves. If you make an object bigger or smaller, the pattern on it should get bigger or smaller. Rotating an object ought to rotate the pattern, too.

Further, it makes sense to be able to transform the patterns themselves, independently of the object. Want your stripes closer together or farther apart? Scale them. Want to change how they are oriented on the object? Rotate them. What to change their phase? Translate them to shift them to one side or the other.

Write the following three tests to sketch out how this behavior should look, and introduce a new method called stripe_at_object(pattern, object, point). It should return the color for the given *pattern*, on the given *object*, at the given world-space *point*, and it should respect the transformations on both the pattern and the object while doing so.

```
features/patterns.feature
Scenario: Stripes with an object transformation
  Given object ← sphere()
    And set_transform(object, scaling(2, 2, 2))
    And pattern ← stripe_pattern(white, black)
  When c ← stripe_at_object(pattern, object, point(1.5, 0, 0))
  Then c = white

Scenario: Stripes with a pattern transformation
  Given object ← sphere()
    And pattern ← stripe_pattern(white, black)
    And set_pattern_transform(pattern, scaling(2, 2, 2))
  When c ← stripe_at_object(pattern, object, point(1.5, 0, 0))
  Then c = white

Scenario: Stripes with both an object and a pattern transformation
  Given object ← sphere()
    And set_transform(object, scaling(2, 2, 2))
    And pattern ← stripe_pattern(white, black)
    And set_pattern_transform(pattern, translation(0.5, 0, 0))
  When c ← stripe_at_object(pattern, object, point(2.5, 0, 0))
  Then c = white
```

Make these tests pass by implementing the stripe_at_object() function. It should do the following:

1. Multiply the given world-space point by the inverse of the object's transformation matrix, to convert the point to object space.

2. Then, multiply the object-space point by the inverse of the pattern's transformation matrix to convert that point to *pattern space*.

3. Pass the resulting point to your original stripe_at() function, and return the result.

It'll look like this in pseudocode:

```
function stripe_at_object(pattern, object, world_point)
  object_point  ← inverse(object.transform) * world_point
  pattern_point ← inverse(pattern.transform) * object_point

  return stripe_at(pattern, pattern_point)
end function
```

Almost there! Now make your program actually use this new function by changing your lighting() and shade_hit() functions as follows:

1. Add object as yet another parameter for your lighting() function. The tests and pseudocode in this book assume the new function signature is lighting(material, object, light, point, eyev, normalv, in_shadow).

2. Modify the implementation of the lighting() function so that it calls stripe_at_object() instead of stripe_at().

3. Modify shade_hit() so that it passes the hit's object property to lighting().

4. Fix your lighting() tests so that they create an object (a sphere is fine—it's just a placeholder for those tests, anyway) and pass it to lighting().

All of your tests should be passing now. Celebrate by giving the stripes pattern another try! See what happens if you rotate the stripes, or scale them, or transform the object they're attached to.

When you're ready, let's talk about how to generalize all of this, in preparation for adding more patterns.

Generalizing Patterns

The idea now is to modify your code so that a material can be assigned *any* pattern, not just stripes. The process for accomplishing this will look a lot like the refactoring you did in *Refactoring Shapes*, on page 117, when you were preparing to support planes as primitives. Specifically, you'll tackle this in five steps:

1. Identify the pieces that every pattern will have in common.

2. Implement an abstract pattern that encapsulates these common pieces and delegates to concrete patterns for their specific bits.

3. Modify the stripes pattern to extend this abstract pattern.

4. Modify your material implementation to depend on the abstract pattern.

5. Make all existing tests pass.

So, the common bits. The good news is that every pattern will be essentially the same, differentiated only by the function that converts points into colors. Besides that function, every pattern will have a transformation matrix, and every pattern will need to use it to help transform a given point from world space to pattern space before producing a color.

As with the shapes refactoring, the way forward here is going to depend a lot on how you've architected your program so far. One way is to follow a similar strategy to that proposed for the shapes, where the base abstraction performs the common functionality and delegates the specific functionality to the concrete implementations.

If you take this route, use the following tests as guidelines for writing your own. These tests assume that the abstract function (the one that transforms the point and delegates to the concrete function) is called pattern_at_shape(pattern, shape, point). The concrete function (to be implemented by each pattern) is here simply called pattern_at(pattern, point).

The tests also assume that there is a function called test_pattern(), which is similar to the test_shape() function from *Refactoring Shapes*, on page 117. Its job will be to help you test the behaviors of the abstract pattern superclass by returning a special implementation used only for the tests.

First, show that this test pattern has a transformation matrix and that the transformation is (by default) the identity matrix.

```
features/patterns.feature
Scenario: The default pattern transformation
  Given pattern ← test_pattern()
  Then pattern.transform = identity_matrix
```

Next, show that the pattern's transformation can be assigned.

```
features/patterns.feature
Scenario: Assigning a transformation
  Given pattern ← test_pattern()
  When set_pattern_transform(pattern, translation(1, 2, 3))
  Then pattern.transform = translation(1, 2, 3)
```

Next, test the pattern_at_shape() function to see that it correctly transforms the points before calling the concrete function. The following tests replace the ones you wrote earlier in the chapter, testing the stripe pattern's transformations.

```
Scenario: A pattern with an object transformation
  Given shape ← sphere()
    And set_transform(shape, scaling(2, 2, 2))
    And pattern ← test_pattern()
  When c ← pattern_at_shape(pattern, shape, point(2, 3, 4))
  Then c = color(1, 1.5, 2)

Scenario: A pattern with a pattern transformation
  Given shape ← sphere()
    And pattern ← test_pattern()
    And set_pattern_transform(pattern, scaling(2, 2, 2))
  When c ← pattern_at_shape(pattern, shape, point(2, 3, 4))
  Then c = color(1, 1.5, 2)

Scenario: A pattern with both an object and a pattern transformation
  Given shape ← sphere()
    And set_transform(shape, scaling(2, 2, 2))
    And pattern ← test_pattern()
    And set_pattern_transform(pattern, translation(0.5, 1, 1.5))
  When c ← pattern_at_shape(pattern, shape, point(2.5, 3, 3.5))
  Then c = color(0.75, 0.5, 0.25)
```

These tests assume the test pattern's concrete function is defined like this:

$$\text{pattern\_at}(pattern, point) = \text{color}(point_x, point_y, point_z)$$

In other words, it takes the given point and returns a new color where the color's red/green/blue components are set to the point's x/y/z components. You can then use the *color* to see that the *point* was transformed!

Once those are passing, update your stripe_pattern() implementation so that it inherits from this abstract pattern. You can remove the code that transforms the points, since that's now taken care of by the abstract pattern_at_shape() function.

Lastly, update your material data structure, so that it references the abstract pattern instead of the stripe pattern, and make lighting() call the pattern_at_shape() function.

Whew! Tidy things up by making sure your tests all pass, and then move on. With this abstract pattern as a foundation, you're ready to start implementing more patterns.

Making a Gradient Pattern

A *gradient* pattern is like stripes, but instead of discrete steps from one color to the next, the function returns a blend of the two colors, linearly interpolating from one to the other as the x coordinate changes. If the first color is red, and the second is blue, the resulting gradient will look like this:

Add the following test to show how a basic linear gradient pattern ought to work.

```
features/patterns.feature
Scenario: A gradient linearly interpolates between colors
  Given pattern ← gradient_pattern(white, black)
  Then pattern_at(pattern, point(0, 0, 0)) = white
    And pattern_at(pattern, point(0.25, 0, 0)) = color(0.75, 0.75, 0.75)
    And pattern_at(pattern, point(0.5, 0, 0)) = color(0.5, 0.5, 0.5)
    And pattern_at(pattern, point(0.75, 0, 0)) = color(0.25, 0.25, 0.25)
```

To make this pass, your gradient_pattern() implementation should use a *blending function*. This is a function that takes two values and interpolates the values between them. A basic linear interpolation looks like this:

$$\mathrm{color}(p, c_a, c_b) = c_a + (c_b - c_a) * (p_x - \mathrm{floor}(p_x))$$

This takes the distance between the two colors, multiplies it by the fractional portion of the x coordinate, and adds the product to the first color. The result is a smooth, linear transition from the first color to the second.

In pseudocode, your gradient's color function should look something like this:

```
function pattern_at(gradient, point)
  distance ← gradient.b - gradient.a
  fraction ← point.x - floor(point.x)

  return gradient.a + distance * fraction
end
```

Once that test is passing, let's have a look at ring patterns.

Making a Ring Pattern

A *ring pattern* depends on two dimensions, x and z, to decide which color to return. It works similarly to stripes, but instead of testing the distance of the point in just x, it tests the distance of the point in both x and z, which results in this pattern of concentric circles as shown in the figure on page 136.

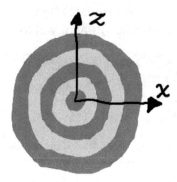

Write the following test for this. You're checking to make sure that these rings extend in both x and z.

```
features/patterns.feature
Scenario: A ring should extend in both x and z
  Given pattern ← ring_pattern(white, black)
  Then pattern_at(pattern, point(0, 0, 0)) = white
    And pattern_at(pattern, point(1, 0, 0)) = black
    And pattern_at(pattern, point(0, 0, 1)) = black
    # 0.708 = just slightly more than √2/2
    And pattern_at(pattern, point(0.708, 0, 0.708)) = black
```

To make that pass, you'll implement the function for a ring pattern, something like this:

$$\text{color}(p, c_a, c_b) = \begin{cases} c_a, & \text{if floor}(\sqrt{p_x^2 + p_z^2}) \bmod 2 = 0 \\ c_b, & \text{otherwise} \end{cases}$$

Make that test pass, and then we'll look at one more pattern: checkers.

Making a 3D Checker Pattern

A two-dimensional *checker* pattern is a repeating pattern of squares, where two squares of the same color are never adjacent, like this:

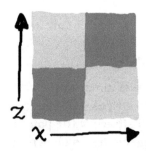

What's cool is that this idea can extend to three dimensions, too, like this:

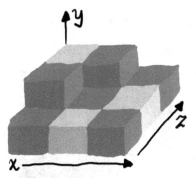

You get a pattern of alternating *cubes*, where two cubes of the same color are never adjacent. This three-dimensional checker pattern is the one you'll implement here.

Go ahead and write the following tests for these 3D checkers, showing that the pattern does indeed repeat in all three dimensions.

features/patterns.feature
```
Scenario: Checkers should repeat in x
  Given pattern ← checkers_pattern(white, black)
  Then pattern_at(pattern, point(0, 0, 0)) = white
    And pattern_at(pattern, point(0.99, 0, 0)) = white
    And pattern_at(pattern, point(1.01, 0, 0)) = black

Scenario: Checkers should repeat in y
  Given pattern ← checkers_pattern(white, black)
  Then pattern_at(pattern, point(0, 0, 0)) = white
    And pattern_at(pattern, point(0, 0.99, 0)) = white
    And pattern_at(pattern, point(0, 1.01, 0)) = black

Scenario: Checkers should repeat in z
  Given pattern ← checkers_pattern(white, black)
  Then pattern_at(pattern, point(0, 0, 0)) = white
    And pattern_at(pattern, point(0, 0, 0.99)) = white
    And pattern_at(pattern, point(0, 0, 1.01)) = black
```

The function for this pattern is very much like that for stripes, but instead of relying on a single dimension, it relies on the sum of all three dimensions, x, y, and z, like this. (Note that $\lfloor x \rfloor$ is the same as floor(x).)

$$\text{color}(p, c_a, c_b) = \begin{cases} c_a, & \text{if } (\lfloor p_x \rfloor + \lfloor p_y \rfloor + \lfloor p_z \rfloor) \bmod 2 = 0 \\ c_b, & \text{otherwise} \end{cases}$$

Once your tests are all passing, read on. We'll wrap this chapter up with some ideas for you to experiment with.

> **Joe asks:**
> ## Why does my checkered sphere look weird?
>
> If you try applying this checker pattern to a sphere, you'll get something like this:
>
>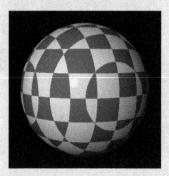
>
> If you were instead expecting the pattern to cover the surface of the sphere in a regular grid pattern, this may have left you scratching your head and wondering what you did wrong. Well, good news! You did nothing wrong. The pattern is working exactly right.
>
> Because patterns convert *points in space* to colors, it's as if you're carving that sphere out of a checker-patterned block, rather than neatly painting the pattern onto the surface of the sphere.
>
> To apply a two-dimensional texture (like checkers) to the surface of an object, you need to implement something called *UV mapping*, which converts a three-dimensional point of intersection (x, y, z) into a two-dimensional surface coordinate (u, v). You'd then map that surface coordinate to a color. It's fun to do, but sadly beyond the scope of this book. Tutorial-style resources are hard to find, but with a bit of reading between the lines and some experimentation, searching for topics like "spherical texture mapping" can bear fruit.

Putting It Together

Okay! You have working implementations of four different patterns: stripes, gradients, rings, and checkers. Your first order of business, then, should be to take them all for a spin! Try them each on planes and spheres, scale them, rotate them, experiment with different colors, and get a feel for how these patterns behave in practice.

Once you feel like you're getting a handle on them, try some deeper experiments. Here are a few ideas to get you started:

Radial gradient pattern

   Consider your ring pattern, which creates a radial pattern of concentric circles. Then, consider your gradient pattern, which interpolates between two colors. How would you combine those two concepts to create a new "radial gradient" pattern that interpolates between two colors, radially?

Nested patterns

Instead of specifying a pair of *colors* when instantiating a pattern, what if you instead specified *other patterns*? So instead of a checker pattern in black and white, make one where the checkers contain alternating patterns of stripes in different orientations, like this:

One way to make this work is to add a new pattern, called solid_pattern(color), which returns the same color for every point. Patterns can then be nested, with the innermost pattern always being one of these solid color patterns.

Blended patterns

This adds a new pattern, blended_pattern(a, b), where a and b are *other patterns*, rather than *colors*. The blend pattern will then evaluate both of its patterns at each point, and blend the resulting colors together. (Blending a color can be as simple as averaging them, if you want, but you could get creative with that formula, too!) For example, here's a blending of two green/white stripe patterns, crossing at ninety-degree angles to one another:

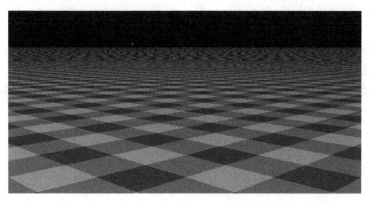

Perturbed patterns

This is another fun one! It's a way to add organic-looking textures to your scenes. The way it works is you use a 3D noise function to "jitter" the point before the pattern consumes it. Look for an implementation of Perlin noise, or Simplex noise. Then, create a new pattern, called perturb(pattern), which uses that noise to jitter each point before delegating it to the given pattern.

"Jittering" a point means moving it by some small amount. With most implementations of Perlin noise, for instance, you can request a range of values for a given three-dimensional point. You scale those numbers by some fraction (maybe 20% or less), and then take the first of those values and add it to the x coordinate. Then, add the second value to the y coordinate, and the third value to the z coordinate. Finally, you treat that as a new point, and pass it to the subpattern.

The result is that each pattern looks *perturbed*, as if someone had stuck their finger in wet paint and swirled it around. Here's an example of perturbed versions of each of the patterns from this chapter:

Implementations of Perlin noise exist for many programming languages. For example, you can review Ken Perlin's original reference implementation, written in Java.[1]

The sky's the limit! Play around with patterns and see what you can come up with. When you're ready to move on, in the next chapter we'll be taking the realism of your scenes up a notch, with reflection and refraction.

---

1.   https://mrl.nyu.edu/~perlin/noise/

## CHAPTER 11

Reflection and Refraction

All right. Hang on to your passenger assist handle, because you're about to add another bit of material finesse to your ray tracer. Check out this sneak preview:

That's right, boys and girls. You're going to make objects *reflective* and *transparent*. Mirrors and glass marbles will be your oyster.

Both of these work through similar means: spawning an additional ray at the point of intersection and recursively following it to determine the color at that point. You'll tackle them one at a time: reflection first, and then transparency and refraction.

Are you ready? Here goes!

Reflection

Look around you. Odds are you'll find something in your vicinity that is reflective to one degree or another. Maybe it's your phone's screen, or a polished table, or a window, or a pair of sunglasses. Whatever it is, that reflection gives you all kinds of clues about what to expect from that surface and helps convince your brain that what you're seeing is *real*.

This works in rendered scenes, too. Adding even just a subtle bit of reflection can make your scene bloom with photorealism. Consider the following two images:

Both depict the same scene, from the same angle and with the same lighting, but the floor on the right is just slightly reflective, making it appear more glossy than the other.

You'll add this feature to your ray tracer with seven tests:

1. Add a reflective attribute to your material data structure.

2. Update prepare_computations() to compute the ray's reflection vector, reflectv.

3. Handle the case where the ray strikes a nonreflective surface.

4. Handle the case where the ray strikes a reflective surface.

5. Make sure shade_hit() calls the function for computing reflections.

6. Make sure your ray tracer can avoid infinite recursion, as when a ray bounces between two parallel mirrors.

7. Show that your code can set a limit to how deeply recursion is allowed to go.

Note that from here on out, the chapters will be a bit more streamlined. Up to this point, you saw tests introduced with a bit of fanfare and discussion. But now the training wheels are coming off. You know the drill by now. You will see the tests, you will get a bit of explanation, and (where necessary) you will walk through the algorithms and perhaps a smattering of pseudocode. You've got this!

Here we go, one test at a time.

Test #1: Add the reflective Material Attribute

Show that your material structure contains a new attribute, called reflective.

When reflective is 0, the surface is completely nonreflective, whereas setting it to 1 produces a perfect mirror. Numbers in between produce partial reflections.

```
features/materials.feature
Scenario: Reflectivity for the default material
  Given m ← material()
  Then m.reflective = 0.0
```

Make sure the new attribute is a floating point value, so that you can implement partial reflection.

Test #2: Compute the reflectv Vector

Show that the prepare_computations() function precomputes the reflectv vector.

Create a plane and position a ray above it, slanting downward at a 45° angle. Position the intersection on the plane, and have prepare_computations() compute the reflection vector.

```
features/intersections.feature
Line 1  Scenario: Precomputing the reflection vector
     2    Given shape ← plane()
     3      And r ← ray(point(0, 1, -1), vector(0, -√2/2, √2/2))
     4      And i ← intersection(√2, shape)
     5    When comps ← prepare_computations(i, r)
     6    Then comps.reflectv = vector(0, √2/2, √2/2)
```

Line 3 creates and orients the ray, and line 4 places the hit $\sqrt{2}$ units away, courtesy of the Pythagorean theorem. Lastly, line 6 asserts that the reflect vector bounces up from the plane at another 45° angle.

Compute reflectv in prepare_computations() by reflecting the ray's direction vector around the object's normal vector, like this:

```
# after negating the normal, if necessary
comps.reflectv ← reflect(ray.direction, comps.normalv)
```

It's just like you did in your lighting() function, in *The Phong Reflection Model*, on page 83, when you computed the light's reflection vector. Here, though, you're reflecting the *ray*, and not the *light*.

Test #3: Strike a Nonreflective Surface

Show that when a ray strikes a nonreflective surface, the reflected_color() function returns the color black.

You're getting to the meat of the reflection algorithm itself, now. This test introduces a new function, reflected_color(world, comps), which will be the core of how your ray tracer computes reflections.

Place a ray inside at the origin of the default world, inside both of the world's spheres. Bounce the ray off the innermost sphere. By setting the sphere's ambient property to 1, you can guarantee that any reflection will have something to reflect—but because the innermost sphere is not reflective, reflected_color() should simply return black.

features/world.feature
```
Scenario: The reflected color for a nonreflective material
  Given w ← default_world()
    And r ← ray(point(0, 0, 0), vector(0, 0, 1))
    And shape ← the second object in w
    And shape.material.ambient ← 1
    And i ← intersection(1, shape)
  When comps ← prepare_computations(i, r)
    And color ← reflected_color(w, comps)
  Then color = color(0, 0, 0)
```

For this test, make your reflected_color() function return black when the material's reflective attribute is 0. The next test will flesh that function out a bit more.

Test #4: Strike a Reflective Surface

Show that reflected_color() returns the color via reflection when the struck surface is reflective.

Add a reflective plane to the default scene, just below the spheres, and orient a ray so it strikes the plane, reflects upward, and hits the outermost sphere.

features/world.feature
```
Line 1   Scenario: The reflected color for a reflective material
    -      Given w ← default_world()
    -        And shape ← plane() with:
    -          | material.reflective | 0.5                  |
    5          | transform           | translation(0, -1, 0) |
    -        And shape is added to w
    -        And r ← ray(point(0, 0, -3), vector(0, -√2/2, √2/2))
    -        And i ← intersection(√2, shape)
    -      When comps ← prepare_computations(i, r)
    10       And color ← reflected_color(w, comps)
    -      Then color = color(0.19032, 0.2379, 0.14274)
```

Lines 3–5 configure the (semi)reflective plane and position it at y = -1. After preparing the hit, the reflected color will be a darker version of the sphere's shade of green, because the plane will only reflect half of the light from the sphere.

Implement reflected_color() by creating a new ray, originating at the hit's location and pointing in the direction of reflectv. Find the color of the new ray via color_at(), and then multiply the result by the reflective value. If reflective is set to something between 0 and 1, this will give you partial reflection.

In pseudocode, it goes like this:

```
function reflected_color(world, comps)
  if comps.object.material.reflective = 0
    return color(0, 0, 0)
  end if

  reflect_ray ← ray(comps.over_point, comps.reflectv)
  color ← color_at(world, reflect_ray)

  return color * comps.object.material.reflective
end function
```

Spawning these secondary rays is how ray tracers can produce such realistic reflections. Just make sure to use the comps.over_point attribute (and not comps.point) when constructing the new ray. Otherwise, floating point rounding errors will make some rays originate just below the surface, causing them to intersect the same surface they should be reflecting from.

Test #5: Update the shade_hit Function

Show that shade_hit() incorporates the reflected color into the final color.

Recycle the previous test, but this time call shade_hit() instead of calling reflected_color() directly. The resulting color should combine the white of the plane with the reflected green of the sphere.

```
features/world.feature
Scenario: shade_hit() with a reflective material
  Given w ← default_world()
    And shape ← plane() with:
      | material.reflective | 0.5                 |
      | transform           | translation(0, -1, 0) |
    And shape is added to w
    And r ← ray(point(0, 0, -3), vector(0, -√2/2, √2/2))
    And i ← intersection(√2, shape)
  When comps ← prepare_computations(i, r)
    And color ← shade_hit(w, comps)
  Then color = color(0.87677, 0.92436, 0.82918)
```

Implement this by making the shade_hit() function call reflected_color(), and adding the color it returns to the surface color. In pseudocode:

```
function shade_hit(world, comps)
  shadowed ← is_shadowed(world, comps.over_point)

  surface ← lighting(comps.object.material,
                     comps.object,
                     world.light,
                     comps.over_point, comps.eyev, comps.normalv,
                     shadowed)

➤    reflected ← reflected_color(world, comps)
➤
➤    return surface + reflected
end function
```

By adding the reflected color to the surface color, the two blend together and produce a believable reflection. However, there's a gotcha hiding here. The shade_hit() function now calls reflected_color(), which calls color_at(), which calls shade_hit()... That's a recursive loop, with the potential to cause some problems. Let's address that next.

Test #6: Avoid Infinite Recursion

Show that your code safely handles infinite recursion caused by two objects that mutually reflect rays between themselves.

Create two parallel mirrors by positioning one plane above another and making them both reflective. Orient a ray so that it strikes one plane and bounces to the other. What will happen?

```
features/world.feature
Scenario: color_at() with mutually reflective surfaces
  Given w ← world()
    And w.light ← point_light(point(0, 0, 0), color(1, 1, 1))
    And lower ← plane() with:
      | material.reflective | 1                   |
      | transform           | translation(0, -1, 0) |
    And lower is added to w
    And upper ← plane() with:
      | material.reflective | 1                   |
      | transform           | translation(0, 1, 0) |
    And upper is added to w
    And r ← ray(point(0, 0, 0), vector(0, 1, 0))
  Then color_at(w, r) should terminate successfully
```

Your ray tracer will probably not handle this well. Because of that recursive loop you made for the previous test, your reflections will bounce back and forth between those two mirrors, right up until your stack explodes.

Infinite recursion is the pits.

\//
∵̆   Joe asks:
How can I test "should terminate successfully"?

Testing "should terminate successfully" can be tricky. Rather than trying to determine whether your program will actually terminate (because good luck with that[a]), it might be better to check for the opposite. Look for what happens when the program *doesn't* terminate. Mostly likely, under infinite recursion, your program will eventually run out of memory. Does your environment raise an exception when this happens? Test for that, if you can. Or, if that's not an option, you might instead assert that the function terminates in some finite amount of time.

---

a.   See Wikipedia's entry on the Halting problem: en.wikipedia.org/wiki/Halting_problem

---

Still, the tests must pass. One way to accomplish this is to limit how deeply the recursion is allowed to go. After all, if a ray can only bounce four or five times, it is unlikely to blow up your call stack. You can implement this constraint by declaring some threshold and then requiring the reflected_color() function to return immediately if the recursion goes deeper than that.

For now, allow this test to fail. The next test will point you in the right direction and will help you get them both passing.

Test #7: Limit Recursion

Show that reflected_color() returns without effect when invoked at the limit of its recursive threshold.

Duplicate the scenario in *Test #5: Update the shade_hit Function*, on page 145. The difference, though, is that here you'll invoke reflected_color(world, comps, remaining) with a new, additional parameter—remaining—which tells the function how many more recursive calls it is allowed to make.

features/world.feature
```
Line 1   Scenario: The reflected color at the maximum recursive depth
    -      Given w ← default_world()
    -        And shape ← plane() with:
    -          | material.reflective | 0.5                  |
    5          | transform           | translation(0, -1, 0) |
    -        And shape is added to w
    -        And r ← ray(point(0, 0, -3), vector(0, -√2/2, √2/2))
    -        And i ← intersection(√2, shape)
    -      When comps ← prepare_computations(i, r)
   10        And color ← reflected_color(w, comps, 0)
    -      Then color = color(0, 0, 0)
```

Line 10 sets the remaining parameter to 0, telling the function that it is not allowed to make any more recursive calls. It should return black instead.

Make this pass by adding another condition to the top of your reflected_color() function. It should return black if remaining is less than 1.

To make this useful, though, you next need to pass that number back and forth between color_at(), shade_hit(), and reflected_color(). Perform the following refactoring:

1. Add a third parameter to color_at(world, ray, remaining).

2. Add a third parameter to shade_hit(world, hit, remaining).

3. Make color_at() pass the remaining value to shade_hit().

4. Make it so that when reflected_color() calls color_at(), it decrements the remaining value before passing it on.

In other words, use something like this:

```
function color_at(world, ray, remaining)
  # ...
  color ← shade_hit(world, comps, remaining)
  # ...
end function

function shade_hit(world, comps, remaining)
  # ...
  reflected ← reflected_color(world, comps, remaining)
  # ...
end function

function reflected_color(world, comps, remaining)
  if remaining <= 0
    return color(0, 0, 0)
  end if

  # ...
  color ← color_at(world, reflect_ray, remaining - 1)
  # ...
end function
```

In this way, your code keeps track of how deep the recursion is allowed to go and avoids nastiness when things get a little carried away.

Be sure to change all existing calls of color_at() and shade_hit() to pass in the maximum recursive depth via the new remaining parameter. If your programming language supports default parameter values, this is a great place for it. Setting remaining's default value to 4 or 5 is empirically pretty safe. Larger numbers will slow down your renderer on scenes with lots of reflective objects.

Once that's done, you should find that all your previous tests are now passing again, including *Test #6: Avoid Infinite Recursion*, on page 146.

Whew!

Take a moment and celebrate with a simple scene. Populate it with spheres, and make some of them reflective. See how the color of a surface affects reflection. Do some colors work better than others? What happens when you vary the ambient, diffuse, and specular parameters on a reflective surface?

When you've got that working to your satisfaction, read on. It's time to talk about transparency and refraction.

Transparency and Refraction

Refraction describes how light bends when it passes from one transparent medium to another. With this added to your ray tracer, you'll be able to render pretty convincing glass, water, and other transparent materials. The following figure is one example, showing how a glass sphere distorts the image of the scene behind it.

Refraction is governed by a property called the *refractive index* (or *index of refraction*). It's a number that determines the degree to which light will bend when entering or exiting the material, compared to other materials. The larger the number, the more strongly light will bend when encountering that material.

You can find various lists online of materials and their corresponding indices of refraction.[1] To save you the search, here are some of the more common materials and their refractive indices:

---

1. Here's one such list: hyperphysics.phy-astr.gsu.edu/hbase/Tables/indrf.html

- Vacuum: 1
- Air: 1.00029
- Water: 1.333
- Glass: 1.52
- Diamond: 2.417

Once again, the key to making this work in your ray tracer is to spawn a secondary ray every time your ray encounters a transparent material, just like you did for reflection. The difference here is really just the math that determines which direction the new ray should go.

You'll implement this in eight tests:

1. Add transparency and refractive_index to material as new attributes.

2. For a given intersection, find the refractive index of the material that the ray is passing *from*, and the refractive index of the material that the ray is passing *to*. We typically refer to these as n_1 and n_2.

3. Add a new attribute in prepare_computations(), called under_point, which determines where the refracted ray will originate.

4. Handle refraction when the surface is opaque.

5. Handle refraction when the maximum recursive depth is reached.

6. Handle refraction under *total internal reflection*. (More on that in a bit!)

7. Handle refraction in the general case, when the surface is transparent.

8. Combine the reflected and refracted colors with the material color to find the final surface color.

You've got this!

Test #1: Add the Material Attributes for transparency and refractive_index

Show that your material structure contains two new attributes, called transparency and refractive_index. transparency defaults to 0, and refractive_index defaults to 1.

```
features/materials.feature
Scenario: Transparency and Refractive Index for the default material
  Given m ← material()
  Then m.transparency = 0.0
    And m.refractive_index = 1.0
```

Defaulting transparency to 0 makes all surfaces opaque by default, and using 1 as the default for refractive_index makes all objects empty, vacuum-filled shells.

With the addition of those two attributes, you can also implement a helper function, glass_sphere(), that creates a sphere with a glassy texture. Add the following test to make sure it works as expected.

features/spheres.feature
```
Scenario: A helper for producing a sphere with a glassy material
  Given s ← glass_sphere()
  Then s.transform = identity_matrix
    And s.material.transparency = 1.0
    And s.material.refractive_index = 1.5
```

This will come in handy for later tests, including the very next one.

Test #2: Determining n_1 and n_2

Show that prepare_computations() determines n_1 and n_2 correctly at six different points of intersection.

As mentioned, n_1 and n_2 are the names given to the refractive indices of the materials on either side of a ray-object intersection, with n_1 belonging to the material being *exited*, and n_2 belonging to the material being *entered*.

For this test, construct a scene which looks something like this in cross-section:

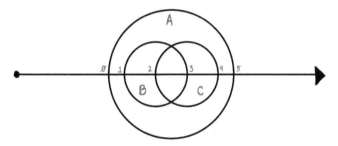

A, B, and C are three glass spheres, with B and C contained by A and overlapping each other slightly. A ray is cast through the center of all three, and your test must check that prepare_computations() can correctly determine n_1 and n_2 at each of the numbered intersections.

This test is presented as a *scenario outline* with certain variable names between angle brackets, like <this>. A table below the scenario, called "Examples," shows what values should be plugged into the test for each variable, with the rows representing separate invocations of the test.

features/intersections.feature

```
Line 1  Scenario Outline: Finding n1 and n2 at various intersections
   -      Given A ← glass_sphere() with:
   -          | transform                | scaling(2, 2, 2) |
   -          | material.refractive_index | 1.5             |
   5      And B ← glass_sphere() with:
   -          | transform                | translation(0, 0, -0.25) |
   -          | material.refractive_index | 2.0                     |
   -      And C ← glass_sphere() with:
   -          | transform                | translation(0, 0, 0.25) |
   10         | material.refractive_index | 2.5                    |
   -      And r ← ray(point(0, 0, -4), vector(0, 0, 1))
   -      And xs ← intersections(2:A, 2.75:B, 3.25:C, 4.75:B, 5.25:C, 6:A)
   -      When comps ← prepare_computations(xs[<index>], r, xs)
   -      Then comps.n1 = <n1>
   15     And comps.n2 = <n2>
   -
   -      Examples:
   -          | index | n1  | n2  |
   -          | 0     | 1.0 | 1.5 |
   20         | 1     | 1.5 | 2.0 |
   -          | 2     | 2.0 | 2.5 |
   -          | 3     | 2.5 | 2.5 |
   -          | 4     | 2.5 | 1.5 |
   -          | 5     | 1.5 | 1.0 |
```

Here, the examples correspond to the intersections to be tested. For instance, the example on line 19 says that when looking at the intersection at index 0, n_1 should be 1.0 and n_2 should be 1.5. Those values are substituted on lines 13–15, replacing the variables <index>, <n1>, and <n2>, and then the test runs. This repeats for each row in the Examples table.

Note in particular the behavior at intersection #3, where n_1 and n_2 are both 2.5. This is a consequence of how spheres B and C overlap. Sphere C is entered at intersection #2, so when sphere B is exited at #3, it turns out that C, with a refractive index of 2.5, is effectively on both sides of the intersection. This won't happen often, but that's why it makes a good test case!

Now, you may have noticed already the new argument being passed to prepare_computations(intersection, ray, xs). The third argument, xs, is the collection of all intersections, which can tell you where the hit is relative to the rest of the intersections. With that, you can decide which object, if any, contains the intersected object.

Adding a new parameter to prepare_computations() will affect any test you've written so far that calls this function, which is more than a few. If that gives you grief, and if your programming language supports optional parameters, consider making the xs parameter optional. If not given, it can default to a collection of one value, the intersection. Just make sure you update (at least) your color_at() function so it sends the actual list of intersections to prepare_computations()!

The algorithm works like this: start with an empty list, called containers, that will record which objects have been encountered but not yet exited. These objects must contain the subsequent intersection. Then, iterating over the collection of intersections, do the following at each intersection.

1. If the intersection is the hit, set n_1 to the refractive index of the last object in the containers list. If that list is empty, then there is no containing object, and n_1 should be set to 1.

2. If the intersection's object is already in the containers list, then this intersection must be exiting the object. Remove the object from the containers list in this case. Otherwise, the intersection is entering the object, and the object should be added to the end of the list.

3. If the intersection is the hit, set n_2 to the refractive index of the last object in the containers list. If that list is empty, then again, there is no containing object and n_2 should be set to 1.

4. If the intersection is the hit, terminate the loop here.

As pseudocode, it looks something like this:

```
containers ← empty list

for i ← each intersection in xs
  if i = hit then
    if containers is empty
      comps.n1 ← 1.0
    else
      comps.n1 ← last(containers).material.refractive_index
    end if
  end if

  if containers includes i.object then
    remove i.object from containers
  else
    append i.object onto containers
  end if
```

```
  if i = hit then
    if containers is empty
      comps.n2 ← 1.0
    else
      comps.n2 ← last(containers).material.refractive_index
    end if

    terminate loop
  end if
end for
```

Add that logic to prepare_computations(), and get that test passing.

Test #3: Computing under_point

Show that prepare_computations() computes a new attribute, under_point, which lies just beneath the intersected surface.

Construct an intersection between a ray and a glass sphere such that the intersection occurs at z=0. After preparing the computations, the under_point attribute should describe a point just beneath the surface of the sphere, barely more than z=0.

features/intersections.feature

```
Scenario: The under point is offset below the surface
  Given r ← ray(point(0, 0, -5), vector(0, 0, 1))
    And shape ← glass_sphere() with:
      | transform | translation(0, 0, 1) |
    And i ← intersection(5, shape)
    And xs ← intersections(i)
  When comps ← prepare_computations(i, r, xs)
  Then comps.under_point.z > EPSILON/2
    And comps.point.z < comps.under_point.z
```

Note that the result is compared against half of EPSILON to make sure that it has been adjusted in the correct direction.

The purpose of this new attribute is to describe where the refracted rays will originate. Remember in *Rendering Shadows*, on page 113, how you computed the over_point attribute so it was offset just a fraction above the surface to prevent objects from shadowing themselves? It's the same thing here, only instead of lifting the point *above* the surface, you push the point *below* the surface.

Compute that attribute exactly as you did for comps.over_point, but instead of adding a fraction of the surface normal vector, you'll subtract it. In pseudocode, it'll look like this:

```
comps.point ← position(ray, comps.t)
# and then, after computing and possibly negating
# the normal vector...
comps.over_point ← comps.point + comps.normalv * EPSILON
comps.under_point ← comps.point - comps.normalv * EPSILON
```

Test #4: Finding the Refracted Color of an Opaque Object

Introduce a new function, refracted_color(world, comps, remaining), and show that it returns the color black when the hit applies to an opaque object.

Intersect a ray with the first sphere of the default world. After preparing the hit, calling refracted_color(world, comps, remaining) should return black, because the sphere is not transparent at all.

features/world.feature
```
Scenario: The refracted color with an opaque surface
  Given w ← default_world()
    And shape ← the first object in w
    And r ← ray(point(0, 0, -5), vector(0, 0, 1))
    And xs ← intersections(4:shape, 6:shape)
  When comps ← prepare_computations(xs[0], r, xs)
    And c ← refracted_color(w, comps, 5)
  Then c = color(0, 0, 0)
```

Making this pass requires refracted_color() to check the material of the hit object, returning black if transparency is 0 . For now, be sure and return some other color (like white) when transparency is *not* 0, like this:

```
function refracted_color(world, comps, remaining)
  if comps.object.material.transparency = 0
    return color(0, 0, 0)
  end if

  return color(1, 1, 1)
end function
```

That helps ensure that the test fails if you get the logic wrong in your code, while you incrementally build out the rest of the refracted_color() function.

Test #5: Finding the Refracted Color at the Maximum Recursive Depth

Show that refracted_color() returns the color black when invoked at the maximum recursive depth, when there are no remaining recursive calls available.

Intersect a ray again with the first sphere of the default world, but this time give the sphere a glassy material. Then, invoke refracted_color() with the remaining parameter set to 0. It should return the color black.

features/world.feature

```
Scenario: The refracted color at the maximum recursive depth
  Given w ← default_world()
    And shape ← the first object in w
    And shape has:
      | material.transparency     | 1.0 |
      | material.refractive_index | 1.5 |
    And r ← ray(point(0, 0, -5), vector(0, 0, 1))
    And xs ← intersections(4:shape, 6:shape)
  When comps ← prepare_computations(xs[0], r, xs)
    And c ← refracted_color(w, comps, 0)
  Then c = color(0, 0, 0)
```

To pass this test, your function must return black if remaining is 0.

Test #6: Finding the Refracted Color under Total Internal Reflection

Show that refracted_color() returns the color black when the conditions are right for total internal reflection.

This case deals with *total internal reflection*. No, it's not the name of a metal band. This is a phenomenon that occurs when light enters a new medium at a sufficiently acute angle, and the new medium has a lower refractive index than the old. For example, a ray of light moving from water to air could experience total internal reflection if it strikes the interface between them at a small enough angle.

When these conditions are true, the ray will reflect off the interface, instead of passing through it, as the following illustration shows.

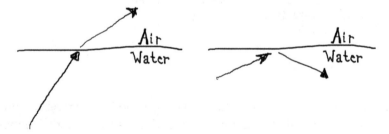

This, incidentally, is what allows things like fiber optic cable to work.

Under total internal reflection, light is not propagated across the interface between the two media. This means that your ray tracer should return the color black when total internal reflection occurs.

Construct a scene where the ray starts inside the first sphere of the default world and strikes that sphere at a sufficiently acute angle. Total internal reflection should result, and the function should return black.

```
features/world.feature
Scenario: The refracted color under total internal reflection
  Given w ← default_world()
    And shape ← the first object in w
    And shape has:
      | material.transparency    | 1.0 |
      | material.refractive_index | 1.5 |
    And r ← ray(point(0, 0, √2/2), vector(0, 1, 0))
    And xs ← intersections(-√2/2:shape, √2/2:shape)
  # NOTE: this time you're inside the sphere, so you need
  # to look at the second intersection, xs[1], not xs[0]
  When comps ← prepare_computations(xs[1], r, xs)
    And c ← refracted_color(w, comps, 5)
  Then c = color(0, 0, 0)
```

The implementation of this depends on a little thing called *Snell's Law*, which describes the relationship between the angle of the incoming ray and the angle of the refracted ray. Given those two angles, θ_i and θ_t (say, "theta i" and "theta t"), Snell's Law declares:

$$\frac{\sin \theta_i}{\sin \theta_t} = \frac{\eta_2}{\eta_1}$$

Now it's a matter of applying a few trigonometric identities to turn this into information you can use in your ray tracer, but don't panic! What you need to do is find θ_i, given θ_t, which goes like this in pseudocode:

```
# Find the ratio of first index of refraction to the second.
# (Yup, this is inverted from the definition of Snell's Law.)
n_ratio ← comps.n1 / comps.n2

# cos(theta_i) is the same as the dot product of the two vectors
cos_i ← dot(comps.eyev, comps.normalv)

# Find sin(theta_t)^2 via trigonometric identity
sin2_t ← n_ratio^2 * (1 - cos_i^2)
```

If sin2_t is greater than 1, then you've got some total internal reflection going on. Go ahead and update your refracted_color() function to check for this case, and return the color black when it does.

Test #7: Finding the Refracted Color

Show that refracted_color() in all other cases will spawn a secondary ray in the correct direction, and return its color.

Start with the default world, but make the first, outermost sphere fully ambient, so that it shows up regardless of lighting. Apply the test pattern from *Generalizing Patterns*, on page 132, to it. The second, innermost sphere is given a glassy material. Then spawn a ray inside the innermost sphere, pointing straight up.

Remember that the test pattern will return a color based on the point of intersection, which means the test can inspect the returned color to determine whether or not the ray was refracted. Sneaky!

```
features/world.feature
Scenario: The refracted color with a refracted ray
  Given w ← default_world()
    And A ← the first object in w
    And A has:
      | material.ambient | 1.0            |
      | material.pattern | test_pattern() |
    And B ← the second object in w
    And B has:
      | material.transparency    | 1.0 |
      | material.refractive_index | 1.5 |
    And r ← ray(point(0, 0, 0.1), vector(0, 1, 0))
    And xs ← intersections(-0.9899:A, -0.4899:B, 0.4899:B, 0.9899:A)
  When comps ← prepare_computations(xs[2], r, xs)
    And c ← refracted_color(w, comps, 5)
  Then c = color(0, 0.99888, 0.04725)
```

To make this test pass, update your refracted_color() function again. It needs to do a few more computations to figure out which direction the ray is refracted and then spawn and evaluate that refracted ray. In pseudocode, it goes like this:

```
# Find cos(theta_t) via trigonometric identity
cos_t ← sqrt(1.0 - sin2_t)

# Compute the direction of the refracted ray
direction ← comps.normalv * (n_ratio * cos_i - cos_t) -
            comps.eyev * n_ratio

# Create the refracted ray
refract_ray ← ray(comps.under_point, direction)

# Find the color of the refracted ray, making sure to multiply
# by the transparency value to account for any opacity
color ← color_at(world, refract_ray, remaining - 1) *
        comps.object.material.transparency
```

Just so.

Test #8: Handling Refraction in shade_hit

Show that your shade_hit() function handles refraction.

Add a glass floor to the default world, positioned just below the two default spheres, and add a new, colored sphere below the floor. Cast a ray diagonally toward the floor, with the expectation that it will refract and eventually strike the colored ball. Because the plane is only semitransparent, the resulting color should combine the refracted color of the ball and the color of the plane.

```
features/world.feature
Scenario: shade_hit() with a transparent material
  Given w ← default_world()
    And floor ← plane() with:
      | transform               | translation(0, -1, 0) |
      | material.transparency    | 0.5                   |
      | material.refractive_index | 1.5                 |
    And floor is added to w
    And ball ← sphere() with:
      | material.color    | (1, 0, 0)              |
      | material.ambient  | 0.5                    |
      | transform         | translation(0, -3.5, -0.5) |
    And ball is added to w
    And r ← ray(point(0, 0, -3), vector(0, -√2/2, √2/2))
    And xs ← intersections(√2:floor)
  When comps ← prepare_computations(xs[0], r, xs)
    And color ← shade_hit(w, comps, 5)
  Then color = color(0.93642, 0.68642, 0.68642)
```

Make this pass by calling refracted_color() from shade_hit() and adding its result to the sum of the reflected and surface colors.

At this point things look pretty good. Your renderer can produce lovely refraction effects, but be careful: the results will be unpleasant when total internal reflection comes into play. Consider the following two images. Each depicts a glass sphere, with an air bubble in the middle of it.

The sphere on the left is what your ray tracer will currently produce, adding the refracted color to the surface color. Sadly, total internal reflection causes the interaction between the glass and the pocket of air to render that black band. The sphere on the right, though, uses a more realistic algorithm that blends reflection and refraction together, mitigating the band. Kind of "night and day," right?

The secret sauce here is the *Fresnel effect*, and the good news is that it's not much more work to add to your ray tracer. Read on to see how it comes together.

Fresnel Effect

The *Fresnel effect* (that's a silent "s," by the way—thank the French for that) is the name for how light behaves on transparent surfaces. If you've ever stood beside a lake, you'll be familiar with it. Looking straight down into the water, you see the rocks and fish below the surface. But as you look up toward the far shore, the water becomes more opaque and reflects more and more of the scenery. The following figure demonstrates this, with a brown/green checkered plane for the bottom of the lake, and a second, transparent plane as the water. A white/gray checkered wall in the far distance stands in for the scenery.

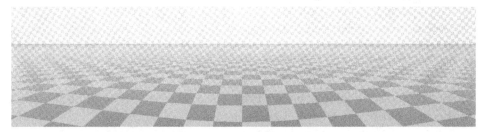

Notice specifically how the "water" strongly reflects the white/gray checkered wall when far away and more weakly close-up. Similarly, the water is strongly transparent close-up, but less so at a distance.

The formulas that describe this behavior were first deduced in the early 1800s by Augustin-Jean Fresnel, a French physicist. The basic idea is this: when the angle between the eye and the surface is large ("looking straight down into the water"), the amount of light reflected is small relative to the amount transmitted through the surface, and when the angle is small ("looking toward the far shore"), the amount of light reflected is larger.

This inverse relationship between reflection and refraction is what fixes that "black out" caused by total internal reflection. It gets filled in by reflections—the refracted and reflected rays complement each other, balancing things out nicely.

The bad news? Fresnel's equations deal with more than our simulation cares about, like the polarization of light. While it's certainly possible to model all of this in software, to do so would be slow.

The good news? Another fellow, Christophe Schlick, came up with an approximation to Fresnel's equations that is much faster, and plenty accurate besides. Hurray for Schlick!

To make this work, you'll implement a new function, schlick(comps), which returns a number between 0 and 1, inclusive. This number is called the *reflectance* and represents what fraction of the light is reflected, given the surface information at the hit.

You'll implement the schlick() function with four tests:

1. Reflectance when total internal reflection occurs.

2. Reflectance when a ray strikes a surface at a 90° angle.

3. Reflectance when n_2 is greater than n_1, and the angle is small.

4. Reflectance always used by shade_hit() when a surface is both reflective and transparent.

Here goes! You're on the final stretch.

Test #1: Determine Reflectance under Total Internal Reflection

Show that schlick() returns a 1 when conditions are right for total internal reflection.

Position a ray inside a glass sphere, offset from the center and pointing straight up. The ray is offset sufficiently to trigger total internal reflection, resulting in schlick() returning 1.

```
features/intersections.feature
Scenario: The Schlick approximation under total internal reflection
  Given shape ← glass_sphere()
    And r ← ray(point(0, 0, √2/2), vector(0, 1, 0))
    And xs ← intersections(-√2/2:shape, √2/2:shape)
  When comps ← prepare_computations(xs[1], r, xs)
    And reflectance ← schlick(comps)
  Then reflectance = 1.0
```

Intuitively, "total internal reflection" means all the light is reflected and none is refracted. The fraction of light that is reflected must be 1 in this case. This is called the *reflectance.*

Make that test pass by implementing a check for total internal reflection. The following pseudocode describes how it works:

```
function schlick(comps)
  # find the cosine of the angle between the eye and normal vectors
  cos ← dot(comps.eyev, comps.normalv)

  # total internal reflection can only occur if n1 > n2
  if comps.n1 > comps.n2
    n ← comps.n1 / comps.n2
    sin2_t = n^2 * (1.0 - cos^2)
    return 1.0 if sin2_t > 1.0
  end if

  # return anything but 1.0 here, so that the test will fail
  # appropriately if something goes wrong.
  return 0.0
end function
```

Remember that total internal reflection can only happen when n_1 is greater than n_2, so the check itself is guarded by that condition. The cos variable, though, will be used later in the function and should be initialized regardless of whether or not total internal reflection occurs.

Test #2: Determine Reflectance of a Perpendicular Ray

Show that reflectance (via schlick()) is small when a ray strikes the surface at a perpendicular angle.

Create a glass sphere and a ray that intersects it. The ray should strike the sphere perpendicular to its surface. The reflectance in this case will be slight.

features/intersections.feature
```
Scenario: The Schlick approximation with a perpendicular viewing angle
  Given shape ← glass_sphere()
    And r ← ray(point(0, 0, 0), vector(0, 1, 0))
    And xs ← intersections(-1:shape, 1:shape)
  When comps ← prepare_computations(xs[1], r, xs)
    And reflectance ← schlick(comps)
  Then reflectance = 0.04
```

Don't worry about making this one pass just now; we'll discuss the implementation at the end of the following test, and you'll make them both pass in one fell swoop!

Test #3: Determine Reflectance when $n_2 > n_1$

Show that reflectance (via schlick()) is significant when $n_2 > n_1$ and the ray strikes the surface at a small angle.

This is the "looking across the lake to the far shore" scenario, and a significant amount of light should be reflected. The test mimics this by preparing a ray so that it glances off a sphere, almost tangent to it.

features/intersections.feature

```
Scenario: The Schlick approximation with small angle and n2 > n1
  Given shape ← glass_sphere()
    And r ← ray(point(0, 0.99, -2), vector(0, 0, 1))
    And xs ← intersections(1.8589:shape)
  When comps ← prepare_computations(xs[0], r, xs)
    And reflectance ← schlick(comps)
  Then reflectance = 0.48873
```

Make this test and the previous test pass by adding a few more computations to your schlick() function. The following pseudocode finishes it off by adding the indicated lines:

```
function schlick(comps)
  # find the cosine of the angle between the eye and normal vectors
  cos ← dot(comps.eyev, comps.normalv)

  # total internal reflection can only occur if n1 > n2
  if comps.n1 > comps.n2
    n ← comps.n1 / comps.n2
    sin2_t = n^2 * (1.0 - cos^2)
    return 1.0 if sin2_t > 1.0

➤    # compute cosine of theta_t using trig identity
➤    cos_t ← sqrt(1.0 - sin2_t)
➤
➤    # when n1 > n2, use cos(theta_t) instead
➤    cos ← cos_t
  end if

➤  r0 ← ((comps.n1 - comps.n2) / (comps.n1 + comps.n2))^2
➤  return r0 + (1 - r0) * (1 - cos)^5
end function
```

This probably all seems like magic, but I promise it's grounded in reality! An excellent paper called "Reflections and Refractions in Ray Tracing," by Bram de Greve,[2] isn't long and is well worth the read if you're curious about the math behind all of this.

Test #4: Employ Reflectance When Combining Reflection and Refraction

Show that the schlick() reflectance value is used by shade_hit() when a material is both transparent and reflective.

This is essentially the same test as *Test #8: Handling Refraction in shade_hit*, on page 158, but the plane is made both transparent *and* reflective. This will cause the color at the point of intersection to incorporate both the reflected

---

2. Many online sites have a copy. Here's one: graphics.stanford.edu/courses/cs148-10-summer/docs/
2006--degreve--reflection_refraction.pdf.

and refracted colors, combining those of the default world's spheres with the sphere that was added below the plane.

features/world.feature

```
Scenario: shade_hit() with a reflective, transparent material
  Given w ← default_world()
    And r ← ray(point(0, 0, -3), vector(0, -√2/2, √2/2))
    And floor ← plane() with:
      | transform              | translation(0, -1, 0) |
      | material.reflective    | 0.5                   |
      | material.transparency  | 0.5                   |
      | material.refractive_index | 1.5                |
    And floor is added to w
    And ball ← sphere() with:
      | material.color    | (1, 0, 0)                |
      | material.ambient  | 0.5                      |
      | transform         | translation(0, -3.5, -0.5) |
    And ball is added to w
    And xs ← intersections(√2:floor)
  When comps ← prepare_computations(xs[0], r, xs)
    And color ← shade_hit(w, comps, 5)
  Then color = color(0.93391, 0.69643, 0.69243)
```

Make this work by changing your shade_hit() function, so that instead of naively returning the sum of the surface, reflected, and refracted colors, you'll first check to see if the surface material is both transparent and reflective. If it is, you'll use the Schlick approximation to combine them. The following pseudocode demonstrates:

```
function shade_hit(world, comps, remaining)
  shadowed ← is_shadowed(world, comps.over_point)

  surface ← lighting(comps.object.material,
                     comps.object,
                     world.light,
                     comps.over_point, comps.eyev, comps.normalv,
                     shadowed)

➤ reflected ← reflected_color(world, comps, remaining)
➤ refracted ← refracted_color(world, comps, remaining)
➤
➤ material ← comps.object.material
➤ if material.reflective > 0 && material.transparency > 0
➤   reflectance ← schlick(comps)
➤   return surface + reflected * reflectance +
➤                   refracted * (1 - reflectance)
➤ else
➤   return surface + reflected + refracted
➤ end
end function
```

There! That ought to do it. Once your tests are all passing, you're set to render bona fide reflections and refractions, complete with Fresnel effects. Impressive!

Putting It Together

Ray tracers are best known for mirrors and glass. Take some time and experiment, to see why. Here are a few tips for figuring out how to employ reflection and refraction effectively in your scenes.

1. We tend to think of glass as exclusively transparent, but no one is surprised to look in a window and see their own ghostly reflection superimposed over the scene. When rendering glass or any similar material, set both transparency and reflectivity to high values, 0.9 or even 1. This allows the Fresnel effect to kick in, and gives your material an added touch of realism!

2. Because the reflected and refracted colors are added to the surface color, they'll tend to make such objects brighter. You can tone down the material's diffuse and ambient properties to compensate. The more transparent or reflective the surface, the smaller the diffuse property should be. This way, more of the color comes from the secondary rays, and less from the object's surface.

3. If you'd like a subtly colored mirror, or slightly tinted glass, use a very *dark* color, instead of a very *light* one. Red glass, for instance, should use a very dark red, almost black, instead of a very bright red. In general, the more reflective or transparent the surface, the darker its surface color should be. Note that if you add color, make sure that you have some diffuse and possibly ambient contribution, too; otherwise, your surface will render as black regardless of what color you give to it.

4. Reflective and transparent surfaces pair nicely with tight specular highlights. Set specular to 1 and bump shininess to 300 or more to get a highlight that really shines.

Also, here's a closing challenge for you: suppose you wanted to render a scene where you were looking through the surface of a pond at some rocks beneath it. In terms of implementation, that would be a transparent plane, with some spheres scattered below it. As your ray tracer is currently implemented, the plane is going to cast a shadow on anything beneath it, which leaves everything under the water in darkness, ruining the effect. You could add a light source beneath the plane, but that will introduce odd shadows and highlights—not a good solution either.

What you really want is for some objects to "opt out" of the shadow calculation. The surface of the pond, for instance, should be ignored when calculating shadows.

How would you go about changing your ray tracer to support that? What would you need to do to allow objects to individually declare that they cast no shadow?

Chew on that one for a bit. When you're ready to move on, turn the page! Next up, you'll add another primitive shape to your ray tracer: the humble cube.

## CHAPTER 12

Cubes

Reflections and refractions were huge, and you totally nailed them! Your scenes are looking more realistic than ever. In this chapter, you're going to increase the scope of what's possible by adding a new primitive shape: the *cube*.

Check it out. Here's a scene rendered *entirely with cubes*.

True, most of the cubes have been stretched and squashed in various ways, but—cross my heart—they all started life as perfect cubes.

In fact, they all started life as a very specific kind of cube, called an *axis-aligned bounding box*. In this chapter, you'll add support for them by implementing a new ray intersection algorithm, as well as the algorithm for finding the normal on the surface of a cube.

An axis-aligned bounding box, or AABB, is a box with a special property: its sides are all aligned with the scene's axes. Two are aligned with the x axis, two with the y axis, and two with the z axis, like the figure on page 168.

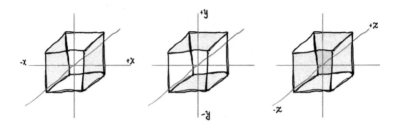

This particular constraint makes the intersection math *much* less complex, which makes the computer happier and ought to make you happier as well. The cube logic in your ray tracer will implement these AABBs, so your cubes will always begin centered at the origin and extend from -1 to +1 along each axis. From there, you can use transformation matrices to scale, rotate, and translate them into any orientation you like.

You've already done most of the hard work in previous chapters, building a framework for supporting, transforming, and intersecting primitive shapes. That's awesome! That means this chapter only needs to focus on two things: the ray-cube intersection algorithm, and the algorithm for finding the normal on the cube.

Let's start with the intersection algorithm.

Intersecting a Ray with a Cube

The intersection algorithm must decide whether a given ray intersects any of the cube's six faces or whether the ray misses the cube altogether. Treat those two cases as tests, starting with the first one: a ray intersecting a cube.

Test #1: A Ray Intersects a Cube

Show that the local_intersect() function for a cube correctly identifies intersections on any face.

This test creates a single cube and then casts a ray at each of its faces to show that the algorithm works correctly from all six directions.

```
features/cubes.feature
Scenario Outline: A ray intersects a cube
  Given c ← cube()
    And r ← ray(<origin>, <direction>)
  When xs ← local_intersect(c, r)
  Then xs.count = 2
    And xs[0].t = <t1>
    And xs[1].t = <t2>
```

Examples:

```
|        | origin            | direction         | t1 | t2 |
| +x     | point(5, 0.5, 0)  | vector(-1, 0, 0)  |  4 |  6 |
| -x     | point(-5, 0.5, 0) | vector(1, 0, 0)   |  4 |  6 |
| +y     | point(0.5, 5, 0)  | vector(0, -1, 0)  |  4 |  6 |
| -y     | point(0.5, -5, 0) | vector(0, 1, 0)   |  4 |  6 |
| +z     | point(0.5, 0, 5)  | vector(0, 0, -1)  |  4 |  6 |
| -z     | point(0.5, 0, -5) | vector(0, 0, 1)   |  4 |  6 |
| inside | point(0, 0.5, 0)  | vector(0, 0, 1)   | -1 |  1 |
```

The test also casts a ray from *inside* the cube, to show that the algorithm handles that case as well.

This works by treating a cube as it were composed of six planes, one for each face of the cube. Intersecting a ray with that cube involves testing it against each of the planes, and if the ray intersects them in just the right way, it means that the ray intersects the cube, as well. Let's consider the algorithm at a simpler level, first, to build some intuition about how it works. Start by looking at the following figure. It shows a ray intersecting a 2D square.

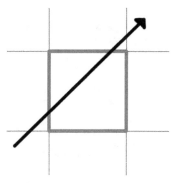

The first step is to find the t values of all the places where the ray intersects those lines, like this:

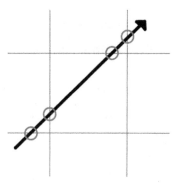

Next, consider them in parallel pairs. The following figure highlights the pairings with two blue intersections on two parallel blue lines, and two yellow intersections on two parallel yellow lines:

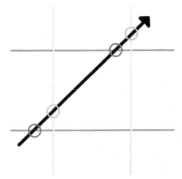

For each pair of lines, there will be a *minimum* t closest to the ray origin, and a *maximum* t farther away. Focus on the *largest* of all the minimum t values and the *smallest* of all the maximum t values, like so:

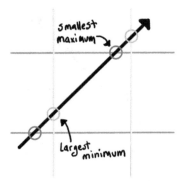

The intersection of the ray with that square will always be those two points: the largest minimum t value and the smallest maximum t value. This works for any number of dimensions, too. In three dimensions, you intersect planes instead of lines, but you still consider them in parallel pairs.

In pseudocode, the intersection routine itself looks like this:

```
function local_intersect(cube, ray)
  xtmin, xtmax ← check_axis(ray.origin.x, ray.direction.x)
  ytmin, ytmax ← check_axis(ray.origin.y, ray.direction.y)
  ztmin, ztmax ← check_axis(ray.origin.z, ray.direction.z)

  tmin ← max(xtmin, ytmin, ztmin)
  tmax ← min(xtmax, ytmax, ztmax)

  return ( intersection(tmin, cube), intersection(tmax, cube) )
end function
```

For each of the x, y, and z axes, you'll check to see where the ray intersects the corresponding planes and return the minimum and maximum t values for each. Once you've found those points of intersection, you find the actual points of intersection by taking the largest of the minimum t values and the smallest of the maximum t values.

The helper function, check_axis(), looks like this in pseudocode:

```
function check_axis(origin, direction)
  tmin_numerator = (-1 - origin)
  tmax_numerator = (1 - origin)

  if abs(direction) >= EPSILON
    tmin ← tmin_numerator / direction
    tmax ← tmax_numerator / direction
  else
    tmin ← tmin_numerator * INFINITY
    tmax ← tmax_numerator * INFINITY
  end if

  if tmin > tmax then swap(tmin, tmax)

  return tmin, tmax
end function
```

This takes the ray-plane intersection formula that you used in Chapter 9, *Planes*, on page 117, and generalizes it to support planes that are offset from the origin. Specifically, each pair of planes is offset 1 unit in opposing directions, hence -1 - origin and 1 - origin.

If the denominator (direction) is effectively zero, though, you don't want to be dividing by it. The previous pseudocode handles this case by multiplying the numerators by infinity, which makes sure tmin and tmax—while both being infinity—have the correct sign (positive or negative).

 If your programming language natively handles infinity and floating-point division by zero, you can avoid most of the song and dance in check_axis() and just divide the numerators by the denominator. No special case needed when direction is zero!

Implement this, and make that first test pass. Once you've got it working, move on to the next test!

Test #2: A Ray Misses a Cube

Show that the local_intersect() function for a cube handles the case where the ray misses the cube.

Once again, the test creates a single cube, but this time the rays are cast in such a way that they miss the cube. Some are cast parallel to different faces, others are just cast diagonally away from the cube.

features/cubes.feature
```
Scenario Outline: A ray misses a cube
  Given c ← cube()
    And r ← ray(<origin>, <direction>)
  When xs ← local_intersect(c, r)
  Then xs.count = 0
```

```
  Examples:
    | origin          | direction                      |
    | point(-2, 0, 0) | vector(0.2673, 0.5345, 0.8018) |
    | point(0, -2, 0) | vector(0.8018, 0.2673, 0.5345) |
    | point(0, 0, -2) | vector(0.5345, 0.8018, 0.2673) |
    | point(2, 0, 2)  | vector(0, 0, -1)               |
    | point(0, 2, 2)  | vector(0, -1, 0)               |
    | point(2, 2, 0)  | vector(-1, 0, 0)               |
```

In each case, though, the ray should miss the cube, resulting in zero intersections.

Consider it from a two-dimensional perspective again. In the following configuration, the ray misses the square:

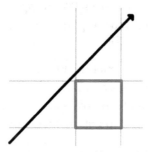

Once again, find the points of intersection with the two pairs of lines, and then find the largest of the minimum t values and the smallest of the maximum t values, like this:

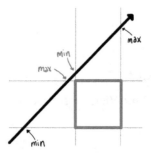

Look closely: the minimum t is farther from the ray origin than the maximum t! Well, that clearly makes no sense, and the contradiction is your clue that the ray misses the square.

The following pseudocode adds one line to the previous implementation, testing for that case.

```
function local_intersect(cube, ray)
  xtmin, xtmax ← check_axis(ray.origin.x, ray.direction.x)
  ytmin, ytmax ← check_axis(ray.origin.y, ray.direction.y)
  ztmin, ztmax ← check_axis(ray.origin.z, ray.direction.z)

  tmin ← max(xtmin, ytmin, ztmin)
  tmax ← min(xtmax, ytmax, ztmax)

➤   return () if tmin > tmax

  return ( intersection(tmin, cube), intersection(tmax, cube) )
end function
```

Once you've got that test passing, you're ready to implement the last bit for cubes: calculating the normal vector.

Finding the Normal on a Cube

Recall that the *normal* is the vector that points outward perpendicularly from a surface. Your ray tracer uses it to compute a variety of effects, including shading, reflection, and refraction. Fortunately, the algorithm for finding the normal on a cube is elegant and short—two delightful attributes!

Let's jump right into the test.

Test #3: The Normal on a Cube

Show that the local_normal_at() function correctly computes the normal at various points on a cube.

Now, each face of a cube is a plane with its own normal. This normal will be the same at every point on the corresponding face. The following test demonstrates this by finding the normal at various points on a cube.

```
features/cubes.feature
Scenario Outline: The normal on the surface of a cube
  Given c ← cube()
    And p ← <point>
  When normal ← local_normal_at(c, p)
  Then normal = <normal>
```

Examples:

point	normal
point(1, 0.5, -0.8)	vector(1, 0, 0)
point(-1, -0.2, 0.9)	vector(-1, 0, 0)
point(-0.4, 1, -0.1)	vector(0, 1, 0)
point(0.3, -1, -0.7)	vector(0, -1, 0)
point(-0.6, 0.3, 1)	vector(0, 0, 1)
point(0.4, 0.4, -1)	vector(0, 0, -1)
point(1, 1, 1)	vector(1, 0, 0)
point(-1, -1, -1)	vector(-1, 0, 0)

Note that this test also demonstrates the normal at two of the cube's corners, to make sure that case is handled consistently. Specifically, it assumes that the corners are treated as positions on either the +x or -x faces, and returns the normal for that face.

To understand how the algorithm for this will work, note that all the points on the +x face have a normal pointing in the +x direction, like this:

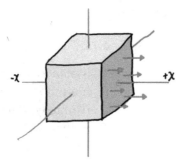

Picking a few points at random from that face gives us the following list:

- (1.0, 0.0, -0.4)
- (1.0, -0.5, 0.6)
- (1.0, 0.1, 0.9)
- (1.0, -0.9, 0.7)

What do you notice here? Perhaps you see that the x component is not only 1, but is also always greater than any of the other components? Hold that thought!

Consider the following list of points on the -y face of a cube:

- (-0.2, -1.0, 0.5)
- (0.1, -1.0, -0.9)
- (0.8, -1.0, 0.9)
- (-0.7, -1.0, 0.0)

Here, the y component is always -1.0, and is *less* than any of the other components.

One more list. Try and figure out which face of a cube each of the following points is from:

- (-1.0, 0.3, -0.5)
- (0.3, -0.9, 1.0)
- (-0.6, 1.0, 0.7)
- (0.4, -1.0, 0.2)

The face is always the one matching the component whose absolute value is a 1!

Now, in practice, you can't trust that the points you get will have components that exactly equal 1.0 (curse you, floating point rounding!), but you can make it work by choosing the component with the largest absolute value. The following pseudocode illustrates how your local_normal_at() function should work for cubes.

```
function local_normal_at(cube, point)
  maxc ← max(abs(point.x), abs(point.y), abs(point.z))

  if maxc = abs(point.x) then
    return vector(point.x, 0, 0)
  else if maxc = abs(point.y) then
    return vector(0, point.y, 0)
  end if

  return vector(0, 0, point.z)
end function
```

In other words, find the component with the largest absolute value. If that's x, return a vector pointing in that direction. If it's y, return a vector pointing in *that* direction, and so forth.

Make that test pass, and your cube is done!

Putting It Together

Your ray tracer now supports spheres, planes, and cubes. How awesome is that? By all means, experiment and see what you can make by combining the three primitives, but first: what can you make using *only* cubes?

Try it out. Form a room out of a large cube. Make a table out of five cubes: four for the legs, and one for the table's surface. Put a box on the table. Scatter some boxes on the floor.

Here's another challenge: using only two cubes, can you make a room whose floor and ceiling have a different texture than the walls?

You can also make these algorithms faster. For example, when comparing a ray with the cube's sides, the algorithm insists on checking all six planes, even if it's clear by the first or second comparison that the ray misses. In a production-quality ray tracer, this kind of wastefulness would be unacceptable. How might you optimize it? What can you do to minimize the number of comparisons it makes?

Ponder that for a bit, if you like. When you're ready, read on. In the next chapter you'll add two more primitives: cylinders and cones.

## CHAPTER 13

Cylinders

Next up is the mighty *cylinder*. It plays nicely with your existing suite of graphics primitives, and it's fantastic for representing all sorts of things: arms, legs, necks, fingers, and torsos, as well as columns, pipes, and table legs. Here's an example of cylinders in various configurations to give you a taste of how versatile this shape can be:

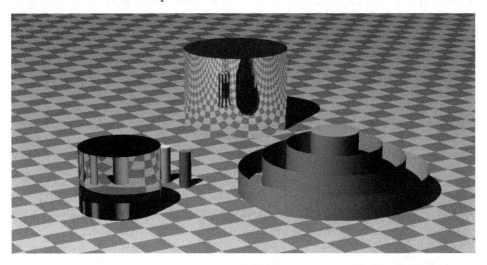

As with all your other shapes, you'll use cylinders by instantiating them at the origin and then transforming them into the size and position you need. For convenience, you'll give the cylinders a default radius of 1, but the way the math works out they'll all be infinitely long, extending to infinity in both +y and -y. Since trying to do anything useful with an infinitely long cylinder is tricky, you'll also implement controls to allow your cylinders to be truncated at one or both ends, and to be either open or capped.

You'll tackle all of this in a few steps:

1. Implement the basic intersection algorithm for an infinite cylinder of radius 1.

2. Compute the normal vector for a cylinder.

3. Add support for truncating the cylinder. By default, a truncated cylinder is *open*, or hollow.

4. Add support for end caps, to allow the cylinder to be *closed*, or solid.

5. Compute the normal vector on the end caps.

Lastly, as a bonus, you'll see, briefly, how to intersect a ray with a cone, the algorithm for which just happens to be very similar to that of a cylinder.

Are you ready for this? Here goes!

Intersecting a Ray with a Cylinder

Either the ray misses the cylinder or it hits the cylinder. Right? This dichotomy neatly describes the tests you'll write first. You'll start by confirming that a ray *misses* a cylinder. Such tests can be made to pass trivially, but rather than passing them by making your local_intersect method do nothing, this provides a good opportunity to start actually implementing the intersection routines.

Test #1: A Ray Misses a Cylinder

Show that the local_intersect() function correctly identifies when a ray misses a cylinder.

This test creates a cylinder and casts three different rays at it. The first ray is positioned on the surface and points along the +y axis, parallel to the cylinder. The second is inside the cylinder and also points along the +y axis. The third ray is positioned outside the cylinder and oriented askew from all axes. All three should miss the cylinder.

```
features/cylinders.feature
Scenario Outline: A ray misses a cylinder
  Given cyl ← cylinder()
    And direction ← normalize(<direction>)
    And r ← ray(<origin>, direction)
  When xs ← local_intersect(cyl, r)
  Then xs.count = 0
```

Examples:

```
| origin           | direction        |
| point(1, 0, 0)   | vector(0, 1, 0)  |
| point(0, 0, 0)   | vector(0, 1, 0)  |
| point(0, 0, -5)  | vector(1, 1, 1)  |
```

The algorithm that implements this shares some features with the ray-sphere intersection algorithm on page 57. As with the sphere algorithm, you'll compute a *discriminant* value, which will be negative if the ray does not intersect. Here's some pseudocode:

```
function local_intersect(cylinder, ray)
  a ← ray.direction.x² + ray.direction.z²

  # ray is parallel to the y axis
  return () if a is approximately zero

  b ← 2 * ray.origin.x * ray.direction.x +
      2 * ray.origin.z * ray.direction.z
  c ← ray.origin.x² + ray.origin.z² - 1

  disc ← b² - 4 * a * c

  # ray does not intersect the cylinder
  return () if disc < 0

  # this is just a placeholder, to ensure the tests
  # pass that expect the ray to miss.
  return ( intersection(1, cylinder) )
end function
```

Note that the last line of the function, returning a single intersection at t=1, ensures that the tests pass because the ray truly misses the cylinder and not simply because the function wasn't doing anything else. You'll flesh that bit out next, in test #2.

Test #2: A Ray Hits a Cylinder

Show that the local_intersect() function correctly identifies when a ray hits a cylinder.

Once again, the scenario outline creates three different rays, each of which is expected to intersect the cylinder. The first is configured to strike the cylinder on a tangent, but even though the actual intersection is at a single point, you'll still make your code return *two* intersections, both at t=5. (This mimics how you handled tangent intersections in Chapter 5, *Ray-Sphere Intersections*, on page 57, and will help with determining object overlaps in Chapter 16, *Constructive Solid Geometry (CSG)*, on page 227.) The second ray intersects the cylinder perpendicularly through the middle and results in two intersections at 4 and 6. The last ray is skewed so that it strikes the cylinder at an angle.

features/cylinders.feature
```
Scenario Outline: A ray strikes a cylinder
  Given cyl ← cylinder()
    And direction ← normalize(<direction>)
    And r ← ray(<origin>, direction)
  When xs ← local_intersect(cyl, r)
  Then xs.count = 2
    And xs[0].t = <t0>
    And xs[1].t = <t1>

  Examples:
    | origin          | direction         | t0      | t1      |
    | point(1, 0, -5) | vector(0, 0, 1)   | 5       | 5       |
    | point(0, 0, -5) | vector(0, 0, 1)   | 4       | 6       |
    | point(0.5, 0, -5) | vector(0.1, 1, 1) | 6.80798 | 7.08872 |
```

Make this pass by using the discriminant to find the t values for the points of intersection. The highlighted lines in the following pseudocode demonstrate the calculation you need:

```
function local_intersect(cylinder, ray)
  a ← ray.direction.x² + ray.direction.z²

  # ray is parallel to the y axis
  return () if a is approximately zero

  b ← 2 * ray.origin.x * ray.direction.x +
      2 * ray.origin.z * ray.direction.z
  c ← ray.origin.x² + ray.origin.z² - 1

  disc ← b² - 4 * a * c

  # ray does not intersect the cylinder
  return () if disc < 0

➤  t0 ← (-b - √(disc)) / (2 * a)
➤  t1 ← (-b + √(disc)) / (2 * a)
➤
➤  return ( intersection(t0, cylinder), intersection(t1, cylinder) )
end function
```

All that's left before you can actually render this cylinder is to compute the normal vector.

Finding the Normal on a Cylinder

Once you know the points of intersection, the normal vector is used to help shade the surface appropriately. You'll only need one scenario to cover this bit.

Test #3: Normal Vector on a Cylinder

Show that the normal vector on the surface of a cylinder is computed correctly.

This scenario chooses four points on the surface of the cylinder, one each at +x, -x, +z and -z, and shows that the normal is the expected value at each point.

```
features/cylinders.feature
Scenario Outline: Normal vector on a cylinder
  Given cyl ← cylinder()
  When n ← local_normal_at(cyl, <point>)
  Then n = <normal>

  Examples:
    | point          | normal          |
    | point(1, 0, 0) | vector(1, 0, 0) |
    | point(0, 5, -1)| vector(0, 0, -1)|
    | point(0, -2, 1)| vector(0, 0, 1) |
    | point(-1, 1, 0)| vector(-1, 0, 0)|
```

To accomplish this, take the point in question and remove the y component. Treating the result as a vector gives you the normal. In pseudocode, it looks like this:

```
function local_normal_at(cylinder, point)
  return vector(point.x, 0, point.z)
end function
```

With those tests passing, your ray tracer can render cylinders! They'll be infinitely long, which might be a bit unwieldy, but with a bit of imagination you can do all kinds of interesting things with them. Give it a try! When you come back, we will look at truncating those cylinders to make them easier to use.

Truncating Cylinders

Imagine a world where table legs stretch forever in both directions, where pencils can never be sharpened because they have no end, and where cars roll around on wheels that are infinitely wide. What a mess! Perhaps Salvador Dalí could make something out of that, but for the rest of us, such cylinders are hard to use well. To make them more useful you can *truncate* them, chopping them off at one or both ends.

For your ray tracer, you'll implement truncated cylinders by permitting a *minimum* and a *maximum* y value to be given for each cylinder. For example, the cylinder only exists between y=-1 and y=2 as shown in the figure on page 182.

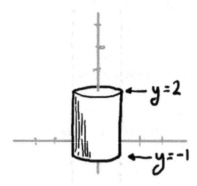

Note that the extents are *exclusive*, meaning if the cylinder is truncated at y=2, the cylinder extends up to—but not including—that limit.

You'll need just two tests for this feature: one that adds the new attributes and one that updates the intersection logic to support the truncated cylinders. Start with the new attributes.

Test #4: Minimum and Maximum Bounds

Demonstrate the default values for a cylinder's minimum and maximum bounds.

This scenario creates a new cylinder and shows that the minimum defaults to negative infinity and the maximum defaults to positive infinity.

```
features/cylinders.feature
Scenario: The default minimum and maximum for a cylinder
  Given cyl ← cylinder()
  Then cyl.minimum = -infinity
    And cyl.maximum = infinity
```

The minimum and maximum always refer to units on the y axis and are defined in object space. The next test shows how you use these attributes to actually truncate a cylinder.

Test #5: Truncated Cylinders

Show that the cylinders in your ray tracer can be truncated at either end.

This scenario sets up a cylinder, truncates it at y=1 and y=2, and then casts several rays at it in order to make sure that the truncated cylinder is being intersected correctly.

```
features/cylinders.feature
Scenario Outline: Intersecting a constrained cylinder
  Given cyl ← cylinder()
    And cyl.minimum ← 1
```

```
    And cyl.maximum ← 2
    And direction ← normalize(<direction>)
    And r ← ray(<point>, direction)
 When xs ← local_intersect(cyl, r)
 Then xs.count = <count>
```

Examples:

		point	direction	count
	1	point(0, 1.5, 0)	vector(0.1, 1, 0)	0
	2	point(0, 3, -5)	vector(0, 0, 1)	0
	3	point(0, 0, -5)	vector(0, 0, 1)	0
	4	point(0, 2, -5)	vector(0, 0, 1)	0
	5	point(0, 1, -5)	vector(0, 0, 1)	0
	6	point(0, 1.5, -2)	vector(0, 0, 1)	2

Specifically, the examples cast the following rays:

- Example 1 casts a ray diagonally from inside the cylinder, with the ray escaping without intersecting the cylinder.

- Examples 2 and 3 cast rays perpendicularly to the y axis, but from above and below the cylinder, and also miss.

- Examples 4 and 5 are edge cases, showing that the minimum and maximum y values are themselves outside the bounds of the cylinder.

- The final example casts a ray perpendicularly through the middle of the cylinder and produces two intersections.

The following figure shows how the scene is configured, with the corresponding rays:

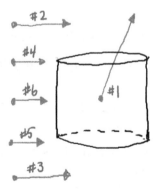

To make this work, change your local_intersect method so that it computes the y coordinate at each point of intersection. If the y coordinate is between the minimum and maxmium values, then the intersection is valid. The following pseudocode shows how this comes together:

```
    t0 ← (-b - √(disc)) / (2 * a)
    t1 ← (-b + √(disc)) / (2 * a)
    if t0 > t1 then swap(t0, t1)
```
➤ `xs = ()`
➤
➤ `y0 ← ray.origin.y + t0 * ray.direction.y`
➤ `if cylinder.minimum < y0 and y0 < cylinder.maximum`
➤   `add intersection(t0, cylinder) to xs`
➤ `end if`
➤
➤ `y1 ← ray.origin.y + t1 * ray.direction.y`
➤ `if cylinder.minimum < y1 and y1 < cylinder.maximum`
➤   `add intersection(t1, cylinder) to xs`
➤ `end if`
➤
➤ `return xs`

With that change, your tests should all be passing. Next up: *solid* cylinders!

Capped Cylinders

If you've played with your new truncated cylinders at all, you'll have noticed that they're hollow, like lengths of PVC pipe or empty toilet paper rolls. This can be exactly the effect you need sometimes, but at other times you really want the cylinders to be *capped*, or closed at each end. To do that, you need to add *end caps*—discs that exactly cover each end of the cylinder.

These discs are planes that are constrained to the cylinder's cross-section—and you implemented planes way back in Chapter 9, *Planes*, on page 117. While you can't exactly reuse your plane code for this, the concepts will (hopefully!) look familiar.

You'll add end caps to your cylinders in three steps:

1. Add a closed attribute to your cylinders, indicating that the cylinders should be capped.

2. Update your cylinder's local_intersect method to add checks for the top and bottom end caps (if closed is true).

3. Update your cylinder's local_normal_at method to compute the normal on the end caps (again, if closed is true).

First, the closed attribute.

Test #6: Closed Cylinders

Show that your cylinders possess a closed attribute, which defaults to false.

Set up a new cylinder and show that the closed attribute is false, by default.

features/cylinders.feature
```
Scenario: The default closed value for a cylinder
  Given cyl ← cylinder()
  Then cyl.closed = false
```

Make that pass, and then you can move on to updating the intersection algorithm.

Test #7: Intersecting a Cylinder's End Caps

Show that your intersection routine correctly finds the points of intersection between a ray and a cylinder's end caps.

This scenario outline sets up the same truncated cylinder as before, between y=1 and y=2, but also makes the cylinder closed before throwing rays at it.

features/cylinders.feature
```
Scenario Outline: Intersecting the caps of a closed cylinder
  Given cyl ← cylinder()
    And cyl.minimum ← 1
    And cyl.maximum ← 2
    And cyl.closed ← true
    And direction ← normalize(<direction>)
    And r ← ray(<point>, direction)
  When xs ← local_intersect(cyl, r)
  Then xs.count = <count>

  Examples:
    |   | point          | direction        | count |
    | 1 | point(0, 3, 0) | vector(0, -1, 0) | 2     |
    | 2 | point(0, 3, -2)| vector(0, -1, 2) | 2     |
    | 3 | point(0, 4, -2)| vector(0, -1, 1) | 2     | # corner case
    | 4 | point(0, 0, -2)| vector(0, 1, 2)  | 2     |
    | 5 | point(0, -1, -2)| vector(0, 1, 1)  | 2     | # corner case
```

The ray in the first example starts above the cylinder and points down through the cylinder's middle, along the y axis. It should intersect both end caps, resulting in two intersections.

Examples 2 and 4 originate (respectively) above and below the cylinder and cast a ray diagonally through it, intersecting one end cap before exiting out the far side of the cylinder. This also results in two intersections.

Examples 3 and 5 are corner cases. These also originate (respectively) above and below the cylinder, intersecting an end cap, but they exit the cylinder at the point where the other end cap intersects the side of the cylinder. In this case, there should still be only two intersections: one with the first end cap and the other where the second end cap meets the cylinder wall.

To implement this, you'll add a new function, intersect_caps(cyl, ray, xs). It checks to see if the given ray intersects the end caps of the given cylinder, and adds the points of intersection (if any) to the xs collection. Here it is in pseudocode:

```
# a helper function to reduce duplication.
# checks to see if the intersection at `t` is within a radius
# of 1 (the radius of your cylinders) from the y axis.
function check_cap(ray, t)
  x ← ray.origin.x + t * ray.direction.x
  z ← ray.origin.z + t * ray.direction.z

  return (x² + z²) <= 1
end

function intersect_caps(cyl, ray, xs)
  # caps only matter if the cylinder is closed, and might possibly be
  # intersected by the ray.
  if cyl is not closed or ray.direction.y is close to zero
    return
  end if

  # check for an intersection with the lower end cap by intersecting
  # the ray with the plane at y=cyl.minimum
  t ← (cyl.minimum - ray.origin.y) / ray.direction.y
  if check_cap(ray, t)
    add intersection(t, cyl) to xs
  end if

  # check for an intersection with the upper end cap by intersecting
  # the ray with the plane at y=cyl.maximum
  t ← (cyl.maximum - ray.origin.y) / ray.direction.y
  if check_cap(ray, t)
    add intersection(t, cyl) to xs
  end if
end function
```

First, the ray is intersected with a plane at the minimum extent. Then, the point of intersection is tested (via the check_cap() helper function) to see if it lies within the radius of the cylinder. If it does, the intersection is added to the collection. The same process follows for the maximum extent.

Make sure your cylinder's local_intersect function calls this new function after it checks for intersections with the cylinder's walls. You'll also need to change the logic at the beginning of the function so it doesn't actually return when a is zero, otherwise your cap intersection will be skipped and at least one of your tests will fail. Instead, if a is zero, skip the cylinder intersection logic and just call intersect_caps().

You're almost done, but before you can render these closed cylinders, you need to update the calculation for the normal vector to account for the end caps. That's the very next test.

Test #8: Computing the Normal Vector at the End Caps

Show that the normal vector calculation accounts for closed cylinders, and returns the correct normal at the end caps.

This scenario outline creates a closed, truncated cylinder and computes the normal at various points on each end cap:

```
features/cylinders.feature
Scenario Outline: The normal vector on a cylinder's end caps
  Given cyl ← cylinder()
    And cyl.minimum ← 1
    And cyl.maximum ← 2
    And cyl.closed ← true
  When n ← local_normal_at(cyl, <point>)
  Then n = <normal>

  Examples:
    | point           | normal          |
    | point(0, 1, 0)   | vector(0, -1, 0) |
    | point(0.5, 1, 0) | vector(0, -1, 0) |
    | point(0, 1, 0.5) | vector(0, -1, 0) |
    | point(0, 2, 0)   | vector(0, 1, 0)  |
    | point(0.5, 2, 0) | vector(0, 1, 0)  |
    | point(0, 2, 0.5) | vector(0, 1, 0)  |
```

The end caps are planes, which means an end cap has the same normal at every point on it. The algorithm must check to see which end cap the point corresponds to, or see if it lies on the cylinder itself, and return the appropriate normal vector. In pseudocode, it looks like this:

```
function local_normal_at(cylinder, point)
  # compute the square of the distance from the y axis
  dist ← point.x² + point.z²

  if dist < 1 and point.y >= cylinder.maximum - EPSILON
    return vector(0, 1, 0)

  else if dist < 1 and point.y <= cylinder.minimum + EPSILON
    return vector(0, -1, 0)

  else
    return vector(point.x, 0, point.z)
  end if
end function
```

If the point lies less than 1 unit from the y axis, and it lies within EPSILON (see *Comparing Floating Point Numbers,* on page 5) of the minimum or maximum extent, then it must be on one of the end caps. It's important that you include EPSILON here; if you don't, you'll wind up with rendering glitches caused by the wrong normal vector being calculated when floating point round-off causes the point to be slightly inside an end cap.

That's it, though. When that passes, you'll be rendering capped, truncated cylinders. Give it a shot!

The feature isn't quite over yet, though. You're going to wrap it up by implementing the cone primitive.

Cones

Okay. Next you're going to add cones to your ray tracer, and it turns out that cones are remarkably similar to cylinders. A true *cone* has these features:

- It is infinite in length, just like a cylinder.
- It can be truncated, just like a cylinder.
- It can be closed, just like a cylinder.

And I really do mean *just like a cylinder.* You may be able to reuse a fair bit of the code you just wrote for cylinders.

Here's where the challenge ramps up, though—I'm going to take the training wheels off. No hand-holding. No safety nets. Just a bit of explanation, a few tests, and a whole heap of confidence in your ability to do just about anything you put your mind to.

You're going to implement what is called a *double-napped cone,* which most folks would actually call *two* cones: one upside down, the other right-side up, with their tips meeting at the origin and extending toward infinity in both directions, as depicted in the following figure.

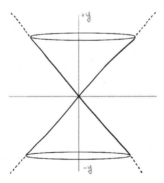

To render this, you'll need to implement its intersection algorithm and the algorithm to compute its normal vector.

The intersection algorithm works almost exactly like the cylinder's, but a, b, and c are computed differently. Given a ray's origin o and direction vector d, the following formulas replace the ones you used for cylinders:

$$a = d_x^2 - d_y^2 + d_z^2$$
$$b = 2o_x d_x - 2o_y d_y + 2o_z d_z$$
$$c = o_x^2 - o_y^2 + o_z^2$$

When a is zero, it means the ray is parallel to one of the cone's halves, like so:

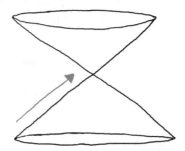

As you can see, this still means the ray might intersect the other half of the cone. In this case the ray will miss when both a and b are zero. If a is zero but b isn't, you'll use the following formula to find the single point of intersection:

$$t = -c/2b$$

If a is nonzero, you'll use the same algorithm, but with the new a, b, and c, that you used for the cylinders.

Here are two tests to help you double-check your cone intersections:

```
features/cones.feature
Scenario Outline: Intersecting a cone with a ray
  Given shape ← cone()
    And direction ← normalize(<direction>)
    And r ← ray(<origin>, direction)
  When xs ← local_intersect(shape, r)
  Then xs.count = 2
    And xs[0].t = <t0>
    And xs[1].t = <t1>

  Examples:
    | origin         | direction           | t0      | t1       |
    | point(0, 0, -5) | vector(0, 0, 1)     | 5       | 5        |
    | point(0, 0, -5) | vector(1, 1, 1)     | 8.66025 | 8.66025  |
    | point(1, 1, -5) | vector(-0.5, -1, 1) | 4.55006 | 49.44994 |
```

```
Scenario: Intersecting a cone with a ray parallel to one of its halves
  Given shape ← cone()
    And direction ← normalize(vector(0, 1, 1))
    And r ← ray(point(0, 0, -1), direction)
  When xs ← local_intersect(shape, r)
  Then xs.count = 1
    And xs[0].t = 0.35355
```

You'll implement end caps for cones much as you did for cylinders, but with one difference: whereas cylinders have the same radius everywhere, the radius of a cone will change with y. In fact, a cone's radius at any given y will be the absolute value of that y. This means the check_cap() function will need to be adjusted to accept the y coordinate of the plane being tested (cone.minimum or cone.maximum, respectively) and treat that as the radius within which the point must lie.

Here's a test for the cone end caps to help you with your implementation:

features/cones.feature
```
Scenario Outline: Intersecting a cone's end caps
  Given shape ← cone()
    And shape.minimum ← -0.5
    And shape.maximum ← 0.5
    And shape.closed ← true
    And direction ← normalize(<direction>)
    And r ← ray(<origin>, direction)
  When xs ← local_intersect(shape, r)
  Then xs.count = <count>

  Examples:
    | origin            | direction       | count |
    | point(0, 0, -5)   | vector(0, 1, 0) | 0     |
    | point(0, 0, -0.25)| vector(0, 1, 1) | 2     |
    | point(0, 0, -0.25)| vector(0, 1, 0) | 4     |
```

Lastly, for the normal vector, compute the end cap normals just as you did for the cylinder, but change the rest to the following, given in pseudocode:

```
y ← √(point.x² + point.z²)
y ← -y if point.y > 0

return vector(point.x, y, point.z)
```

Again, here's a test to help you out:

features/cones.feature
```
Scenario Outline: Computing the normal vector on a cone
  Given shape ← cone()
  When n ← local_normal_at(shape, <point>)
  Then n = <normal>
```

Examples:

```
| point            | normal           |
| point(0, 0, 0)   | vector(0, 0, 0)  |
| point(1, 1, 1)   | vector(1, -√2, 1)|
| point(-1, -1, 0) | vector(-1, 1, 0) |
```

As with the infinite cylinder, a double-napped cone is a bit unwieldy, but thanks to truncation, you can cut off any bits of those double cones that you don't want. If you want a traditional unit cone, for example, you can truncate it at y=-1 and y=0, and then translate it up 1 unit in y.

Putting It Together

You're now armed with quite a variety of graphics primitives: spheres, planes, cubes, cylinders, and cones. What can you make with them? Here are some ideas:

- An ice cream cone with one (or more!) scoops.
- The US Capitol building.
- An arrow.
- A lightbulb.
- Stonehenge.
- A spiral staircase.
- A picture frame.
- The Saturn V rocket.
- A pencil.

If you're feeling particularly ambitious, you might consider trying a (simplified!) model of something organic: a tree, a dog, or even a stick-figure person.

When you're ready, turn the page. You'll learn an easier way to construct complex models, as well as an optimization you can use to potentially reduce the number of intersection tests required to render your scenes.

## CHAPTER 14

Groups

Here you are, just a few more chapters to go before the end of the book. By now you've spent some time playing with your renderer, experimenting with shapes, patterns, and composition, and you've probably figured out that building a scene with the primitives at your disposal involves a lot of fiddling with transformations. Add a shape, scale it, translate it, rotate it *just so*, and then repeat for every other shape you need in your scene.

As your scenes grow in complexity, so too does the effort needed to model them. Have you wished for a way to streamline things? Wouldn't it be nice if you could group shapes together and transform them as a unit?

Here's an example that does just that. The following figure shows three different views of a complex shape composed of spheres, cylinders, and cones.

With your ray tracer in its current state, each sphere, cylinder, and cone must be painstakingly transformed into place, requiring careful tracking of each component and where it needs to end up. But by grouping shapes together, complex shapes can be constructed at the origin and then transformed as a unit wherever and however you want.

In this chapter you'll add support for groups of shapes, allowing them to be nested as deeply you need, and as a bonus, you'll also read about how they can be used to optimize your ray tracer.

Implementing Groups

Groups are abstract shapes with no surface of their own, taking their form instead from the shapes they contain. This allows you to organize them in trees, with groups containing both other groups and concrete primitives. The real killer feature of groups, though, is that groups may be transformed just like any other shape, and those transforms then apply implicitly to any shapes contained by the group. You just put shapes in a group, transform the group, and *voilà*—it all applies as a single unit.

Let's make this happen. You'll tackle this in several steps:

1. Create a new shape subclass called Group.

2. Add a new attribute to Shape, called parent, which refers to the group that contains the shape (if any).

3. Write a function for adding shapes to a group.

4. Implement the ray-group intersection algorithm.

5. Implement the necessary changes to compute the normal on a shape that is part of a group.

 This section describes a bidirectional tree structure, where parent nodes reference child nodes and child nodes reference parent nodes. Not all programming languages make this easy to implement. If your language makes this challenging, consider reading through the entire chapter first, and then implement the feature in your own way. If you get stuck, you can always ask for tips on the forum.[1]

Start by creating your new Group class for aggregating shapes.

Test #1: Creating a New Group

A group is a shape, which starts as an empty collection of shapes.

This test introduces a new function, group(), which returns a new Group instance. The test then shows that the group has its own transformation (unsurprising,

---

1. forum.raytracerchallenge.com

as it ought to be a Shape subclass), and the collection it represents should be empty.

```
features/groups.feature
Scenario: Creating a new group
  Given g ← group()
  Then g.transform = identity_matrix
    And g is empty
```

Make that pass by adding a Group class, making it a container of shapes, and making it behave like a Shape itself. The next test will address the Shape side of things by adding a parent attribute.

Test #2: A Shape Has a Parent Attribute

A shape has an optional parent, which is unset by default.

This test requires a new attribute on Shape, called parent, which may be either unset (the default) or may be set to a Group instance. You'll see your old test_shape() function from *Refactoring Shapes*, on page 117, used here as a generic shape to demonstrate the addition of the new attribute.

```
features/shapes.feature
Scenario: A shape has a parent attribute
  Given s ← test_shape()
  Then s.parent is nothing
```

Next up, you'll write a function for adding shapes as children of a group, linking them together in a kind of tree.

Test #3: Adding a Child to a Group

Adding a child to a group makes the group the child's parent and adds the child to the group's collection.

This test adds a new function, add_child(group, shape) and shows how it is used to add a child shape to a group.

```
features/groups.feature
Scenario: Adding a child to a group
  Given g ← group()
    And s ← test_shape()
  When add_child(g, s)
  Then g is not empty
    And g includes s
    And s.parent = g
```

Make that pass, and you can start moving on to the fun stuff! It's time to intersect rays with these groups of shapes.

Tests #4 and 5: Intersecting a Ray with a Group

Two tests show that a ray intersects a group if and only if the ray intersects at least one child shape contained by the group.

The first test is the trivial case—casting a ray and checking to see if it intersects an empty group. The resulting collection of intersections should be empty.

features/groups.feature
```
Scenario: Intersecting a ray with an empty group
  Given g ← group()
    And r ← ray(point(0, 0, 0), vector(0, 0, 1))
  When xs ← local_intersect(g, r)
  Then xs is empty
```

The second test builds a group of three spheres and casts a ray at it. The spheres are arranged inside the group so that the ray will intersect two of the spheres but miss the third. The resulting collection of intersections should include those of the two spheres.

features/groups.feature
```
Scenario: Intersecting a ray with a nonempty group
  Given g ← group()
    And s1 ← sphere()
    And s2 ← sphere()
    And set_transform(s2, translation(0, 0, -3))
    And s3 ← sphere()
    And set_transform(s3, translation(5, 0, 0))
    And add_child(g, s1)
    And add_child(g, s2)
    And add_child(g, s3)
  When r ← ray(point(0, 0, -5), vector(0, 0, 1))
    And xs ← local_intersect(g, r)
  Then xs.count = 4
    And xs[0].object = s2
    And xs[1].object = s2
    And xs[2].object = s1
    And xs[3].object = s1
```

To make both of these tests pass, implement the local_intersect() function for your Group shape and have it iterate over all of the group's children, calling intersect() on each of them in turn. It should aggregate the resulting intersections into a single collection and sort them all by t.

Test #6: Group Transformations

Demonstrate that group and child transformations are both applied.

This test creates a group and adds a single sphere to it. The new group is given one transformation, and the sphere is given a different transformation. A ray is then cast in such a way that it should strike the sphere, as long as the sphere is being transformed by both its own transformation and that of its parent.

features/groups.feature
```
Scenario: Intersecting a transformed group
  Given g ← group()
    And set_transform(g, scaling(2, 2, 2))
    And s ← sphere()
    And set_transform(s, translation(5, 0, 0))
    And add_child(g, s)
  When r ← ray(point(10, 0, -10), vector(0, 0, 1))
    And xs ← intersect(g, r)
  Then xs.count = 2
```

The lovely thing about this test is that it should already pass if your group's local_intersect() function calls intersect() on its children. Make sure this is so.

When you're ready, read on! The next piece of this puzzle requires finding the normal vector on a child object.

Finding the Normal on a Child Object

Remember back in *Transforming Normals*, on page 79, when you used the shape's transformation matrix to manipulate the normal vector? The same thing needs to happen when computing the normal on a child object of a group, but now there's a complication: when an intersection is found with a *group*, the intersection record itself references the intersected *child*. As your ray tracer is currently implemented, this means that when you compute the normal vector on that child object, only the child's transforms are considered, and not the transforms of any group the child may belong to.

This is what you'll work on next, in three steps:

- Write a function that converts a point from world space to object space, recursively taking into consideration any parent object(s) between the two spaces.

- Write a function that converts a normal vector from object space to world space, again recursively taking into consideration any parent object(s) between the two spaces.

- Update the normal_at() function so that it calls these two new functions to transform the incoming point and outgoing vector appropriately.

Got it? Here goes!

Test #7: Convert a Point from World Space to Object Space

Take a point in world space and transform it to object space, taking into consideration any parent objects between the two spaces.

This test constructs an outer group, which contains an inner group, which in turn contains a sphere. Each is given its own transformation before calling a new function, world_to_object(shape, point), to convert a world-space point to object space.

features/shapes.feature
```
Scenario: Converting a point from world to object space
  Given g1 ← group()
    And set_transform(g1, rotation_y(π/2))
    And g2 ← group()
    And set_transform(g2, scaling(2, 2, 2))
    And add_child(g1, g2)
    And s ← sphere()
    And set_transform(s, translation(5, 0, 0))
    And add_child(g2, s)
  When p ← world_to_object(s, point(-2, 0, -10))
  Then p = point(0, 0, -1)
```

Make this test pass by implementing world_to_object(shape, point). If shape has a parent, the function should first convert the point to its parent's space, by calling world_to_object(parent, point). The result is then multiplied by the inverse of the shape's transform. In pseudocode, it looks like this:

```
function world_to_object(shape, point)
  if shape has parent
    point ← world_to_object(shape.parent, point)
  end if

  return inverse(shape.transform) * point
end function
```

Next up, you'll convert a vector from object to world space.

Test #8: Convert a Normal Vector from Object Space to World Space

Take a normal vector in object space and transform it to world space, taking into consideration any parent objects between the two spaces.

This sets up two nested groups like in the previous test. Again, each is given its own transformation, and then another new function, normal_to_world(shape, normal), is used to transform a vector to world space.

features/shapes.feature
```
Scenario: Converting a normal from object to world space
  Given g1 ← group()
    And set_transform(g1, rotation_y(π/2))
```

```
      And g2 ← group()
      And set_transform(g2, scaling(1, 2, 3))
      And add_child(g1, g2)
      And s ← sphere()
      And set_transform(s, translation(5, 0, 0))
      And add_child(g2, s)
    When n ← normal_to_world(s, vector(√3/3, √3/3, √3/3))
    Then n = vector(0.2857, 0.4286, -0.8571)
```

You can make this test pass by first converting the given normal to the parent object space using the algorithm you implemented in *Transforming Normals*, on page 79. Take the inverse of the shape's transform, transpose the result, and multiply it by the vector. Normalize the result. Then, if the shape has a parent, recursively pass the new vector to normal_to_world(parent, normal). Here's the implementation in pseudocode:

```
function normal_to_world(shape, normal)
  normal ← transpose(inverse(shape.transform)) * normal
  normal.w ← 0
  normal ← normalize(normal)

  if shape has parent
    normal ← normal_to_world(shape.parent, normal)
  end if

  return normal
end function
```

Once those tests are passing, you're ready to find the normal on a child object.

Test #9: Find the Normal on an Object in a Group

Find the normal on a child object of a group, taking into account transformations on both the child object and the parent(s).

As with the previous two tests, this one sets up a hierarchy of two groups and a sphere and assigns them each a transformation. It then find the normal vector at a point on the sphere (in world space), using the normal_at() function.

```
features/shapes.feature
Scenario: Finding the normal on a child object
  Given g1 ← group()
    And set_transform(g1, rotation_y(π/2))
    And g2 ← group()
    And set_transform(g2, scaling(1, 2, 3))
    And add_child(g1, g2)
    And s ← sphere()
    And set_transform(s, translation(5, 0, 0))
    And add_child(g2, s)
  When n ← normal_at(s, point(1.7321, 1.1547, -5.5774))
  Then n = vector(0.2857, 0.4286, -0.8571)
```

Next, update your normal_at() function to use your new world_to_object() and normal_to_world() functions, calling the former to convert the world-space point to object space before calculating the normal, and then calling the latter to convert the normal back to world space. In pseudocode, your updated normal_at() function should come together like this:

```
function normal_at(shape, world_point)
  local_point ← world_to_object(shape, world_point)
  local_normal ← local_normal_at(shape, local_point)
  return normal_to_world(shape, local_normal)
end function
```

You're just about done with groups, but there's one more bit to address. In *Transforming Patterns*, on page 130, you allowed patterns to be transformed by converting points from world space to object space, and from there to pattern space, before computing the color. For those patterns to behave nicely when applied to objects in groups, you'll need to use this new world_to_object() function when converting points from world space to object space. Otherwise, the patterns won't apply the group transformations and won't look like you expect. You're on your own for this one; make it so!

> **Joe asks:**
> ## Where is the group's local_normal_at function?
>
> Ah, you noticed it was missing! Well done, but it's not a mistake or oversight. Because normals are always computed by calling the concrete shape's local_normal_at() function, the group itself doesn't need one. In fact, if your code ever tries to call local_normal_at() on a group, that means there's a bug somewhere.
>
> Consider implementing local_normal_at() for groups, but having the implementation throw an exception or otherwise cause an error. This can help you catch those bugs earlier and makes it explicit that groups are abstract and don't have normal vectors.

That should about do it for your implementation of groups. You'll work through an exercise shortly to get familiar with how to use them, but first, let's take a quick look at how these groups can be used to optimize your ray tracer.

Using Bounding Boxes to Optimize Large Scenes

One of the most computationally expensive things a ray tracer does is find the intersections between a ray and an object, and what makes things even worse is that it has to do this repeatedly for every pixel. To render a scene of ten objects to a small 200×200 canvas, your ray tracer must perform *at least* 400,000 intersection tests, plus however many additional intersections are needed to generate shadows, reflections, and refraction. Adding insult to injury, the majority of those rays won't even come close to most of the objects in a typical scene.

What a waste, right? If only you could test just the objects that were reasonably close to any given ray...

The good news is that there are a variety of different techniques for teaching your ray tracer how to do this. They're all a bit beyond the scope of this book, but let's take a quick look at one of the least complicated: *bounding boxes*.

If that term seems familiar, it's probably because you saw it used back in Chapter 12, *Cubes*, on page 167, when the cubes were called *axis-aligned bounding boxes* (AABB). The idea behind this optimization is to use these cubes, or bounding boxes, to contain a group of other objects. Then, when intersecting the group with a ray, you first test the ray against the bounding box. If the ray misses, testing anything inside the box is pointless, because it would have to miss them as well.

The following figure illustrates this with a bounding box that contains three shapes. Since ray A misses the bounding box, there's no need to see if it intersects any of the shapes inside it. However, because ray B *does* intersect the box, you'd need to try that ray against the shapes it contains.

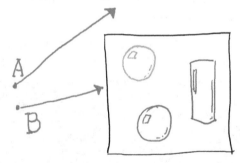

I won't walk you through this one, but give it a try anyway. Although implementing this definitely has some fiddly bits, I have faith in you! Here's a basic outline of what you'll need to do:

1. Create a Bounds structure that describes the minimum and maximum extents (coordinates) for the box. You can store these as two points, where one has the minimum x, y, and z coordinates and the other has the maximum.

2. Make a bounds(shape) function that returns the bounds for the given shape, in object space. This is the *untransformed* bounds, so a sphere (for example) will always extend from -1 to 1 in x, y, and z. Some shapes

(planes, untruncated cylinders, and others) will extend to infinity in one or more dimensions, so make sure you can handle that case.

3. Make a bounds(group) function that converts the bounds of all the group's children into "group space," and then combines them into a single bounding box. This is one of those fiddly bits! Here are two tips, though. First, to convert a point from object space to its parent space, multiply the point by the object's transformation matrix. Second, when transforming an entire bounding box, first transform all eight of the cube's corners, and then find a single bounding box that fits them all. If you can't quite see why you'd need to transform all eight points, imagine rotating the box 45° around any axis, and then figure out what the new *axis-aligned* bounding box ought to look like.

4. Reuse your cube's intersection algorithm, changing it so that it accepts AABBs at arbitrary (but still axis-aligned) locations. To do this, you'll need to change the -1 and the 1 in the check_axis() function to be, respectively, the minimum and maximum value for the axis being tested. So, if you are testing the z axis, and the bounding box goes from z=-5 to z=3, you'd use -5 instead of -1, and 3 instead of 1.

5. Make the local_intersect(group, ray) function first test the ray against the group's bounding box. Only if the ray intersects the bounding box should the ray be tested against the children.

As an example of how much this technique can help, I put together the following scene of more than 280 marbles with glass and metallic textures:

Rendered without bounding boxes at 1200x600 pixels, this image required more than *1.8 billion* intersection tests, of which only 1% ever actually hit anything. By using sixteen bounding boxes, though, and arranging them in a 4x4 grid so that all the marbles were covered, the render required only a bit more than *180 million* intersection tests, with 10% hitting something. That's an order of magnitude better, just by adding bounding boxes!

Here's the caveat, though: as with any optimization, it's not a guaranteed win in every situation. Not every scene will benefit from bounding boxes, and some might even see *worse* performance (depending on the objects in the scene and how you organize them).

Still, it's a useful optimization, and it will earn its keep in the next chapter, Chapter 15, *Triangles*, on page 207. Give it a shot!

Putting It Together

Let's wrap this up with an example of how you can use groups in your scenes. You are going to build a model of a hexagon using cylinders and spheres, like this:

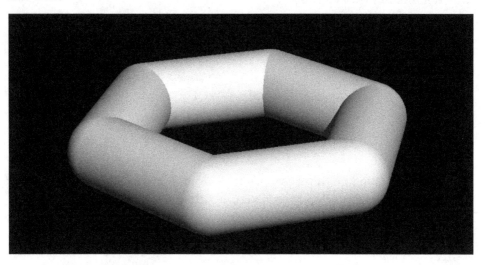

You'll build this by first defining a single instance of each component: one sphere (to become the corners of the hexagon), and one cylinder (to become the edges). You'll transform each into place once, and add them to a group. Then, you'll create duplicates of that group, rotating each duplicate around the y axis until the whole hexagon is constructed.

Start by writing a function that creates the prototypical sphere component, scaling it by 25% and translating it -1 unit in z. The following pseudocode shows this as a function named hexagon_corner().

```
function hexagon_corner()
  corner ← sphere()
  set_transform(corner, translation(0, 0, -1) *
                        scaling(0.25, 0.25, 0.25))
  return corner
end function
```

 Remember that when you combine matrix transformations, you do so in *reverse order*. Thus, though the pseudocode for hexagon_corner() multiplies the translation by the scaling, the result is that the sphere is scaled first and *then* translated.

Next, write a function that creates the prototypical cylinder component. Limit it to a minimum of y=0 and a maximum of y=1, and scale it by 25% in x and z. Rotate it $-\pi/2$ radians in z (to tip it over) and $-\pi/6$ radians in y (to orient it as an edge). Then, translate it -1 unit in z. In pseudocode, this hexagon_edge() function might look like this:

```
function hexagon_edge()
  edge ← cylinder()
  edge.minimum ← 0
  edge.maximum ← 1
  set_transform(edge, translation(0, 0, -1) *
                      rotation_y(-π/6) *
                      rotation_z(-π/2) *
                      scaling(0.25, 1, 0.25))
  return edge
end function
```

The next step is to join those two primitives into a group, forming one side of the hexagon. The following hexagon_side() function demonstrates this in pseudocode.

```
function hexagon_side()
  side ← group()

  add_child(side, hexagon_corner())
  add_child(side, hexagon_edge())

  return side
end function
```

Once you've got a function that can return a single side of the hexagon, you can write the final function, hexagon(), which calls hexagon_side() six times and rotates each piece into place, like so:

```
function hexagon()
  hex ← group()

  for n ← 0 to 5
    side ← hexagon_side()
    set_transform(side, rotation_y(n*π/3))
    add_child(hex, side)
  end for

  return hex
end function
```

From there, you can add a light source and a camera, and go nuts with it!

What other composite shapes can you build? Try creating a stick figure or an automobile. Trees and plants are definitely possible, too, and lend themselves well to fractal algorithms like Lindenmayer systems.

Also, you may soon realize that materials applied to a group have no effect at all on the shapes it contains. What if you wanted the shapes in your ray tracer to be able to "inherit" materials from their parents? How might you extend your code to make that happen?

Give it some thought. Then, once you've played with this new feature enough, read on. You'll add your final primitive in the next chapter: the triangle.

## CHAPTER 15

Triangles

The final primitive in your ray tracer might seem an odd choice: the *triangle*. By itself, its utility is perhaps questionable, but where it really shines is when you use hundreds or thousands of them together to construct a surface.

Here's an example of a scene composed of more than *fifteen thousand* triangles:

In the purple teddy bear, you can clearly see the facets and planes that betray the model's triangular composition. Even the cow, if you take a magnifying glass to the image, would show similar (if finer) faceting. But that teapot, now! Is it truly composed of triangles as well?

Oh, yes, it is. And in this chapter you'll not only add support for polygonal models like the teddy bear and the cow, but also normal interpolation to make models like the teapot appear flawlessly smooth.

Let's jump into it!

Triangles

While it's certainly possible to implement a triangle primitive at the origin, with unit dimensions, and then transform it into place like you've done with every other primitive you've implemented, it turns out that it makes these triangles really difficult to use well. So, your triangle primitive will actually accept three parameters, describing the location of each of its corners in object space. You can still transform the triangle as well, if needed.

Your implementation of triangles will follow these steps:

1. Create the triangle shape itself, precomputing several values to optimize the intersection calculations.

2. Implement the local_normal_at() function to compute the normal vector for triangles.

3. Implement the Möller–Trumbore ray-triangle intersection algorithm. This will occupy several tests.

Ready, set, go!

Test #1: Creating a Triangle

A triangle is a shape composed of three points. The constructor ought to precompute two edge vectors and the triangle's normal.

Given three points, instantiate a triangle. Then show that each point is initialized and that two edge vectors and the normal vector are all precomputed.

```
features/triangles.feature
Scenario: Constructing a triangle
  Given p1 ← point(0, 1, 0)
    And p2 ← point(-1, 0, 0)
    And p3 ← point(1, 0, 0)
    And t ← triangle(p1, p2, p3)
  Then t.p1 = p1
    And t.p2 = p2
    And t.p3 = p3
    And t.e1 = vector(-1, -1, 0)
    And t.e2 = vector(1, -1, 0)
    And t.normal = vector(0, 0, -1)
```

Your ray tracer will eventually use those two edge vectors, e1 and e2, to determine if and where the ray intersects the triangle. It will also use that normal vector as the normal at every point of intersection. While you could certainly calculate those three values for every hit, they'll always be the same everywhere on the triangle. Save your ray tracer some work and precompute them when the shape is constructed, as follows:

$$e_1 = p_2 - p_1$$
$$e_2 = p_3 - p_1$$
$$normal = \text{normalize}(\text{cross}(e_2, e_1))$$

With the normal vector precomputed, the next test almost writes itself.

Test #2: Normal Vector for a Triangle

The triangle's precomputed normal is used for every point on the triangle.

Once you've got your triangle() function precomputing the normal vector, the local_normal_at(triangle, point) function should simply return that vector for every point it is given.

```
features/triangles.feature
Scenario: Finding the normal on a triangle
  Given t ← triangle(point(0, 1, 0), point(-1, 0, 0), point(1, 0, 0))
  When n1 ← local_normal_at(t, point(0, 0.5, 0))
    And n2 ← local_normal_at(t, point(-0.5, 0.75, 0))
    And n3 ← local_normal_at(t, point(0.5, 0.25, 0))
  Then n1 = t.normal
    And n2 = t.normal
    And n3 = t.normal
```

Go ahead and make this pass by implementing local_normal_at() for triangles and have it return the precomputed normal vector.

The next five tests will all deal with the intersection algorithm.

Tests #3 to 7: Intersecting a Ray with a Triangle

A ray that misses a triangle should not add any intersections to the intersection list. A ray that strikes a triangle should add exactly one intersection to the list.

These five tests introduce the behavior of the ray-triangle intersection algorithm. The specific algorithm that you'll implement is the *Möller–Trumbore* algorithm,[1] which is fast, short, and has the handy side effect of precomputing a few values that you'll use later in the chapter for implementing smooth triangles. You'll build your implementation of this algorithm in pieces, with each test exercising a bit more of it.

For this first test, start by creating a triangle. Then, position a ray such that it is cast parallel to the surface of the triangle. The ray should miss the triangle.

---

1. www.tandfonline.com/doi/abs/10.1080/10867651.1997.10487468

```
Scenario: Intersecting a ray parallel to the triangle
  Given t ← triangle(point(0, 1, 0), point(-1, 0, 0), point(1, 0, 0))
    And r ← ray(point(0, -1, -2), vector(0, 1, 0))
  When xs ← local_intersect(t, r)
  Then xs is empty
```

Make that test pass by crossing the ray direction with e2, and then dotting the result with e1 to produce the determinant. If the result is close to zero, then the ray is parallel to the triangle and misses. Here's some pseudocode for the first part of the algorithm, handling this specific case.

```
function local_intersect(triangle, ray)
  dir_cross_e2 ← cross(ray.direction, triangle.e2)
  det ← dot(triangle.e1, dir_cross_e2)
  return () if abs(det) < EPSILON

  # a bogus intersection to ensure the result isn't a false positive
  return ( intersection(1, triangle) )
end function
```

Note the bogus intersection being returned at the end; this is purely to prevent false positives when testing. Without that, if you have an error in your function and it fails to recognize that the ray misses, it would (at this point) *still* return without adding an intersection, which the test would take to mean that the function is working correctly. Adding the bogus intersection ensures that the test fails if your implementation is wrong. You'll remove that bogus line soon, after you've implemented the entire algorithm.

The next three tests set up the same triangle and then configure a ray so that it misses the triangle over one of its edges. For the first test, the ray passes beyond the p1-p3 edge.

```
Scenario: A ray misses the p1-p3 edge
  Given t ← triangle(point(0, 1, 0), point(-1, 0, 0), point(1, 0, 0))
    And r ← ray(point(1, 1, -2), vector(0, 0, 1))
  When xs ← local_intersect(t, r)
  Then xs is empty
```

To make this pass, add the following calculations just before the bogus intersection in your local_intersect() function.

```
f ← 1.0 / det

p1_to_origin ← ray.origin - triangle.p1
u ← f * dot(p1_to_origin, dir_cross_e2)
return () if u < 0 or u > 1
```

If that u value is not between 0 and 1, inclusive, the ray misses.

The next two tests configure the ray to pass beyond the p1-p2 and p2-p3 edges of the triangle.

features/triangles.feature
```
Scenario: A ray misses the p1-p2 edge
  Given t ← triangle(point(0, 1, 0), point(-1, 0, 0), point(1, 0, 0))
    And r ← ray(point(-1, 1, -2), vector(0, 0, 1))
  When xs ← local_intersect(t, r)
  Then xs is empty

Scenario: A ray misses the p2-p3 edge
  Given t ← triangle(point(0, 1, 0), point(-1, 0, 0), point(1, 0, 0))
    And r ← ray(point(0, -1, -2), vector(0, 0, 1))
  When xs ← local_intersect(t, r)
  Then xs is empty
```

You can make these pass by implementing the following calculations, again putting them just before the bogus intersection at the end of your function.

```
origin_cross_e1 ← cross(p1_to_origin, triangle.e1)
v ← f * dot(ray.direction, origin_cross_e1)
return () if v < 0 or (u + v) > 1
```

Finally, you need to handle the case where the ray actually strikes the triangle. This last test creates the triangle again, but arranges the ray so that it intersects it, and confirms that an intersection exists at the correct distance.

features/triangles.feature
```
Scenario: A ray strikes a triangle
  Given t ← triangle(point(0, 1, 0), point(-1, 0, 0), point(1, 0, 0))
    And r ← ray(point(0, 0.5, -2), vector(0, 0, 1))
  When xs ← local_intersect(t, r)
  Then xs.count = 1
    And xs[0].t = 2
```

Replace the bogus intersection at the end of the triangle's local_intersect() function with the following logic, to produce the *actual* intersection.

```
t = f * dot(triangle.e2, origin_cross_e1)
return ( intersection(t, triangle) )
```

Once those tests are all passing, you should be able to render some triangles. Feel free to render them singly if you want, but they become much more interesting in groups. Think about how you would construct a three- or four-sided pyramid from triangles. How about an octahedron? Or if you want to get really ambitious, consider more complex polyhedra, like the dodecahedron in the image on page 212.

Ultimately, though, arranging triangles by hand is difficult to do well. It's far easier to use a 3D modeling tool to construct a shape, and then export it to

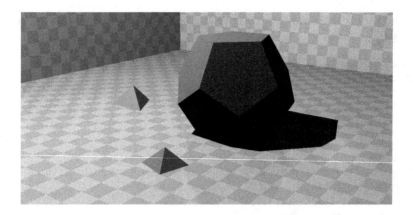

a file. The next section will walk you through the process of implementing a parser for one of the most common 3D model file formats, which will allow you to import more complex models into your scenes.

Wavefront OBJ Files

The Wavefront OBJ file format is a common format for storing and sharing 3D graphics data. Like the PPM image format that you implemented way back in Chapter 2, *Drawing on a Canvas*, on page 15, the OBJ format is plain text, which means you can view, edit, and even create these files in any text editor, though it's much easier to model something in a 3D modeling tool and then export it to OBJ.

The OBJ format consists of statements, each of which occupies a single line. Each statement is prefaced with a command, followed by a space-delimited list of arguments. For example, the following OBJ file defines three vertices (v), and a triangle (f, for "face") that references those vertices.

```
v 1.5 2 1.3
v 1.4 -1.2 0.12
v -0.1 0 -1.3

f 1 2 3
```

There are quite a few other statement types as well, but you only need to recognize a handful of them in your ray tracer. You'll implement this parser in six steps:

1. Begin with a parser that silently ignores all unrecognized statements.

2. Add support for vertices to the parser.

3. Add support for triangles.

4. Implement triangulation of convex polygons, so that your parser can import those, too.

5. Add support for groups of polygons within a model.

6. Export the entire model as a Group instance, so that you can add it to a scene to be rendered.

Let me reiterate that you'll be using Group instances to represent these groups of triangles. While this technique is straightforward to explain, it's unfortunately *not* the most optimal way to represent this kind of data. If you're interested in optimizing your ray tracer, you might investigate a structure called a *triangle mesh*, which can be stored and processed a bit more efficiently.

For now, though, groups of triangles will be fine. Let's get started!

Test #8: OBJ Parser with Gibberish Input

The parser should silently ignore any unrecognized statements.

Since your parser will only handle a subset of the OBJ format, you need to make sure it doesn't choke when given a model that contains statements you haven't implemented yet. The following test introduces a function called parse_obj_file(file), which returns a data structure encapsulating the contents of the (ostensibly OBJ-formatted) file.

```
features/obj_file.feature
Scenario: Ignoring unrecognized lines
  Given gibberish ← a file containing:
    """

    There was a young lady named Bright
    who traveled much faster than light.
    She set out one day
    in a relative way,
    and came back the previous night.
    """

  When parser ← parse_obj_file(gibberish)
  Then parser should have ignored 5 lines
```

In this case, it parses a file containing gibberish, and the resulting parser notes how many lines were ignored.

Test #9: OBJ File with Vertex Data

The parser should process vertex data from the given input.

Here, the parser is given a file containing four vertex statements. Each vertex statement starts with a "v," followed by a space character, and then three integer or floating point numbers delimited by spaces.

```
features/obj_file.feature
Scenario: Vertex records
  Given file ← a file containing:
    """
    v -1 1 0
    v -1.0000 0.5000 0.0000
    v 1 0 0
    v 1 1 0
    """
  When parser ← parse_obj_file(file)
  Then parser.vertices[1] = point(-1, 1, 0)
    And parser.vertices[2] = point(-1, 0.5, 0)
    And parser.vertices[3] = point(1, 0, 0)
    And parser.vertices[4] = point(1, 1, 0)
```

The resulting parser should have an array of vertices, each recorded as a point. Note: it is significant that the array is 1-based, and not 0-based! When you get to the next test, you'll see that faces (triangles and polygons) refer to these vertices by their index, starting with 1.

Test #10: OBJ File with Triangle Data

The parser should process triangle data from the given input.

The parser is now given a file containing four vertex statements and two triangles. The triangles are introduced with the f command (for "face"), followed by three integers referring to the corresponding vertices. Note that these indices are 1-based, and *not* 0-based! That is, vertex number 1 is the first vertex encountered in the file, not the second.

```
features/obj_file.feature
Scenario: Parsing triangle faces
  Given file ← a file containing:
    """
    v -1 1 0
    v -1 0 0
    v 1 0 0
    v 1 1 0

    f 1 2 3
    f 1 3 4
    """
  When parser ← parse_obj_file(file)
    And g ← parser.default_group
    And t1 ← first child of g
    And t2 ← second child of g
  Then t1.p1 = parser.vertices[1]
    And t1.p2 = parser.vertices[2]
    And t1.p3 = parser.vertices[3]
    And t2.p1 = parser.vertices[1]
```

```
    And t2.p2 = parser.vertices[3]
    And t2.p3 = parser.vertices[4]
```

Note also the test references a default_group property on the parser. This Group instance receives all generated geometry. Your parser should add the two triangles to this group.

Test #11: OBJ File with Polygon Data

The parser should process and triangulate polygonal data from the given input.

Pushing the envelope a bit now, you'll give your parser a file containing five vertex statements and a single pentagonal face consuming them all. Your ray tracer only knows how to render triangles, though, so it needs to be able to break that polygon apart into triangles.

```
features/obj_file.feature
Scenario: Triangulating polygons
  Given file ← a file containing:
    """

    v -1 1 0
    v -1 0 0
    v 1 0 0
    v 1 1 0
    v 0 2 0

    f 1 2 3 4 5
    """
  When parser ← parse_obj_file(file)
    And g ← parser.default_group
    And t1 ← first child of g
    And t2 ← second child of g
    And t3 ← third child of g
  Then t1.p1 = parser.vertices[1]
    And t1.p2 = parser.vertices[2]
    And t1.p3 = parser.vertices[3]
    And t2.p1 = parser.vertices[1]
    And t2.p2 = parser.vertices[3]
    And t2.p3 = parser.vertices[4]
    And t3.p1 = parser.vertices[1]
    And t3.p2 = parser.vertices[4]
    And t3.p3 = parser.vertices[5]
```

This will come up fairly often in OBJ files, whether found online or exported yourself. It's often more efficient (space-wise) to describe a planar polygon than to describe the same polygon as a series of triangles. This is fine, but it means you need to explicitly *triangulate*—convert to triangles—the polygons before you can render them.

To keep things simple, just assume the incoming data always describes convex polygons—those whose interior angles are all less than or equal to 180°. When this is the case you can break them into triangles using a *fan triangulation*. Visually, the process looks like this:

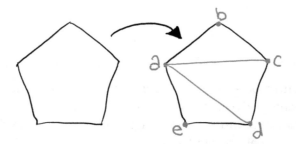

The idea is that you pick one starting vertex, a, and then create a triangle by combining it with the next two vertices in the list, b and c. Then, starting with a again, create another triangle with c and d. Continue in this fashion, starting each triangle with vertex a, adding the last vertex of the previous triangle and the next vertex in the list, and proceeding until all vertices have been used.

In pseudocode, it looks like this:

```
# vertices is a 1-based array of at least three vertices
function fan_triangulation(vertices)
  triangles ← empty list

  for index ← 2 to length(vertices) - 1
    tri ← triangle(vertices[1], vertices[index], vertices[index+1])
    add tri to triangles
  end for

  return triangles
end function
```

Note that the pseudocode here expects a 1-based array of points, because that's what the OBJ file format assumes. If your parser is translating the OBJ 1-based indices to 0-based, then you can feel free to implement your fan triangulation accordingly.

That's the key to making this test pass—apply a fan triangulation to the list of vertices and add the resulting triangles to the default group.

Test #12: Named Groups in OBJ Files

The parser should recognize a group statement and add subsequent triangles to the named group.

Models can get fairly complex, and might be composed of different pieces. Rather than a single model of a person, for instance, the model might be composed of groups like "arm," "leg," and "head." These groups are identified in an OBJ file with the g command.

This test reads an OBJ file, and then shows that the given named groups are present and contain the expected triangles.

```
features/obj_file.feature
Scenario: Triangles in groups
  Given file ← the file "triangles.obj"
  When parser ← parse_obj_file(file)
    And g1 ← "FirstGroup" from parser
    And g2 ← "SecondGroup" from parser
    And t1 ← first child of g1
    And t2 ← first child of g2
  Then t1.p1 = parser.vertices[1]
    And t1.p2 = parser.vertices[2]
    And t1.p3 = parser.vertices[3]
    And t2.p1 = parser.vertices[1]
    And t2.p2 = parser.vertices[3]
    And t2.p3 = parser.vertices[4]
```

Create the following triangles.obj file as well, so you can feed it to the test:

```
files/triangles.obj
v -1 1 0
v -1 0 0
v 1 0 0
v 1 1 0

g FirstGroup
f 1 2 3
g SecondGroup
f 1 3 4
```

To make the test pass, you'll need to keep track of which group was most recently referenced and add all subsequent triangles to that group.

Test #13: Converting an OBJ Model to a Group

The parser should convert a parsed OBJ model to a Group instance.

Once you've parsed the OBJ file, you still need to add the model to your scene. This test adds a function, obj_to_group(parser), which converts a parsed OBJ file to a Group instance that you can then add to your scene. It uses the same triangles.obj file as the previous test, for input.

```
features/obj_file.feature
Scenario: Converting an OBJ file to a group
  Given file ← the file "triangles.obj"
    And parser ← parse_obj_file(file)
  When g ← obj_to_group(parser)
  Then g includes "FirstGroup" from parser
    And g includes "SecondGroup" from parser
```

With that piece done, you should be able to take some simple OBJ files, parse them, and render them in your scenes! You can find many online, searching for things like "simple obj file." One such site is this minimal page from an MIT computer graphics class: groups.csail.mit.edu/graphics/classes/6.837/F03/models. Another, which includes both high- and low-resolution versions of the teapot, is from a computer graphics class at the University of Utah: graphics.cs.utah.edu/courses/cs6620/fall2013/?prj=5.

 Many OBJ models you'll find online consist of thousands of triangles. Don't be surprised if your ray tracer bogs down under that kind of load! To speed things up, consider researching some optimizations, like the bounding box technique mentioned in Chapter 14, *Groups*, on page 193, and subdividing the triangles in a group into smaller groups. This can reduce the number of triangles that need to be intersected by each ray.

Your renders are looking good, now, but they could still look better. Those models, as rendered, are pretty obviously made up of triangles. It's time to teach your ray tracer how to smooth those edges by lying about the normal vectors.

Smooth Triangles

Assuming everything was successful so far, you've got your ray tracer rendering complex polygonal models that you've imported from OBJ files! A glaringly obvious drawback, though, is that these models are polygonal. The teapot in the following figure is probably typical of what you're seeing:

After the initial thrill of "Oh my gosh! It works!" wears off, you're left wondering what you can do to make that chunky teapot look a bit more glossy.

Well, one thing you can do is find a higher resolution model. The first one used about 240 triangles. The teapot in the following figure uses closer to 6,400.

The difference is striking! It's much cleaner looking, but it's *still* not perfect. It also takes much, much more work to render, thanks to using twenty-five times as many triangles.

Fortunately, there's a handy technique called *normal interpolation*, which works by assigning a normal vector to each vertex. Then, those vertex normals are used to interpolate the normal vector at any given point on the triangle, basically *lying* about the normal vector to trick the shading routines! Done correctly, the result can mimic a flawlessly curved surface. The following figure shows that high-resolution teapot again, rendered without normal interpolation on the left, and with it on the right.

Those triangles have been smoothed right over! It works for lower resolution models, too. Check out the figure on page 220, demonstrating smooth triangles with the low-resolution teapot.

In this case, though, you can see the weakness of this technique: it doesn't change the geometry—only the normal vector at the point of intersection.

Thus, the image silhouette remains blocky and angular, giving the lie to the smooth appearance of the surface.

To make this work, you'll do the following things:

1. Add a new primitive, called smooth_triangle(p1, p2, p3, n1, n2, n3).

2. Add u and v properties to the intersection object. They'll be used to represent a location on the surface of a triangle, relative to its corners.

3. Populate the u and v properties of the intersection when intersecting a triangle.

4. Accept an intersection object as a parameter to both normal_at() and local_normal_at(), and implement the normal calculation for smooth triangles, with normal interpolation.

5. Pass the hit intersection when calling normal_at() and local_normal_at().

That seems like a lot, but it will come together fairly quickly.

Each of the smooth_triangle() tests assumes that the triangle to test, tri, is prepared by the following setup:

features/smooth-triangles.feature
```
Background:
  Given p1 ← point(0, 1, 0)
    And p2 ← point(-1, 0, 0)
    And p3 ← point(1, 0, 0)
    And n1 ← vector(0, 1, 0)
    And n2 ← vector(-1, 0, 0)
    And n3 ← vector(1, 0, 0)
  When tri ← smooth_triangle(p1, p2, p3, n1, n2, n3)
```

Once that's ready, start with making sure it constructs the triangle correctly.

Test #14: Creating a Smooth Triangle

A smooth triangle should store the triangle's three vertex points, as well as the normal vector at each of those points.

Assuming the background has already set up the smooth triangle tri, this test just asserts that each of the properties has been set correctly.

```
features/smooth-triangles.feature
Scenario: Constructing a smooth triangle
  Then tri.p1 = p1
    And tri.p2 = p2
    And tri.p3 = p3
    And tri.n1 = n1
    And tri.n2 = n2
    And tri.n3 = n3
```

Next, you'll enhance your intersection() structure.

Test #15: Adding u and v Properties to Intersections

An intersection record may have u and v properties, to help identify where on a triangle the intersection occurred, relative to the triangle's corners.

These u and v properties will be floating point numbers between 0 and 1. They are specific to triangles, so intersections with any other shape won't use them. Still, for triangles—and especially for *smooth* triangles—they're relevant. The following test demonstrates how to construct an intersection record that encapsulates the u and v properties, using a new intersection_with_uv(t, shape, u, v) function.

```
features/intersections.feature
Scenario: An intersection can encapsulate `u` and `v`
  Given s ← triangle(point(0, 1, 0), point(-1, 0, 0), point(1, 0, 0))
  When i ← intersection_with_uv(3.5, s, 0.2, 0.4)
  Then i.u = 0.2
    And i.v = 0.4
```

It's safe to leave the u and v properties undefined when intersections are constructed in any other way.

Test #16: Populate u and v on Triangle Intersections

When intersecting triangles, preserve the u and v values in the resulting intersection.

Back to smooth triangles, this test shows what happens when you intersect one with a ray. The resulting intersection should have the u and v properties set.

```
features/smooth-triangles.feature
Scenario: An intersection with a smooth triangle stores u/v
  When r ← ray(point(-0.2, 0.3, -2), vector(0, 0, 1))
    And xs ← local_intersect(tri, r)
  Then xs[0].u = 0.45
    And xs[0].v = 0.25
```

This is actually really great, because you've already computed both u and v! Remember when I said the Möller–Trumbore algorithm had a feature that would come in handy later? Well, now it's later. That triangle intersection routine defined two variables, u and v. Take those two variables and pass them to the new intersection_with_uv() function, in place of the existing call to intersection().

For finding the intersection with a ray and a smooth triangle, use the triangle intersection routine. It really is the same calculation, but with the addition of storing u and v on the intersection. If this requires some refactoring to happen in your code, make sure you take care of that now, too.

Once you've got those u and v properties being stored in the intersection, read on. You're about to put them to use.

Test #17: Normal Interpolation

When computing the normal vector on a smooth triangle, use the intersection's u and v properties to interpolate the normal.

This test sets up an intersection with u and v and then passes that intersection to normal_at(). The point is intentionally set to the origin to reinforce the fact that it isn't used here—only u and v should have any effect.

```
features/smooth-triangles.feature
Scenario: A smooth triangle uses u/v to interpolate the normal
  When i ← intersection_with_uv(1, tri, 0.45, 0.25)
    And n ← normal_at(tri, point(0, 0, 0), i)
  Then n = vector(-0.5547, 0.83205, 0)
```

Make this pass by adding the intersection object representing the hit as a parameter to both normal_at() and local_normal_at(). To preserve a consistent API, add this parameter to the local_normal_at() function for every shape, even though it's only actually used for the smooth triangles.

Once you've got that parameter passed to the smooth triangle's local_normal_at() function, you interpolate the normal by combining the normal vectors of the triangle's vertices according to the hit's u and v properties, as given in the following pseudocode:

```
function local_normal_at(tri, point, hit)
  return tri.n2 * hit.u +
```

```
        tri.n3 * hit.v +
        tri.n1 * (1 - hit.u - hit.v)
end function
```

Once that's passing, the last bit for making this work is to make sure the hit gets passed to the normal calculation.

Test #18: Pass the Hit to the normal_at Function

The prepare_computations() function should pass the hit itself to the call to normal_at().

Construct an intersection with tri, and some u and v values. When prepare_computations() is called on that intersection, the normal should be calculated according to the rules for the smooth triangle, which requires that the intersection be passed to normal_at().

features/smooth-triangles.feature
```
Scenario: Preparing the normal on a smooth triangle
  When i ← intersection_with_uv(1, tri, 0.45, 0.25)
    And r ← ray(point(-0.2, 0.3, -2), vector(0, 0, 1))
    And xs ← intersections(i)
    And comps ← prepare_computations(i, r, xs)
  Then comps.normalv = vector(-0.5547, 0.83205, 0)
```

Once that's passing, it's time to revisit your OBJ parser and plug these smooth triangles in there.

Smooth Triangles in OBJ Files

Your OBJ parser is already quite close to supporting smooth triangles. All it needs now is to support the *vertex normal* (vn) command and to update the way it parses the f ("face") command.

Test #19: OBJ File with Vertex Normal Data

Vertex normal data should be correctly imported from an OBJ file.

This test sets up an OBJ file that contains four vertex normal statements ("vn"), and then shows that each of them is imported as a vector. Note that the normals collection is 1-based, just as the vertices collection was.

features/obj_file.feature
```
Scenario: Vertex normal records
  Given file ← a file containing:
    """
    vn 0 0 1
    vn 0.707 0 -0.707
    vn 1 2 3
    """
```

```
When parser ← parse_obj_file(file)
Then parser.normals[1] = vector(0, 0, 1)
  And parser.normals[2] = vector(0.707, 0, -0.707)
  And parser.normals[3] = vector(1, 2, 3)
```

The normals are imported as is, with no normalization or other processing done. Once those are imported, it's just a matter of associating each of those vertex normals with a vertex, which you'll do next.

Test #20: Faces with Normal Vectors

Vertex normal data should be correctly associated with face data from an OBJ file.

The f command that you implemented earlier is only half done, really. The following test demonstrates a more complete version of the syntax, permitting the vertices of a face to be associated with normal vectors.

features/obj_file.feature
```
Scenario: Faces with normals
  Given file ← a file containing:
    """
    v 0 1 0
    v -1 0 0
    v 1 0 0

    vn -1 0 0
    vn 1 0 0
    vn 0 1 0

    f 1//3 2//1 3//2
    f 1/0/3 2/102/1 3/14/2
    """
  When parser ← parse_obj_file(file)
    And g ← parser.default_group
    And t1 ← first child of g
    And t2 ← second child of g
  Then t1.p1 = parser.vertices[1]
    And t1.p2 = parser.vertices[2]
    And t1.p3 = parser.vertices[3]
    And t1.n1 = parser.normals[3]
    And t1.n2 = parser.normals[1]
    And t1.n3 = parser.normals[2]
    And t2 = t1
```

It turns out that the f command supports the following variations, the first of which you've already implemented:

```
f 1 2 3
f 1/2/3 2/3/4 3/4/5
f 1//3 2//4 3//5
```

The forward slash is used to delimit up to three different kinds of information per vertex. The first number in each triple is the vertex index itself. The second is an optional *texture vertex* (which you won't implement for this feature and can be ignored). The third is an optional index into the list of vertex normals, corresponding to the vn command you just implemented.

To make this test pass, your f command needs to check to see if vertex normals are present for the vertices, and if they are, the command should call smooth_triangle() instead of triangle().

Make that test pass. Once everything is good, you're ready to sign off on this chapter!

Putting It Together

You can find 3D models to render in a lot of places online by searching for "free 3D models." Here are a few of the first hits I found with that search:

- TurboSquid[2] (paid, but has a section of free models)
- Free3D[3]
- cgtrader[4] (paid, but has a free section)
- ClaraIO[5]

NASA has a library of free 3D resources, including models, at nasa3d.arc.nasa.gov. Many of them are quite large (hundreds of thousands of triangles), but I was able to find several models with just a few thousand, including this adorable little guy:

---

2.   www.turbosquid.com/Search/3D-Models/free
3.   free3d.com
4.   www.cgtrader.com/free-3d-models
5.   clara.io/library

Some caveats apply to any model you find online, though:

- Many of these models are in formats other than OBJ. Online conversion tools vary (just search for "convert 3D formats" or something similar), but I can't vouch for any of them. It's best, when possible, to find OBJ files directly, rather than relying on converting. (Still, I converted the previous astronaut model from a 3DS format to OBJ using the convertor at www.greentoken.de/onlineconv/.)

- These models are *not* of uniform size and are rarely centered conveniently at the origin. My advice is to have your OBJ parser print the minimum and maximum extents of each model it imports, which you can then use to translate and scale the model in your scene.

- These models often have the y and z axes swapped from what this book presents, with z being the "up" axis instead of y. If you find this to be the case, a quick rotation around x by $-\pi/2$ should do the trick.

Lastly, you can have a lot of fun if you can get your hands on a 3D modeling program. Blender[6] is a free, cross-platform option which is incredibly powerful and can export models in OBJ format. Blender has a correspondingly challenging learning curve, but if you're up to it, Blender can be wonderful to play with. You can use it to create your own models or just convert existing models to OBJ. You can even (with Blender's "decimate" modifier) simplify existing models so they use fewer triangles.

Once you're done having fun with polygonal models, read on. The last feature awaits: constructive solid geometry.

---

6. blender.org

## CHAPTER 16

Constructive Solid Geometry (CSG)

You've made it through matrix transformations, Phong illumination, reflection, refraction, and ray-object intersections for a variety of primitive shapes. For this last feature, you'll implement *constructive solid geometry*, or CSG—a method of combining those primitives via set operations. This lets you create much more complex shapes, like these:

It's true that any of those shapes could have been assembled in a 3D modeling app and then exported to an OBJ file, which you could have imported and rendered. Using CSG is better in this case for two significant reasons:

1. To get per-triangle coloring to work, you'd need to implement a parser for Wavefront MTL material files, and make your OBJ parser implement vertex textures to map material definitions to vertices. (Whew!) With CSG, you can strategically apply textures and colors to different surfaces within the model, using only what you've already implemented.

2. You'd need hundreds or even thousands of triangles to render these shapes, while CSG lets you use far fewer primitives. The tricylinder on the left of the previous image required only three cylinders; the carved

cube in the middle is just three cylinders, a cube, and a sphere; and the hollow sphere on the right is a sphere and twelve cubes. Add the cube representing the room, and the entire scene consists of just 22 shapes!

CSG works by taking two or more primitive shapes and combining them using any of three different set operations: union, intersection, and difference.

Union combines the inputs into a single shape, preserving all external surfaces. Here's a cube and a sphere, which have been combined via a union.

 Joe asks:

Why use a CSG union instead of a group?

Good question! In many instances, a group is definitely simpler, but when you're dealing with transparent and reflective objects, like glass, their interior surfaces can contribute unwanted reflections. Here's an example with two overlapping glass spheres. On the left, they were combined using a group. On the right, a CSG union was used.

The picture doesn't lie; using a union instead of a group gets rid of those interior surfaces and gives you a truer transparency.

Intersection preserves the portion of the inputs that share a volume (where the shapes intersect each other), resulting in a single shape with those combined surfaces. This is the intersection between the cube and sphere from the previous image.

Difference preserves only the portion of the first shape where it's not overlapped by the others. Here's the difference between the original cube and sphere, effectively carving the sphere out of the cube.

Your implementation of CSG will support all three of these operations, and you'll learn how to use them together to generate an enormous variety of different shapes and effects.

Are you ready? Here we go.

Implementing CSG

For simplicity's sake, your implementation will treat all CSG operations as strictly binary, meaning that each one takes exactly two shapes as input. This may seem restrictive, but since a CSG object is itself a shape, you can build arbitrarily complex CSG operations by combining them in a hierarchy, like this:

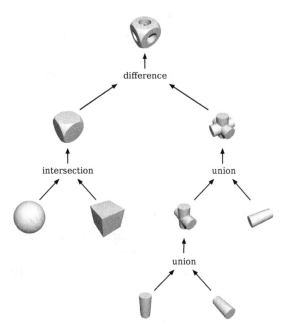

You'll render these shapes by intersecting them with a ray, as you've done with every other shape you've implemented. Intersecting a ray with a CSG shape begins just like intersecting one with a Group: you first intersect the ray with the shape's children. Then, you iterate over the resulting intersection records, tracking which ones are inside which child and filtering out those that don't conform to the current operation. The resulting list of intersections is then returned.

The devil, as ever, is in the details. We'll walk through this process one bit at a time, following these steps:

1. Create a CSG shape by providing an operation and two operand shapes, left and right.

2. Implement the rules for union, intersection, and difference.

3. Filter a list of intersections using the rules from step 2.

4. Demonstrate what happens when a ray misses a CSG object.

5. Demonstrate what happens when a ray hits a CSG object.

Begin by creating the CSG shape itself.

Test #1: Creating a CSG Shape

A CSG shape is composed of an operation and two operand shapes.

Instantiate a new CSG shape. For the sake of the test, use the union operation and give it a sphere and a cube for the two operands.

```
features/csg.feature
Scenario: CSG is created with an operation and two shapes
  Given s1 ← sphere()
    And s2 ← cube()
  When c ← csg("union", s1, s2)
  Then c.operation = "union"
    And c.left = s1
    And c.right = s2
    And s1.parent = c
    And s2.parent = c
```

The operands are referred to as left and right, mirroring the structure of a binary tree where the two children of a parent are arranged with one on the left and one on the right. Note that your code should set the parent attribute of both child shapes to the CSG shape itself, just as if they were part of a group.

Test #2: Evaluating the Rule for a CSG Union Operation

A CSG union preserves all intersections on the exterior of both shapes.

Consider the following illustration, showing a ray intersecting two overlapping spheres. If the two spheres represent a union operation, the highlighted intersections are the ones to be preserved; the rest are ignored.

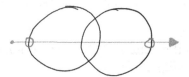

You'll encode this rule in a new function, called intersection_allowed(op, lhit, inl, inr). The arguments are interpreted as follows:

- op is the CSG operation being evaluated.
- lhit is true if the left shape was hit, and false if the right shape was hit.

- inl is true if the hit occurs inside the left shape.
- inr is true if the hit occurs inside the right shape.

Referring to the previous figure, and assuming the ray moves from left to right, you would evaluate the four intersections with the following calls to intersection_allowed:

- intersection_allowed("union", true, false, false)—the hit is on the outside of the left shape.

- intersection_allowed("union", false, true, false)—the hit is on the outside of the right shape, while inside the left shape.

- intersection_allowed("union", true, true, true)—the hit is on the inside of the left shape, while inside the right shape.

- intersection_allowed("union", false, false, true)—the hit is on the inside of the right shape.

You can arrange the arguments in those calls to form a *truth table*, a method of showing boolean input values and the expected output of some operation on them. The following test describes the basic outline you'll use to exercise all three operations, as well as a truth table to describe how the intersection_allowed() function works with the union operation.

```
features/csg.feature
Scenario Outline: Evaluating the rule for a CSG operation
  When result ← intersection_allowed("<op>", <lhit>, <inl>, <inr>)
  Then result = <result>

  Examples:
  | op    | lhit  | inl   | inr   | result |
  | union | true  | true  | true  | false  |
  | union | true  | true  | false | true   |
  | union | true  | false | true  | false  |
  | union | true  | false | false | true   |
  | union | false | true  | true  | false  |
  | union | false | true  | false | false  |
  | union | false | false | true  | true   |
  | union | false | false | false | true   |
```

The goal is to implement intersection_allowed in such a way as to make sure it returns the correct answer for all possible combinations of inputs, thus allowing only the correct intersections.

To make the test pass, consider what the union operation actually *means*. You only want the intersections that are not inside another object. If the hit is on the left object, it must not also be inside the right, and if it is on the right, it must not simultaneously be inside the left. In pseudocode, the logic looks something like this:

```
function intersection_allowed(op, lhit, inl, inr)
  if op is "union"
    return (lhit and not inr) or (not lhit and not inl)
  end if

  # default answer
  return false
end function
```

Implement that to make the test pass. Next you'll tackle the rule for the intersect operation.

Test #3: Evaluating the Rule for a CSG Intersect Operation

A CSG intersect preserves all intersections where both shapes overlap.

Take a look at the next illustration, again showing a ray intersecting two overlapping spheres. This time, though, the highlights show which intersections are kept by a CSG intersect operation.

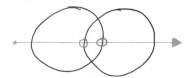

The intersections are chosen in such a way as to preserve the volume that the shapes have in common. Add the following truth table to the end of the one you started in the previous test, showing how the intersection_allowed() function ought to behave in this case.

features/csg.feature
```
# append after the union examples...
| intersection | true  | true  | true  | true  |
| intersection | true  | true  | false | false |
| intersection | true  | false | true  | true  |
| intersection | true  | false | false | false |
| intersection | false | true  | true  | true  |
| intersection | false | true  | false | true  |
| intersection | false | false | true  | false |
| intersection | false | false | false | false |
```

To make those examples pass, you want to allow only those intersections that strike one object while inside the other. If a ray hits the object on the left, the intersection must be inside the right, and vice versa. In pseudocode, that logic looks like this:

```
function intersection_allowed(op, lhit, inl, inr)
  if op is "union"
    return (lhit and not inr) or (not lhit and not inl)
  else if op is "intersect"
    return (lhit and inr) or (not lhit and inl)
  end if

  return false
end function
```

Get those new examples passing, and then move on to the third CSG operation: difference.

Test #4: Evaluating the Rule for a CSG Difference Operation

A CSG difference preserves all intersections not exclusively inside the object on the right.

Take a look at the following diagram of two overlapping spheres. The intersections are now highlighted to represent a CSG difference operation.

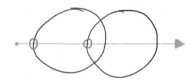

Add this last truth table to the end of the other two, to show how the difference operation should work.

features/csg.feature

```
# append after the intersection examples...
| difference | true  | true  | true  | false |
| difference | true  | true  | false | true  |
| difference | true  | false | true  | false |
| difference | true  | false | false | true  |
| difference | false | true  | true  | true  |
| difference | false | true  | false | true  |
| difference | false | false | true  | false |
| difference | false | false | false | false |
```

The difference operation will keep every intersection on left that *is not* inside right, *and* every intersection on right that *is* inside left. Written as pseudocode, it looks like this:

```
function intersection_allowed(op, lhit, inl, inr)
  if op is "union"
    return (lhit and not inr) or (not lhit and not inl)
  else if op is "intersect"
    return (lhit and inr) or (not lhit and inl)
```

```
➤   else if op is "difference"
➤      return (lhit and not inr) or (not lhit and inl)
    end if

    return false
end function
```

Great! Once those tests are all passing, you're ready to start filtering intersections based on those rules.

Test #5: Filtering a List of Intersections

Given a set of intersections, produce a subset of only those intersections that conform to the operation of the current CSG object.

Once you have the intersection_allowed() function working, you get to use it in the next part of your implementation of CSG: intersection filtering. In the big scheme of things, when your renderer intersects a ray with a CSG object, the CSG object will produce a list of intersections between that ray and its children. This filter_intersections(csg, xs) function accepts that list (xs), evaluates each intersection with the intersection_allowed() function, and returns a new intersection list consisting of those that pass.

The following test creates a csg object composed of two shapes. Then it creates a list of intersections (xs) and calls filter_intersections(). Finally, it checks that the two result intersections are what is expected for the current operation.

features/csg.feature
```
Scenario Outline: Filtering a list of intersections
  Given s1 ← sphere()
    And s2 ← cube()
    And c ← csg("<operation>", s1, s2)
    And xs ← intersections(1:s1, 2:s2, 3:s1, 4:s2)
  When result ← filter_intersections(c, xs)
  Then result.count = 2
    And result[0] = xs[<x0>]
    And result[1] = xs[<x1>]

  Examples:
    | operation    | x0 | x1 |
    | union        | 0  | 3  |
    | intersection | 1  | 2  |
    | difference   | 0  | 1  |
```

For this to work, your filter_intersections() function needs to loop over each intersection in xs, keeping track of which child the intersection hits and which children it is currently inside, and then passing that information to intersection_allowed(). If the intersection is allowed, it's added to the list of passing intersections.

Here it is in pseudocode:

```
function filter_intersections(csg, xs)
  # begin outside of both children
  inl ← false
  inr ← false

  # prepare a list to receive the filtered intersections
  result ← empty intersection list

  for each intersection "i" in xs
    # if i.object is part of the "left" child, then lhit is true
    lhit ← csg.left includes i.object

    if intersection_allowed(csg.operation, lhit, inl, inr) then
      add i to result
    end if

    # depending on which object was hit, toggle either inl or inr
    if lhit then
      inl ← not inl
    else
      inr ← not inr
    end if
  end for

  return result
end function
```

Note the line with csg.left includes i.object, just at the start of the for loop. The implementation of this will be up to you, but A includes B should behave like this:

- If A is a Group, the includes operator should return true if child includes B for any child of A.

- If A is a CSG object, the includes operator should return true if either child of A includes B.

- If A is any other shape, the includes operator should return true if A is equal to B.

In other words, it should recursively search a subtree, looking for the given object, to see whether or not the intersection occurred on the left side of the CSG tree. If it did, then lhit must be true.

Go ahead and make that test pass. Once you do, you can move on to the last two tests: making sure that the actual intersection routine functions correctly.

Tests #6 and 7: Intersecting a Ray with a CSG Object

A ray should intersect a CSG object if it intersects any of its children.

The following tests set up a CSG object and a ray and check to see whether or not the ray intersects. The first test makes sure that a ray misses when it should miss, and the second test makes sure that it hits when it should hit. The second test also applies a transformation to one of the primitives to ensure that the resulting intersections are being filtered correctly.

features/csg.feature

```
Scenario: A ray misses a CSG object
  Given c ← csg("union", sphere(), cube())
    And r ← ray(point(0, 2, -5), vector(0, 0, 1))
  When xs ← local_intersect(c, r)
  Then xs is empty

Scenario: A ray hits a CSG object
  Given s1 ← sphere()
    And s2 ← sphere()
    And set_transform(s2, translation(0, 0, 0.5))
    And c ← csg("union", s1, s2)
    And r ← ray(point(0, 0, -5), vector(0, 0, 1))
  When xs ← local_intersect(c, r)
  Then xs.count = 2
    And xs[0].t = 4
    And xs[0].object = s1
    And xs[1].t = 6.5
    And xs[1].object = s2
```

Make this pass by intersecting the ray with the left and right children and combining the resulting intersections into a single (sorted!) list. The combined intersections should be passed to filter_intersections(), and the filtered collection should then be returned.

In pseudocode, it looks like this:

```
function local_intersect(csg, ray)
  leftxs ← intersect(csg.left, ray)
  rightxs ← intersect(csg.right, ray)

  xs ← combine leftxs and rightxs
  xs ← sort xs by t

  return filter_intersections(csg, xs)
end function
```

And that completes your implementation of CSG shapes! You don't even need to compute a normal vector; the intersection records always point to the primitive object that was hit, and not the parent CSG shape, which means the primitive shape itself will always perform the normal computation. Neat!

One last thing to talk about is how to apply color to CSG shapes.

Coloring CSG Shapes

You may recall that at the beginning of this chapter I said that it was possible to strategically color portions of a CSG shape. It's true—the key is to remember that intersecting a ray with a CSG shape preserves the original intersections with the original primitive shapes. Think about how your ray tracer determines the color to use for a given intersection. In Chapter 6, *Light and Shading*, on page 75, you stored a material structure on each object and used the material from the intersected object to determine what color the intersection should be.

This still holds true with CSG intersections. Consider again this illustration of a red sphere subtracted from a yellow cube.

The faces of the cube remain yellow, but the portion that was subtracted away retains the red of the sphere! This is because those intersections were from the sphere and not the cube and so keep the original coloring of the sphere.

This works even with reflective and transparent surfaces, which means you can make certain faces "disappear" by making their corresponding shape transparent. By default, transparent surfaces will still cast shadows, but if you hark back to *Putting It Together*, on page 165, you'll see one of the optional things to consider is for shapes to "opt out" of casting shadows. Implementing that, and then subtracting transparent shapes from solids, lets you do nifty things like this sphere with a wedge removed from it:

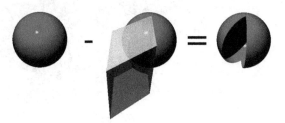

You can form the wedge by rotating a cube 45 degrees around the y axis and then making it narrower by scaling it smaller in z. Make the wedge transparent, position it so it intersects the sphere, and then subtract it from the sphere. It's a fun trick!

Putting It Together

Thinking in terms of CSG can be challenging if you're not used to it. It takes some practice to learn to see the world around you as unions, intersections, and differences of primitive shapes. Here are some things you can do with CSG and some hints for how to construct them.

- A lens. (The intersection of two spheres.)

- A six-sided die. (A cube, mostly, but using CSG difference operations with scaled spheres to form the pips.)

- A block letter or number. (Perhaps from a flattened cube, with pieces shaved off using differences with cubes and cylinders.)

- A flower. (Perhaps form the petals out of spheres, strategically scaled and shaped by intersecting other spheres.)

- The planet Saturn. (Form each ring by subtracting one cylinder from another.)

If you're feeling ambitious, think of how you might increase the realism for each of these. For example, dice in real life are not perfect cubes, but instead have rounded edges and corners. How would you create that effect, using just what you've implemented so far in your ray tracer?

What else can you imagine? Furniture? Buildings? Dragons, knights, and castles? Trains, planes, or automobiles? Might as well make a spaceship or two, because the sky is the limit!

At this point, you're as good as done with the Ray Tracer Challenge, but go ahead and turn the page anyway. Let's talk about where you might take your ray tracer next, because like all the best projects, there's always another feature you can add.

## CHAPTER 17

Next Steps

Here you are at the end. What a ride, eh? From tuples and matrices, you've proceeded all the way through ray-sphere intersections, shading and shadows, patterns, reflections and refractions, and on up to constructive solid geometry. You've built something to be proud of.

As with any good project, though, the "end" is just a line drawn in the sand. The book ends here, but you can add *so much more* to your ray tracer, and the path you take is entirely up to you. New features are limited only by your imagination (and, maybe, your perseverance in the face of a bit more math). Here are some ideas that you might use as jumping-off points for your own experimentation and research.

Let's start by casting light on some light source variations.

Area Lights and Soft Shadows

Your ray tracer currently implements *point lights*, which exist at a single point and have no size. These lights cast sharp, crisp shadows with perfectly defined outlines. But in the physical world, a point light doesn't actually exist. Light sources have dimension, and the shadows they cast tend to be fuzzy around the edges as a result.

Consider the illustration on page 240, which compares shadows cast by a point light (on the left), with shadows cast by an *area light* (on the right).

Those blurred shadows don't come cheap. Recall from Chapter 8, *Shadows*, on page 109, that your current shadow test casts a single ray from the point of intersection to the light source. This results in a boolean "yes/no" result, answering the question of whether the point is in shadow. For an area light, you must cast *multiple* shadow rays, and the answer is no longer "yes" or "no," but an intensity value telling you *how much* shadow exists at that point.

To implement an area light, follow these steps:

1. Decide how many shadow rays you want to cast for each area light. The more you cast, the nicer the shadow looks, but it also means your ray tracer has to do more work per pixel.

2. Cast each ray from the point of intersection to a different point on your area light.

3. Compute the light's intensity as the average number of rays that weren't blocked by any intervening surfaces.

Light sources are of many types, though. Read on for another one.

Spotlights

Another feature of point lights is that they shine equally in every direction. But it can be fun to break that assumption and have your lights focus on a particular point. The result is a *spotlight*, like this:

To make this work, assign your light a direction and an angle that describes the beam's width. Then, any point that falls outside the light's cone is considered to be in shadow. If you want the beam to have a soft boundary, you can define a second "fade" angle, inside of which the beam blends from full intensity to none.

Implementing Spotlights

 Remember, the dot product of two unit vectors is the same as the cosine of the angle between them. If you take the dot product of the light's direction vector, and the vector from the point of intersection to the light, you'll end up with the cosine of the angle between them. Relate that to the angle of the spotlight itself, and you've got the feature half done!

Spotlights are an effective way to focus attention on a specific point in your scene, but they're not the only way. Here's another.

Focal Blur

Focal blur helps bring the viewer's attention to the subject of the image by making it appear sharply in focus. Objects that are too far from—or too near to—the camera will appear out of focus. Here's an example:

The focus here is on the three balls in the foreground; the smaller balls in the background and the reflections on the walls are blurred to emphasize their distance and lack of importance.

To make this work, you need to simulate a camera with a larger *aperture*—the hole through which light enters the camera. By default, your ray tracer mimics a pinhole camera, with a hole exactly large enough for a single ray of light. This allows the entire scene to appear crisply in focus. By making the aperture larger, light can arrive from multiple points at once, blurring the picture at those places.

To implement this you need to specify the size of the aperture and the focal length of the camera. Anything situated at the camera's focal length will be in focus, so you generally put the subject of the picture there. And the wider the aperture, the blurrier things get.

In *Implementing a Camera*, on page 100, you set your canvas 1 unit in front of the camera. This effectively hard-coded your focal length to 1. Changing the focal length basically positions your canvas that distance from the camera. Once you've got your canvas situated, you cast multiple rays for each pixel, and the more, the better. Instead of casting them all from a single point at the origin, you'll place your *aperture* at the origin and choose several points on its surface. Then, for each of those points, construct a ray that passes from the point through the current pixel on the canvas and out into the scene. Average the colors for each of the rays you cast per pixel, and there's your focal blur!

We can summarize:

1. Choose a size for the aperture.

2. Choose a distance for the canvas.

3. Cast multiple rays from random points on the aperture, through the pixel on the canvas.

4. Set the pixel to the average of all rays cast through it.

Casting multiple rays per pixel like this is computationally expensive, though, working a lot harder for each pixel. Still, it's a versatile technique that can create a variety of effects. Read on for another one!

Motion Blur

Motion blur is the effect you see in photographs of a quickly moving object, where it appears blurred because it was in motion while the camera's shutter was open. Not only can this draw a viewer's attention, it can make your scenes more dynamic by adding a sense of action. A skilled artist can do this with just a few strokes of a pen, but for the rest of us, there's motion blur, like this:

In ray tracing, you *could* simulate this effect by rendering your scene multiple times, moving one or more objects a bit in each frame, and then averaging all the frames together. Here's another way, though: for each pixel of your image, cast multiple rays and assign them each a time value. When a ray intersects a moving object, your ray tracer transforms the object according to the associated time value before intersecting it with the ray. The resulting color for each ray is then averaged before being written to your canvas.

You can make optimizations, as well. If you define a bounding box around the moving object, completely containing it at every point of its motion, then you only need to cast additional rays if the first ray happens to intersect that bounding box. This prevents one small moving object from bogging down the entire scene unnecessarily.

Anti-aliasing

Because pixels are not infinitely small, diagonal lines will tend to be rendered as stairsteps, or *jaggies*. The following illustration shows a zoomed-in view:

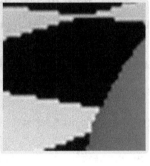

This phenomenon is called *aliasing*, and a lot of effort goes into working around it in production-quality imagery. One such *anti-aliasing* technique renders the image at much higher resolution (double, triple, or more), and then requires a separate image editor to *resample* the picture to a smaller resolution. This essentially averages the values of adjacent pixels, and helps smooth those jagged stairsteps.

You can anti-alias in a single step, though, using a technique called *supersampling*. Instead of casting a single ray for each pixel, you cast multiple rays, each passing through a different (and perhaps random) point offset from the center of the pixel, and average their results. Once again, the more rays you cast, the higher the quality of the result. The image on page 244 is an anti-aliased example of the previous image, rendered using this supersampling technique.

More rays equals more work, so don't expect this technique to come cheaply. You can optimize it, though. For instance, instead of always casting the same number of rays per pixel, you can start by casting one at each corner of the pixel, and one in the pixel's center. If any of the corners differ from the center by more than some threshold amount, you can subdivide that quarter of the pixel and repeat the process, recursively. Even then, because of the time and energy cost, you'll want to save this for the end of the production process.

You can do plenty of other things to your ray tracer that don't require casting more rays. For instance, you can wallpaper textures and imagery onto shapes with texture maps.

Texture Maps

In addition to the solid textures (checkers, rings, and so forth) that you've already implemented, it's possible to apply an external image to an object as a *texture map*. Here's an example using a planar mapping, a cylindrical mapping, and a spherical mapping:

For a planar mapping, you take an image and map an (x, y) pair in object space to a corresponding pixel on the image. You'll usually need to do some interpolation as well, since the point in question will often lie between adjacent pixels.

The cylindrical mapping is a bit trickier, since you need to convert a point on the surface of a cylinder to an image, much like the label on a soup can. You can save yourself a headache if you assume you're always mapping onto a unit cylinder between y=0 and y=1.

The spherical mapping is similar to the cylindrical mapping, but with different behavior at the poles, where an entire row of the image maps to a single point on the sphere. You'll need to convert a 3D point in space into a 2D point on the surface of the sphere, much like finding the latitude and longitude for a point on the earth's surface.

You can do other mapping types as well: cubical, toroidal, and so forth. In each case, target a shape of a constant size (radius of 1, for instance) and make the math work that way. Then, with a bit of scaling, the result can be quite convincing!

In fact, mucking with the surface features of your primitives is a tried and true way to make your scenes shine. Here's another fun technique, in which you lie (in a perfectly moral way) to your renderer.

Normal Perturbation

Hark back to *Smooth Triangles*, on page 218, when you made triangles appear curved by modifying the normal that was reported to the renderer. It turns out that this technique can be used in a variety of ways, basically "lying" to the renderer so that the surface shading is done with modified normals. Check out the image on page 246, showing this technique applied to spheres and a plane.

By attaching a function to the shape (perhaps directly, or maybe via the material), you can have your normal_at() function call the attached function to *perturb*, or add a small vector to, the normal at the given point. In the preceding image, the red sphere uses a sine function to make the surface appear wavy, the blue sphere uses another function to give the surface a quilted appearance, and the green sphere and the plane are both using three-dimensional noise to make the surface look deformed.

This technique can be applied to glass to make it appear etched or frosted, too. And you can even combine it with texture mapping to let an image file define a *normal map* that describes how the normal should be perturbed at any given point.

Besides textures, you can also explore new shape primitives, to increase the variety of your scenes. One such primitive you might try is the torus.

Torus Primitive

A *torus* is a ring or donut shape, like this:

They make really neat, versatile primitives, but they're a bit more advanced than the primitives you've implemented so far. Spheres, cylinders, and cones are called *quadric* surfaces, which means they can be described by second-degree equations (those where no variable is raised to a power higher than 2). A torus, though, is a *quartic* surface, with variables raised to the fourth power. This means you need a quartic equation solver to find the intersection between a torus and a ray.

But that just means you get to dig deeper than you have before, right? If you don't already have access to a quartic equation solver, you might take a look at the Durand-Kerner method.[1] It's not the fastest, but is less intimidating

---

1.   en.wikipedia.org/wiki/Durand-Kerner_method

than some other methods. And Marcin Chwedczuk has written an article called "Ray tracing a torus"[2] that may help cast some light on the topic for you.

See what other primitive shapes you can implement!

Wrapping It Up

As exhaustive as that list might have seemed, it was still just a sampling of what you can try. You can do so much more, like volumetric effects such as smoke, fog, clouds, and fire. Or maybe radiosity and photon mapping for more realistic lighting effects, or parallelization for faster rendering on multi-processor machines. You're never truly done, but that's the wonderful thing about projects like this!

The rest is up to you. Pursue the features that excite you most. Explore your own interests. Make this ray tracer your own. But most important of all: *have fun!*

---

2. marcin-chwedczuk.github.io/ray-tracing-torus

Rendering the Cover Image

The cover image for this book was rendered using the very ray tracer that the book describes, which means that once you've implemented the necessary features, you can render it too!

To render the cover image, your ray tracer must support the features described up through Chapter 12, *Cubes*, on page 167. The actual cover image was rendered using two light sources, though the second is optional.

The cover image scene is described here in YAML[1] format. If a YAML parser exists for your programming language, you may be able to build the scene from this description directly; otherwise, you'll need to translate this description into whatever API you've built for your own renderer.

If rendered as described, you'll get something that looks like this:

___

1.   yaml.org

And here's the scene description itself:

cover.yml

```
# ==========================================================
# the camera
# ==========================================================

- add: camera
  width: 100
  height: 100
  field-of-view: 0.785
  from: [ -6, 6, -10 ]
  to: [ 6, 0, 6 ]
  up: [ -0.45, 1, 0 ]

# ==========================================================
# light sources
# ==========================================================

- add: light
  at: [ 50, 100, -50 ]
  intensity: [ 1, 1, 1 ]

# an optional second light for additional illumination
- add: light
  at: [ -400, 50, -10 ]
  intensity: [ 0.2, 0.2, 0.2 ]

# ==========================================================
# define some constants to avoid duplication
# ==========================================================

- define: white-material
  value:
    color: [ 1, 1, 1 ]
    diffuse: 0.7
    ambient: 0.1
    specular: 0.0
    reflective: 0.1

- define: blue-material
  extend: white-material
  value:
    color: [ 0.537, 0.831, 0.914 ]

- define: red-material
  extend: white-material
  value:
    color: [ 0.941, 0.322, 0.388 ]

- define: purple-material
  extend: white-material
  value:
    color: [ 0.373, 0.404, 0.550 ]
```

```
- define: standard-transform
  value:
    - [ translate, 1, -1, 1 ]
    - [ scale, 0.5, 0.5, 0.5 ]
- define: large-object
  value:
    - standard-transform
    - [ scale, 3.5, 3.5, 3.5 ]
- define: medium-object
  value:
    - standard-transform
    - [ scale, 3, 3, 3 ]
- define: small-object
  value:
    - standard-transform
    - [ scale, 2, 2, 2 ]
# ============================================================
# a white backdrop for the scene
# ============================================================
- add: plane
  material:
    color: [ 1, 1, 1 ]
    ambient: 1
    diffuse: 0
    specular: 0
  transform:
    - [ rotate-x, 1.5707963267948966 ] # pi/2
    - [ translate, 0, 0, 500 ]
# ============================================================
# describe the elements of the scene
# ============================================================
- add: sphere
  material:
    color: [ 0.373, 0.404, 0.550 ]
    diffuse: 0.2
    ambient: 0.0
    specular: 1.0
    shininess: 200
    reflective: 0.7
    transparency: 0.7
    refractive-index: 1.5
  transform:
    - large-object
```

```
- add: cube
  material: white-material
  transform:
    - medium-object
    - [ translate, 4, 0, 0 ]
- add: cube
  material: blue-material
  transform:
    - large-object
    - [ translate, 8.5, 1.5, -0.5 ]
- add: cube
  material: red-material
  transform:
    - large-object
    - [ translate, 0, 0, 4 ]
- add: cube
  material: white-material
  transform:
    - small-object
    - [ translate, 4, 0, 4 ]
- add: cube
  material: purple-material
  transform:
    - medium-object
    - [ translate, 7.5, 0.5, 4 ]
- add: cube
  material: white-material
  transform:
    - medium-object
    - [ translate, -0.25, 0.25, 8 ]
- add: cube
  material: blue-material
  transform:
    - large-object
    - [ translate, 4, 1, 7.5 ]
- add: cube
  material: red-material
  transform:
    - medium-object
    - [ translate, 10, 2, 7.5 ]
- add: cube
  material: white-material
  transform:
    - small-object
    - [ translate, 8, 2, 12 ]
```

```
- add: cube
  material: white-material
  transform:
    - small-object
    - [ translate, 20, 1, 9 ]
- add: cube
  material: blue-material
  transform:
    - large-object
    - [ translate, -0.5, -5, 0.25 ]
- add: cube
  material: red-material
  transform:
    - large-object
    - [ translate, 4, -4, 0 ]
- add: cube
  material: white-material
  transform:
    - large-object
    - [ translate, 8.5, -4, 0 ]
- add: cube
  material: white-material
  transform:
    - large-object
    - [ translate, 0, -4, 4 ]
- add: cube
  material: purple-material
  transform:
    - large-object
    - [ translate, -0.5, -4.5, 8 ]
- add: cube
  material: white-material
  transform:
    - large-object
    - [ translate, 0, -8, 4 ]
- add: cube
  material: white-material
  transform:
    - large-object
    - [ translate, -0.5, -8.5, 8 ]
```

Give it a try. Experiment with it. Apply different materials, patterns, and lighting. Try different shapes and perspectives. See what you can come up with!

Index

Thank you!

How did you enjoy this book? Please let us know. Take a moment and email us at support@pragprog.com with your feedback. Tell us your story and you could win free ebooks. Please use the subject line "Book Feedback."

Ready for your next great Pragmatic Bookshelf book? Come on over to https://pragprog.com and use the coupon code BUYANOTHER2019 to save 30% on your next ebook.

Void where prohibited, restricted, or otherwise unwelcome. Do not use ebooks near water. If rash persists, see a doctor. Doesn't apply to *The Pragmatic Programmer* ebook because it's older than the Pragmatic Bookshelf itself. Side effects may include increased knowledge and skill, increased marketability, and deep satisfaction. Increase dosage regularly.

And thank you for your continued support,

Andy Hunt, Publisher

SAVE 30%!
Use coupon code
BUYANOTHER2019

The Joy of Mazes and Math

Rediscover the joy and fascinating weirdness of mazes and pure mathematics.

Mazes for Programmers

A book on mazes? Seriously?

Yes!

Not because you spend your day creating mazes, or because you particularly like solving mazes.

But because it's fun. Remember when programming used to be fun? This book takes you back to those days when you were starting to program, and you wanted to make your code do things, draw things, and solve puzzles. It's fun because it lets you explore and grow your code, and reminds you how it feels to just think.

Sometimes it feels like you live your life in a maze of twisty little passages, all alike. Now you can code your way out.

Jamis Buck
(286 pages) ISBN: 9781680500554. $38
https://pragprog.com/book/jbmaze

Good Math

Mathematics is beautiful—and it can be fun and exciting as well as practical. *Good Math* is your guide to some of the most intriguing topics from two thousand years of mathematics: from Egyptian fractions to Turing machines; from the real meaning of numbers to proof trees, group symmetry, and mechanical computation. If you've ever wondered what lay beyond the proofs you struggled to complete in high school geometry, or what limits the capabilities of the computer on your desk, this is the book for you.

Mark C. Chu-Carroll
(282 pages) ISBN: 9781937785338. $34
https://pragprog.com/book/mcmath

Level Up

From data structures to architecture and design, we have what you need.

A Common-Sense Guide to Data Structures and Algorithms

If you last saw algorithms in a university course or at a job interview, you're missing out on what they can do for your code. Learn different sorting and searching techniques, and when to use each. Find out how to use recursion effectively. Discover structures for specialized applications, such as trees and graphs. Use Big O notation to decide which algorithms are best for your production environment. Beginners will learn how to use these techniques from the start, and experienced developers will rediscover approaches they may have forgotten.

Jay Wengrow

(220 pages) ISBN: 9781680502442. $45.95

https://pragprog.com/book/jwdsal

Design It!

Don't engineer by coincidence—design it like you mean it! Grounded by fundamentals and filled with practical design methods, this is the perfect introduction to software architecture for programmers who are ready to grow their design skills. Ask the right stakeholders the right questions, explore design options, share your design decisions, and facilitate collaborative workshops that are fast, effective, and fun. Become a better programmer, leader, and designer. Use your new skills to lead your team in implementing software with the right capabilities—and develop awesome software!

Michael Keeling

(358 pages) ISBN: 9781680502091. $41.95

https://pragprog.com/book/mkdsa

Learn Why, Then Learn How

Help introduce Elixir in your organization where it makes most sense, and learn Elixir on the web with the Phoenix framework.

Adopting Elixir

Adoption is more than programming. Elixir is an exciting new language, but to successfully get your application from start to finish, you're going to need to know more than just the language. You need the case studies and strategies in this book. Learn the best practices for the whole life of your application, from design and team-building, to managing stakeholders, to deployment and monitoring. Go beyond the syntax and the tools to learn the techniques you need to develop your Elixir application from concept to production.

Ben Marx, José Valim, Bruce Tate
(242 pages) ISBN: 9781680502527. $42.95
https://pragprog.com/book/tvmelixir

Programming Phoenix 1.4

Don't accept the compromise between fast and beautiful: you can have it all. Phoenix creator Chris McCord, Elixir creator José Valim, and award-winning author Bruce Tate walk you through building an application that's fast and reliable. At every step, you'll learn from the Phoenix creators not just what to do, but why. Packed with insider insights and completely updated for Phoenix 1.4, this definitive guide will be your constant companion in your journey from Phoenix novice to expert, as you build the next generation of web applications.

Chris McCord, Bruce Tate and José Valim
(325 pages) ISBN: 9781680502268. $45.95
https://pragprog.com/book/phoenix14

Dive Deep in to OTP and Absinthe

Put it all together with Elixir, OTP, and Phoenix. Dive into GraphQL for better APIs in Elixir. It's all here.

Functional Web Development with Elixir, OTP, and Phoenix

Elixir and Phoenix are generating tremendous excitement as an unbeatable platform for building modern web applications. For decades OTP has helped developers create incredibly robust, scalable applications with unparalleled uptime. Make the most of them as you build a stateful web app with Elixir, OTP, and Phoenix. Model domain entities without an ORM or a database. Manage server state and keep your code clean with OTP Behaviours. Layer on a Phoenix web interface without coupling it to the business logic. Open doors to powerful new techniques that will get you thinking about web development in fundamentally new ways.

Lance Halvorsen
(218 pages) ISBN: 9781680502435. $45.95
https://pragprog.com/book/lhelph

Craft GraphQL APIs in Elixir with Absinthe

Your domain is rich and interconnected, and your API should be too. Upgrade your web API to GraphQL, leveraging its flexible queries to empower your users, and its declarative structure to simplify your code. Absinthe is the GraphQL toolkit for Elixir, a functional programming language designed to enable massive concurrency atop robust application architectures. Written by the creators of Absinthe, this book will help you take full advantage of these two groundbreaking technologies. Build your own flexible, high-performance APIs using step-by-step guidance and expert advice you won't find anywhere else.

Bruce Williams and Ben Wilson
(302 pages) ISBN: 9781680502558. $47.95
https://pragprog.com/book/wwgraphql

Fix Your Hidden Problems

From technical debt to deployment in the very real, very messy world, we've got the tools you need to fix the hidden problems before they become disasters.

Software Design X-Rays

Are you working on a codebase where cost overruns, death marches, and heroic fights with legacy code monsters are the norm? Battle these adversaries with novel ways to identify and prioritize technical debt, based on behavioral data from how developers work with code. And that's just for starters. Because good code involves social design, as well as technical design, you can find surprising dependencies between people and code to resolve coordination bottlenecks among teams. Best of all, the techniques build on behavioral data that you already have: your version-control system. Join the fight for better code!

Adam Tornhill
(274 pages) ISBN: 9781680502725. $45.95
https://pragprog.com/book/atevol

Release It! Second Edition

A single dramatic software failure can cost a company millions of dollars—but can be avoided with simple changes to design and architecture. This new edition of the best-selling industry standard shows you how to create systems that run longer, with fewer failures, and recover better when bad things happen. New coverage includes DevOps, microservices, and cloud-native architecture. Stability antipatterns have grown to include systemic problems in large-scale systems. This is a must-have pragmatic guide to engineering for production systems.

Michael Nygard
(376 pages) ISBN: 9781680502398. $47.95
https://pragprog.com/book/mnee2

JavaScript and more JavaScript

JavaScript is back and better than ever. Rediscover the latest features and best practices for this ubiquitous language.

Rediscovering JavaScript

JavaScript is no longer to be feared or loathed—the world's most popular and ubiquitous language has evolved into a respectable language. Whether you're writing frontend applications or server-side code, the phenomenal features from ES6 and beyond—like the rest operator, generators, destructuring, object literals, arrow functions, modern classes, promises, async, and metaprogramming capabilities—will get you excited and eager to program with JavaScript. You've found the right book to get started quickly and dive deep into the essence of modern JavaScript. Learn practical tips to apply the elegant parts of the language and the gotchas to avoid.

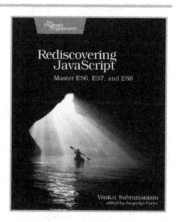

Venkat Subramaniam
(286 pages) ISBN: 9781680505467. $45.95
https://pragprog.com/book/ves6

Simplifying JavaScript

The best modern JavaScript is simple, readable, and predictable. Learn to write modern JavaScript not by memorizing a list of new syntax, but with practical examples of how syntax changes can make code more expressive. Starting from variable declarations that communicate intention clearly, see how modern principles can improve all parts of code. Incorporate ideas with curried functions, array methods, classes, and more to create code that does more with less while yielding fewer bugs.

Joe Morgan
(282 pages) ISBN: 9781680502886. $47.95
https://pragprog.com/book/es6tips

The Pragmatic Bookshelf

The Pragmatic Bookshelf features books written by developers for developers. The titles continue the well-known Pragmatic Programmer style and continue to garner awards and rave reviews. As development gets more and more difficult, the Pragmatic Programmers will be there with more titles and products to help you stay on top of your game.

Visit Us Online

This Book's Home Page
https://pragprog.com/book/jbtracer
Source code from this book, errata, and other resources. Come give us feedback, too!

Keep Up to Date
https://pragprog.com
Join our announcement mailing list (low volume) or follow us on twitter @pragprog for new titles, sales, coupons, hot tips, and more.

New and Noteworthy
https://pragprog.com/news
Check out the latest pragmatic developments, new titles and other offerings.

Save on the eBook

Save on the eBook versions of this title. Owning the paper version of this book entitles you to purchase the electronic versions at a terrific discount.

PDFs are great for carrying around on your laptop—they are hyperlinked, have color, and are fully searchable. Most titles are also available for the iPhone and iPod touch, Amazon Kindle, and other popular e-book readers.

Buy now at *https://pragprog.com/coupon*

Contact Us

Online Orders:	*https://pragprog.com/catalog*
Customer Service:	*support@pragprog.com*
International Rights:	*translations@pragprog.com*
Academic Use:	*academic@pragprog.com*
Write for Us:	*http://write-for-us.pragprog.com*
Or Call:	+1 800-699-7764

CPSIA information can be obtained
at www.ICGtesting.com
Printed in the USA
JSHW041932210920
8103JS00007B/371